The Short Oxford History of Italy

Italy since 1945

The Short Oxford History of Italy

General Editor: John A. Davis

Italy in the Nineteenth Century
edited by John A. Davis

Italy since 1945
edited by Patrick McCarthy

The Short Oxford History of Italy

General Editor: John A. Davis

Italy since 1945

Edited by Patrick McCarthy

OXFORD
UNIVERSITY PRESS

OXFORD

UNIVERSITY PRESS

Great Clarendon Street, Oxford OX2 6DP

Oxford University Press is a department of the University of Oxford.
It furthers the University's objective of excellence in research, scholarship,
and education by publishing worldwide in

Oxford New York

Athens Auckland Bangkok Bogotá Buenos Aires Calcutta
Cape Town Chennai Dar es Salaam Delhi Florence Hong Kong Istanbul
Karachi Kuala Lumpur Madrid Melbourne Mexico City Mumbai
Nairobi Paris São Paulo Shanghai Singapore Taipei Tokyo Toronto Warsaw
with associated companies in Berlin Ibadan

Oxford is a registered trade mark of Oxford University Press
in the UK and in certain other countries

Published in the United States
by Oxford University Press Inc., New York

© Oxford University Press, 2000

British Library Cataloguing in Publication Data

Data available

Library of Congress Cataloging in Publication Data

Data available

ISBN 0–19–873170–1 (hbk)
ISBN 0–19–873169–8 (pbk)

10 9 8 7 6 5 4 3 2 1

Typeset in Minion
by RefineCatch Limited, Bungay, Suffolk
Printed in Great Britain by
T.J. International Ltd., Padstow, Cornwall

General Editor's Preface

Over the last three decades historians have begun to interpret Europe's past in new ways. In part this reflects changes within Europe itself, the declining importance of the individual European states in an increasingly global world, the moves towards closer political and economic integration amongst the European states, and Europe's rapidly changing relations with the non-European world. It also reflects broader intellectual changes rooted in the experience of the twentieth century that have brought new fields of historical inquiry into prominence and have radically changed the ways in which historians approach the past.

The new *Oxford Short History of Europe* series, of which this *Short History of Italy* is part, offers an important and timely opportunity to explore how the histories of the contemporary European national communities are being rewritten. Covering a chronological span from late antiquity to the present, the *Oxford Short History of Italy* is organized in seven volumes, to which over seventy specialists in different fields and periods of Italian history will contribute. Each volume will provide clear and concise accounts of how each period of Italy's history is currently being redefined, and their collective purpose is to show how an older perspective that reduced Italy's past to the quest of a nation for statehood and independence has now been displaced by different and new perspectives.

The fact that Italy's history has long been dominated by the modern nation-state and its origins simply reflects one particular variant on a pattern evident throughout Europe. When from the eighteenth century onwards Italian writers turned to the past to retrace the origins of their nation and its quest for independent nationhood, they were doing the same as their counterparts elsewhere in Europe. But their search for the nation imposed a periodization on Italy's past that has survived to the present, even if the original intent has been lost or redefined. Focusing their attention on those periods—the middle ages, the *Renaissance*, the *Risorgimento* that seemed to anticipate the modern, they carefully averted their gaze from those that did not—the Dark Ages, and the centuries of foreign occupation and conquest after the sack of Rome in 1527.

Paradoxically, this search for unity segmented Italy's past both chronologically and geographically, since those regions (notably the South) deemed to have contributed less to the quest for nationhood were also ignored. It also accentuated the discontinuities of Italian history caused by foreign conquest and invasion, so that Italy's successive rebirths—the *Renaissance* and the *Risorgimento*—came to symbolize all that was distinctive and exceptional in Italian history. Fascism then carried the cycle of triumph and disaster forward into the twentieth century, thereby adding to the conviction that Italy's history was exceptional, the belief that it was in some essential sense also deeply flawed. Post-war historians redrew Italy's past in bleaker terms, but used the same retrospective logic as before to link fascism to failings deeply rooted in Italy's recent and more distant past.

Seen from the end of the twentieth century this heavily retrospective reasoning appears anachronistic and inadequate. But although these older perspectives continue to find an afterlife in countless textbooks, they have been displaced by a more contemporary awareness that in both the present and the past the different European national communities have no single history, but instead many different histories.

The volumes in the *Short History of Italy* will show how Italy's history too is being rethought in these terms. Its new histories are being constructed around the political, cultural, religious and economic institutions from which Italy's history has drawn continuities that have outlasted changing fortunes of foreign conquest and invasion. In each period their focus is the peoples and societies that have inhabited the Italian peninsula, on the ways in which political organization, economic activity, social identities, and organization were shaped in the contexts and meanings of their own age.

These perspectives make possible a more comparative history, one that shows more clearly how Italy's history has been distinctive without being exceptional. They also enable us to write a history of Italians that is fuller and more continuous, recovering the previously 'forgotten' centuries and geographical regions while revising our understanding of those that are more familiar. In each period Italy's many different histories can also be positioned more closely in the constantly changing European and Mediterranean worlds of which Italians have always been part.

John A. Davis

For all children, spouses, and friends who have been forced to cohabit with Massimo D'Alema, Enrico Cuccia, Linda Christian, and Gino Bartali

Contents

List of contributors

PERCY ALLUM teaches political science at the Istituto universitario orientale of Naples.

ROBERT S. C. GORDON teaches in the Italian Department of Cambridge University.

STEPHEN GUNDLE teaches Italian history, politics, and cultural studies at London University.

JOHN L. HARPER teaches American foreign policy at Johns Hopkins University, Bologna.

SALVATORE LUPO teaches contemporary history at the University of Palermo.

PATRICK MCCARTHY teaches European studies at Johns Hopkins University, Bologna.

GIANFRANCO PASQUINO teaches political science at the Facoltà di Bologna.

STEFANO PIVATO teaches contemporary history at the University of Urbino.

SIMONETTA TUNESI works as an environmental chemist and as a consultant.

VERA ZAMAGNI teaches economics at the Facoltà di Bologna.

Abbreviations

AC	Azione cattolica	Catholic Action
ACLI	Associazione cattolica dei lavoratori italiani	Association of Italian Catholic Workers
AN	Alleanza nazionale	National Alliance
BOT	Buoni ordinari del Tesoro	Treasury Bonds
BR	Brigate rosse	Red Brigades
Casmez	Cassa per il Mezzogiorno	Bank for Development of the South
CCD	Centro cristiano democratico	Christian Democratic Centre
CEI	Conferenze episcopale italiana	Italian Council of Bishops
CGIL	Confederazione generale italiana del lavoro	Italian General Confederation of Labour
CISL	Confederazione italiana dei sindacati dei lavoratori	Italian Confederation of Labour Unions
CLN	Comitato di liberazione nazionale	Committee of National Liberation
COBAS	*comitati di base*	autonomous unions
Comit	Banca commerciale italiana	Italian Bank of Commerce
CSM	Consiglio superiore della magistratura	Supreme Council of Magistrates
DC	Democrazia cristiana	Christian Democrat Party
DS	Democratici di sinistra	Democrats of the Left
ECSC	European Coal and Steel Community	
EDC	European Defence Community	
EFIM	Ente di finanziamento industrie mecchaniche	Fund to finance mechanical engineering
ENI	Ente nazionale idrocarburi	National Petroleum Company
ERP	European Recovery Program (Marshall Plan)	
FI	Forza Italia	Let's go Italy!

FUCI	Federazione degli Universitari italiani	Federation of Italian university students
IGC	Inter-Governmental Conference	
IRI	Istituto per la ricostruzione industriale	Institute for Industrial Reconstruction
Istat	Istituto centrale di statistica	Statistics Institute
MSI	Movimento sociale italiano	Italian Social Movement
PCI	Partito comunista italiana	Italian Communist Party
PDS	Partito democratico della sinistra	Democratic Party of the Left
PPI	Partito popolare italiano	Italian People's Party
PRI	Partito repubblicano italiano	Italian Republican Party
PSI	Partito socialista italiana	Italian Socialist Party
RC	Rifondazione comunista	Communist Refoundation
UDR	Unione per la difesa della repubblica	Union for the Defence of the Republic

Introduction

Patrick McCarthy

In their attempt to legitimize the post-war republic, Italian politicians claimed that it was democratic and that it was born of the Resistance, the anti-fascist struggle against the Mussolini and Hitler regimes. The first of these statements was correct, even if the method chosen for citizens to express their views was proportional representation. This offers the advantage that all shades of opinion are represented in parliament and the disadvantage that it is difficult for citizens to vote into power efficient, long-lasting governments. Moreover there could be no alternation of parties in power because the major opposition party, the Partito comunista italiano (PCI), was considered undemocratic. The combination of these two ills meant that, as the years went by, too much power was held by the ruling Christian Democrats, especially by the party apparatus rather than by elected representatives. This power was also fragmented: spread among the party's factions and among their allies and clients in other parties and in the country. The result was that criticism of Italian democracy grew, as Gianfranco Pasquino explains. Such criticism should not, however, make us forget that the post-war republic was more democratic than any previous government.

The second defence requires more discussion. First, there are many kinds of continuity between the republic and the Mussolini years. Vera Zamagni lists the names of people, such as Donato Menichella and Raffaele Mattioli, who held important posts in the fascist economy and went on to play leading roles in the post-war reconstruction. It must be added that contemporary economic historians tend to downplay the specifically fascist elements in Mussolini's handling of the economy and to emphasize the role of necessity. In the cultural sphere Robert Gordon mentions that, although the post-war wave of populism was left-wing and partially inspired by Gramsci, its roots were in second-generation fascism, in works like Elio Vittorini's *Conversazioni in Sicilia*.

Major forces that influenced the early years of the republic cannot be described as anti-fascist. The Catholic Church, perhaps the most important midwife at the birth of the Christian Democrat-led regime, had struck an advantageous bargain with Mussolini: the Lateran Pacts and the Concordat ended the Church's alienation from the *Risorgimento* (Unification) state and gave it much power over education and marriage. That a period of rivalry between the Church and fascism ensued and that the Vatican cordially despised Mussolini's rule, does not mean the Church was anti-fascist. Rather it bided its time and in 1943 it inherited some of the power of the dying regime. It was able to appeal to people who had not opposed fascism and who saw in the Resistance a threat.

The Resistance, which attracted the most civic-minded as well as the bravest Italians, was limited in space and in time. It never reached the South which was liberated by the Anglo-Saxons. Not that the South remained passive: there were bitter struggles in the post-war years as the peasants fought to gain possession of the land. But, without the impulse of a national uprising, these struggles could influence but not shake the new order. The South became the bastion of Christian Democrat (Democrazia cristiana, DC) rule and in the most restive regions like Sicily repression took the forms of banditry, Mafia, and massacres. Salvatore Lupo argues against facile notions of an old and a new Mafia but he emphasizes the Mafia's decision to abandon the pre-fascist ruling notables, many of them Liberals, in order to embrace the DC.

In the North and Centre Mussolini's popularity had waned as he drew closer to Hitler after 1938. One manifestation was the movement of many educated, young people, like the future PCI leader, Pietro Ingrao, towards a more critical view of the regime and then towards anti-fascism. But it was not until the war, which never aroused enthusiasm once the initial illusion of an easy victory vanished, was clearly lost and the northern cities were exposed to Allied bombing, that open opposition developed.

Even then the big strikes in Turin in March 1943 were protests againt hardship rather than against fascism. The workers could, however, be guided towards political opposition by the PCI organizers who were now returning to Italy. Yet Mussolini was removed from power on 25 July not as the result of massive popular pressure but because a segment of the élite—King Vittorio-Emanuele III, the king's supporters within the army, and a large group of dissidents among the fascist leaders—judged that he had become a liability. They replaced him with a government headed by Marshal Badoglio, a soldier with no particular love for democracy, much less for partisan uprisings.

The new rulers were willing, in order to gain support, to release Mussolini's opponents from prison. They also wished to end the lost war before it provoked a general rebellion. However, they moved so clumsily, and the Allies were so unhelpful, that the Nazi armies swept down the peninsula and occupied Rome before Eisenhower's troops could get there. On 8 September Badoglio annouced an armistice and then he and the king promptly fled, thus contributing to the defeat of the monarchy in the 1946 referendum. Pope Pius XII stayed and saw the Church's prestige rise.

As it had been for much of its history, Italy was divided. In the North the Germans rescued Mussolini from prison and installed him as head of government at Salò, a little town on the west side of Lake Garda. Although he was largely a puppet ruler, Salò's official doctrine marked a return to the social themes of early fascism and it attracted a certain number of young supporters. But more importantly the Nazis began systematically to round up and deport Italian Jews, with scant opposition from the Italian authorities.

The Nazi occupation triggered the Resistance. It was small, numbering only 9,000 at the end of 1943 and growing to around 30,000 by the spring of 1944. The partisans were also divided: the largest group were the Communists, who had kept alive a skeleton organization throughout the fascist period, who could take advantage of the myth of the Red Army, present among peasants and workers even before the PCI leaders returned from prison or exile, and who were accustomed to clandestine struggle. Next came the units of the Partito d'azione, a fairly new organization that was democratic, accepted capitalism, but sought to reform it and seemed to be the party of gradual change that Italy needed but had never had. Three other parties had a small number of partisans but belonged to the Resistance umbrella organization, the Comitato di liberazione nazionale (National Liberation Committee or CLN), which was founded at

Rome. These were the Socialists, who could not compete with the Communists in a guerrilla war; the Liberals, who had been the pre-fascist party of government, and the new, Church-backed DC.

The CLN jostled with the Badoglio government and with the Milan-based CLN for Upper Italy which it founded but which had more contact with the partisans. Recent research on the Resistance has distinguished various, very different strands: a national struggle against the German occupier; a civil war against the Italian fascists; and a class-based uprising of peasants against landlords and workers against owners. The three overlapped: in the province of Emilia many landlords had gone over to fascism and they now found themselves confronted by a Communist-dominated Resistance. The goal of an Italy without fascists merged with the dream of an Italy without bosses.

The cruelty of the Nazis, the bitterness of the struggle, and the solidarity that the combat created among the partisans blurred these distinctions and created an idealized Resistance. Honoured with monuments, celebrated annually on 25 April with speeches, demonstrations, and ballads, promoted by organizations of now ageing partisans, and endowed with not very generous funding for historical research, this is the anti-fascist Resistance that legitimized the republic. It played an important role in the early post-war years because it provided the new regime with a model of struggle and sacrifice. It was something of which Italians could be proud and, if its role was exaggerated, it was no more exaggerated than the role of the French Resistance.

The legitimacy furnished by the Resistance was, however, inadequate in several ways. First, the PCI appropriated it, emphasizing the national struggle led by itself, and downplaying the component of class. This was PCI policy from March 1944, when Togliatti returned from the USSR to launch his new party at Salerno. He distrusted not merely the revolutionary hopes but also the bold economic and social thinking of the Resistance, preferring to seek an alliance with the Catholics. But this did not prevent non-communists from seeing the Resistance as a red threat to property and honest folk. Secondly, since the Partito d'azione quickly broke up, there was no non-communist party that could plausibly invoke the Resistance. When the DC did so, it merely sounded rhetorical.

In short, Italians were happy to break with fascism which had brought on them great hardship and, as several contributors to this book emphasize, they were ready and able to enter the post-war world of economic modernization (Vera Zamagni), an increasingly united Europe (John Harper), and an Americanized popular culture (Stephen Gundle). Over the longer term the republic was legitimized by its success in, or association with, this modernization. It was able to offer its citizens the spectacle of Tyrone Power's marriage to Linda Christian! Among politically aware Italians the Partito d'azione hovered like a ghost over the public arena. But the Christian Democrats owed their electoral triumphs to their ability to mediate the transition from a past which included fascism, although this could not be stated openly, to a very different present.

Meanwhile a fascist party was formed in December 1946 under the name Movimento sociale italiano (MSI). It was tolerated so that the other parties could assert their anti-fascist credentials by shunning it. In the 1990s it was able to legitimize itself with an ease which casts further doubt on the authenticity of anti-fascism.

The new Italy was dynamic and enterprising. Percy Allum demonstrates in his account of internal migration that Italians were willing to make great sacrifices in order to better themselves. People left their farms and came flooding into alien Milan and Turin in search of jobs. Economically Italy was playing catch-up and, although it did not start from as far back as is often said, its success in becoming one of Europe's wealthiest nations was amazing. Nor was this success just a matter of cheap labour. Italy could—and can—boast a wealth of entrepreneurial ability that Britain might envy. Its best-known manifestation is the number of small industries which have deep roots in Italian history, which helped lead the country through the difficult 1970s and which are thriving and exporting today.

But the *piccole imprese* (small enterprises) are all too famous and they overshadow Italy's other economic achievements. These include seemingly uncharacteristic successes: a state sector that was well run in the 1950s by men like Oscar Sinigaglia and a notable spell of disinflation by the Prodi government in preparation for entering the EU's monetary union. The price Italy has paid for its achievements is described by Simonetta Tunesi: the destruction of its environment, which is all the graver because the balance between man and nature, an essential trait of traditional Italian culture, has been damaged.

The underlying problem, often posed and never satisfactorily solved, is illustrated here by the contrast between Zamagni's chapter (and to a lesser extent Allum's) and Pasquino's chapter (and to a lesser extent Harper's). Although he is by no means totally pessimistic, Pasquino emphasizes the shortcomings of political culture. Between 1945 and 1979 these are alleviated by the DC's self-confident belief that its role is to spread democracy among the masses. Even so the shortcomings are significant: no alternation of parties in power, in the later years partly because the PCI ignored the chance to break with the USSR offered by the crushing of the Prague Spring; the systematic use of clientelism by a DC determined to remain in power; the unfailing support given to the DC, however reluctantly, by a Church obsessed with anti-communism, only half-attracted by Vatican II, and equally determined to retain its power; the alienation of the citizen from government by a variety of devices ranging from threatened *coups d'état* and all too real massacres, via the accumulation of power in the hands of party nomenclatura, to the use of a special kind of language instantly intelligible to insiders but far removed from the Italian spoken by the ordinary voter.

After the kidnapping and murder of Aldo Moro and the failure of Enrico Berlinguer's strategy of the historic compromise in 1978–79, the Italian political system turned in on itself. Again this is in contrast with Italian society, where Percy Allum sees the many movements of May 1968 as forces, not for messianic Marxism, but for individual freedom. In politics these were the years of Bettino Craxi, who sought only to exploit the introversion of democracy in order to gain power for himself and his Socialist party. After Craxi there could come only a crisis of the political system.

By the 1980s the PCI's lack of vision and strategy was masked only by the charisma of Enrico Berlinguer, who died in 1984. The decline of the left as a matrix of culture is a theme of both Robert Gordon and Stephen Gundle. Gordon follows the figure of the left-wing intellectual from the post-war on. He shapes populism and neo-realism but goes into crisis in the 1960s. Italo Calvino ends his life as a postmodernist; Pier Paolo Pasolini as a prophet of doom. Gundle argues that Berlinguer's funeral was the last time that the PCI held the nation's attention and also that many young people who formed part of the huge crowd experienced the funeral as a spectacle.

In the sphere of sport Stefano Pivato traces a different but related evolution. From its association in the Mussolini years with war and strength, symbolized in the figure of the (in fact highly dubious) world heavyweight boxing champion, Primo Carnera, sport ends up in the 1990s in the form of the ever more popular gymnasium, where the body is pampered and beautified. Along the way sport has gone through the heroic period of the cyclists Coppi and Bartali, whose rivalry was elevated by the fans into the personification of the post-war struggle between the Communists and the Catholics. Together, however, they symbolized the Italy of reconstruction: their triumphs were the exaltation of the peasant values of work, endurance, and courage.

After they retired cycling gave way to soccer and the Italian national and club sides grew ever better and ever more entwined with politics. The 1982 World Cup triumph was described by Aurelio Lepre as the apotheosis of the sporting nation which had outlived the nation. Berlusconi turned AC Milan into a trampoline from which he hurled himself into politics at the head of a movement called Forza Italia (Let's go Italy!). Meanwhile Sergio Cragnotti has taken Lazio onto the stockmarket and other such ventures are planned.

The transformation of the PCI into a non-communist party of the left, the domestic counterpart of the collapse of the Berlin Wall, was one of the causes of the 1992 crisis. Another cause, which leads us back to the debate within the early chapters of this book, is the contrast between Italy's dynamic economy and society and its political stasis. Our explanation of this divide would have to go deep into Italian history (which is the task of other books in this series). We would argue that politics requires national unity as a framework, whereas the dynamism of the economy may be seen precisely as a reaction against the lack of unity and as an outlet for local or group energies.

Other reasons are specific to the post-1945 period. Politics started out ahead of economic development thanks precisely to the Resistance and the new Constitution. But gradually the lack of the prerequisites of healthy political life—a strong and positive national identity, agreement of all social groups on certain underlying principles, trust that one's opponents will obey the rules—brought politics to a stasis masked by a fierce struggle for spoils that was moderated only by a careful concern to cut all parties and pressure groups in on all deals. These defects damaged economic and social life too. They prevented development of the stockmarket and they brought civil society to a halt as micro-organizations, whether parent–teacher associations or neighbourhood groups, decided that involving everyone in a non-decision was more important than making a decision. But economic and social initiatives can be taken by selected groups whose agreement is real rather than contrived.

By the 1990s the economy could not thrive without a government that could impose austerity to meet the Maastricht requirements and to compete with Italy's main trading partners. The results were an electoral setback for the DC–PSI coalition in 1992 and the rise of the Lega Nord. In turn this left the politicians unable to block the Clean Hands operation and led to an exposure of *Tangentopoli*, the organized corruption on which the political system was based. Salvatore Lupo notes at this time a change of tactics by the Mafia which ceases to defer to the state. By their aggression—the murders of Falcone and Borsellino—the Corleonesi drive the state to fight back.

All these phenomena are linked: the delicate agreements between the political class and the Mafia break down in part because pressure from other European countries makes it impossible for the DC negotiators to keep their promises. Yet it would be a mistake to see too much control over the developments of the 1990s. The lira is forced out of the EMS because of international speculation against weak currencies. There is no plot against Italy.

For this reason there is no determinism shaping the likely outcome. Many Italians can see nothing in the past seven years but familiar forms of *Trasformismo*. This is one possibility but there are others. The key seems still to be electoral reform but the referendum on 18 April 1999 to strike out the one-quarter of the House seats awarded by proportional representation did not arouse the interest of the 1993 referendum.

It is our belief that there have emerged at least in northern and central Italy social groups less tied to the splits in Italy and hence less concerned about balancing acts and cutting everyone in on every decision. They seek a stronger state that will interfere less but regulate more. They are willing to be left out of power for the lifetime of one parliament in order to be able to govern in the next parliament. The question remains: will these groups ever present a majority?

While we debate this subtle and taxing question, let me take this opportunity to thank Anthony DiPaola, who worked as an editorial assistant on this book. No blame should be attributed to Anthony for the failure to obtain a quorum in the April referendum. Rather Anthony succeeded in overcoming the editor's computer illiteracy and in enabling such questions to be posed. He gave generously of his time and energy, for which all readers and contributors will undoubtedly be grateful.

1

Italian society transformed

Percy Allum

'Dai tempi di Virgilio ad oggi, non era mai avvenuto un così
profondo cambiamento'.

(Christian Democrat minister, 1965)

Introduction

The last half of the twentieth century has witnessed greater changes
in Italian society than at any time in the previous history of the
peninsula. What was a relatively poor industrializing society suffering
the ravages of war in 1945 has become, fifty years later, one of the
most powerful and prosperous countries in the world (national
income grew fivefold; individual income fourfold) and a member of
the G7.

The transformation from a largely agrarian, if urbanized, society to
an industrial society within in the space of twenty years was followed
by a further transformation into a post-industrial society with the
service sector replacing industry as the major economic activity in an
accelerating time span. Thus, if almost half of the working population was engaged in agriculture in the 1940s, it was nearer 5 per cent
in the 1990s; industry, which represented roughly a third in 1945, rose
to a peak of 40 per cent in 1970 to decline to *circa* 30 per cent in 1995.
On the other hand, the service sector, which accounted for about a
quarter of the working population at the end of hostilities, made a

dramatic surge to about 60 per cent, almost doubling in the last twenty years.

The path from an agrarian society to an industrial and then a service society, defined in terms of the employment shares was, as Goran Therborn (1995, 68) has argued, a specific European phenomenon. Given the significance of the experience of industrial society in moulding the social structure of European societies, two preliminary points are in order regarding Italy. The first concerns the brevity of the industrial society experience, namely a society dominated by 'large work place units with a clearly demarcated, collectively patterned division of labour producing material commodities' (ibid. 71). In fact, Therborn limits the industrial society experience in the case of Italy to the 1960s. However, this brevity must be tempered with a further observation, and this is the second point, that industrial work often dominated the non-agrarian economy for a longer period; in Italy's case certainly since the 1870s. Indeed, Italian industrialization was characterized by the small workshop, which in the form of the small family firm is largely the basis of the country's present prosperity. It has also been an important factor in Italy's social structure.

The dramatic economic transformation of Italy has not occurred, as it could not, in isolation. It was accompanied by a profound social revolution: rural exodus, urbanization, mass literacy, consumerism, secularization. The result, as Henri Mendras (1997, 55) has written in the wider European context, was that

the major social classes and the big symbolic institutions have lost their organizing function; they no longer prescribe ways of life or practical moral conduct. Churches, unions, parties, bourgeois conventions, working-class and peasant cultures no longer furnish models which all are obliged to observe if they do not wish to be ostracized. Today, one can build one's own life on the models of one's choice.

To understand how this happened, it is necessary to bear in mind the global political and economic context: on the one hand the Cold War divided the continent with Italy in the Western camp; while on the other hand the *trente glorieuses*, a golden age for international trade and economic growth, meant specifically the 'economic miracle' for Italy. This is not the place to consider these phenomena (see Vera Zamagni's chapter), but it is necessary to mention that the economic miracle had its origin in Italy's successful integration in the world economy as a low-wage economy, which in turn set in motion a virtuous cycle of export-led growth, because of its connection with the first of the significant post-war trends in Italian society: the 'great migration'.

The great migration

Emigration was an endemic feature of Italian society in the first hundred years of the nation's history. Some 13 million persons left Italy, mainly to the New World, between 1871 and 1920 when transoceanic emigration started to be controlled. It was seen by the Italian government at the time as a necessary safety-valve to relieve demographic pressure. Although emigration to northern Europe and Australia resumed in the post-war period for a couple of decades, what was new in the 1950s was massive internal migration, first from the countryside to the cities (rural exodus) and later, as the economic miracle got under way, from the South to Rome and the North (the great migration). It demonstrated that there was widespread underemployment in the countryside. Indeed, the end of mass transoceanic emigration in the 1920s and overpopulation in the countryside explains the Fascists' rabid opposition to urbanization and the cultivation of the myth of 'rural' life. Urbanization would have boosted unemployment in the towns and created a serious social problem. Hence, labour mobility was discouraged.

It has been estimated that unemployed persons numbered about 2 million or 10 per cent of the working population in the 1950s. In addition, the number of underemployed, especially in agriculture and the services, has been calculated as nearly as high for the simple reason that the mass rural exodus had no adverse effect on agricultural production (Ricossa 1976, 297–8). The role of this 'industrial reserve army' was to keep wage rates down—an essential ingredient of the miracle—because demand for work far exceeded supply. The motivation of the poor peasant was: *Chi non ha, non è* (a Calabrian saying meaning 'He who has nothing, does not exist').

In the two decades between 1953 and 1973, it is claimed that some 9 million Italians were involved in inter-regional migration (Ginsborg

1990*a*, 219). The peak migration periods were the 'miracle' years of 1958–63 and the late 1960s recovery (1967–71), interrupted by a brief halt for the first post-war recession (1964–6), at the annual rate of up to several hundred thousand persons. Moreover, migration patterns were complex. It was generally not a case of persons or families making a single move. It was the result of individual family strategies. If the predominant direction was from the rural areas to the prosperous urban ones in all parts of the peninsula, the move from the southern countryside to the northern industrial triangle often took several steps, via either southern urban centres (particularly Naples and Palermo) or northern rural areas (See Table 1.1). Thus, for example, poor southern peasants rarely made the jump from unemployment at home to factory jobs in the industrial triangle. Indeed, in the early years, the rural exodus from the north-east and centre was as strong as from the poor south and islands, even if the former moved as often to their own regional centres as to the industrial north-west. Hence, the southern peasants often initially took the places of southern urban migrants or northern-central rural migrants, like those of the flower-growers of the Ligurian coastal villages; later on they moved to Turin, Milan, and their hinterlands.

Furthermore, we need to bear in mind that if the vast majority of migrants came from the poor hill and mountain villages of the Southern interior, the small landholders actually outnumbered the farm labourers (*braccianti*). In this connection, we should remember that the land reform, which formed part of the southern programme of 1950, whatever its real intentions, in fact encouraged migration from the rural sector by only supporting what were defined as 'viable' farms. Finally, and somewhat paradoxically, the various government

TABLE 1.1 Migration balance sheet for main areas of Italy, 1951–1971 ('000)

	1951–61	1961–71
Northern Italy	+616	+956
Central Italy	+124	+205
Southern Italy	−1772	−2318
ALL ITALY	−1033	−1157

Source: Acquaviva and Santuccio 1976, 33.

policies to aid the South expanded the market for northern goods and so production by increasing southern incomes.

The first to move were the single young males for whom the lure of the city, often as a result of television from the mid-1950s, became irresistible. They used what is known as the 'migratory chain' (*la catena migratoria*): usually someone with relatives or contacts in the destination moved first to find work and accommodation; once settled he helped others and his family to follow creating local community networks. The result was that people from the same southern village were found living in the same street or district of the northern town, while residents in the next street or nearby district came from a completely different southern region.

Conditions were often appalling. Housing was overcrowded, with often four to five persons living in a room in squalid attics in the city centres or in tin shacks in shanty towns on the outskirts, while labour consisted of unskilled jobs on building sites, or later, those who were lucky aspired to semi-skilled work in engineering factories and flats in ugly high-rise blocks in new districts. Migrants suffered from isolation, when not outright hostility, from the host population who despised the *terroni* (literally people from the land) owing to language and cultural differences.

Bettering themselves and providing for their families ('the strongest expression of solidarity in Italy') was the principal motivation. This meant that they worked hard for long hours, tolerating conditions deemed unacceptable by most indigenous workers to save money either to send to their families or to bring their families to the North, or again to buy a little land for their return south. Not all migrants, however, ended up in the industrial sector or doing 'dirty jobs'. Many aspired to open shops and workshops of their own, while others ended up in the public service as postmen and caretakers (Ginsborg 1990a, 224).

All the studies of the phenomenon have remarked on the dramatic cultural and psychological impact: peasants who were often illiterate and had never been outside their local village suddenly found themselves in the big city with a regular income for the first time in their lives. Despite the dislocation, however, many migrants became permanent and managed to integrate in their new communities, as is attested by the part that many played in the Hot Autumn of 1969 and the social struggles of the following years. In this they held a trump card which their fellow emigrants to other western European countries did not possess, namely they had equal citizenship rights, so they could not be expelled and therefore had the possibility, in a liberal democratic regime, of influencing political organizations such as parties and unions. Indeed, when the unions embraced their demands for better working conditions in 1969, they became fully integrated in the mainstream of working-class radicalism (Slater 1979, 90). The second generation often considered themselves northerners and ironically behaved towards the next wave of immigrants (foreigners this time) with the same hostility as the northerners had shown to their parents.

The social consequences of this massive transfer of population were naturally different in the two areas affected: departure and arrival. The northern cities were absolutely unprepared for this influx: housing was insufficient and chronically overcrowded, and social services such as schools, hospitals, and transport, etc. were inadequate. The former, for example, resulted in the creation of shanty towns on the outskirts of the major cities. This in turn led to large-scale building programmes, creating unsightly urban sprawl round the major agglomerations. Whole new suburban districts were constructed, usually lacking the basic amenities which, alas, were not limited to the North, as an inspection of the hinterland of Rome, Naples, and Palermo reveals.

In the South the hill and mountain villages were left to their fate. With so many young men leaving and only the old and women remaining, they slumped into irreversible decline and degradation. The Church became concerned at this pauperization because of its effect on the integrity of the family but the DC-led governments did little to alleviate this situation. Indeed, Ginsborg (1990a, 232) has noted that the two 'Green Plans' of the 1960s channelled public spending towards capitalist farms in the fertile regions. For the first time in living memory significant amounts of arable land were withdrawn from cultivation.

A further consequence of the great migration, although it has to be taken in conjunction with the economic miracle, was mass consumer society. Television which became a mass phenomenon in the late 1950s, and the automobile, specifically the Fiat 600 launched in 1955, both of which southerners were able to enjoy thanks *inter alia* to migrant remittances, were to promote a certain cultural unification of the country. Television, in particular, was responsible for the spread of a colloquial Italian which could be understood, even if it was not spoken, by everyone. Moreover, Pasolini (1975) in a famous article explained that the programme *Carosello* was unwittingly the vehicle during which the new consumer 'world' open to Italians exploded nightly on their screens. A new world that quickly became a desirable goal for the young which could be achieved through migration. In addition, the car, in the wake of the scooter, became available to the lower middle and upper working classes; it gave many Italians a new conception of space, mobility, and sense of liberation. Indeed, initially it was an important element of democratization before becoming a status symbol. They were just two indicators of 'modernization'.

In this situation, we can well understand the young southerners watching *Carosello* in the village bar and reflecting: 'We are like beasts, not like them, who dress like lords' (Lepore 1995, 186); and feel the pressure to emigrate. The end of the peasant world was mourned by the peasants least of all.

The great migration provoked, as part and parcel of the economic miracle not only modernization (in the form of urbanization and secularization), but substantial changes in the country's social structure to which we now turn.

The changing social structure

The transformation of Italian society, as noted above, followed a specifically European path from agrarian society to industrial and to post-industrial society. However, to appreciate the significance of these changes we need to take account also the specificities of the Italian situation which led Bagnasco to assert (Ginsborg 1994, 226) that Italian society is now 'not only a complex society, but a complicated society'. He was referring first to the fact that Italy is a young nation and in the bare one hundred years of national unity it has not overcome marked regional differences. These are not simply those between industrial North and agrarian South; there are also those between the northern industrial triangle and the north-east and the centre which certain analysts have invested with different social formations: north-west (contemporary); north-east and centre (modern); south (traditional) (Gallino 1971). Secondly, the industrial society phase, in comparison with northern Europe, was extremely brief and too territorially limited to ensure the social and cultural homogeneity of the nation. The result was that post-war developments gave rise to different patterns in the various macro-areas of the country. In this connection, we need to remember that national trends often mask significant regional differences because national statistics represent the average of these differences. Finally, similar trends in different areas often have different meanings as a result of the difference in context. Indeed, it has been claimed that social structures in Italy can only be studied on a local or regional basis (Mendras 1997, 219).

From what has been said and from Table 1.2, it is clear that the forty years of increasing prosperity in the second half of this century break down into two roughly equal periods of some twenty years in which the watershed marking the end of the post-war boom (*trente glorieuses*) can be fixed between the 'Hot Autumn' of 1969 and the first energy crisis of 1973–74. At the outset Italy was a sharply stratified society with 'great differences in income levels, living conditions, cultural values, life styles and consumption patterns between bourgeois and blue collar workers, peasants and clerks, artisans and state employees' (Martinelli 1998, 30).

TABLE 1.2 Major social classes, 1901–1991 (%)

	1901	1936	1951	1971	1991
Upper middle class[a]	2	2	2	3	3
Other middle classes	51	55	57	50	58
Urban middle classes	14	16	24	33	46
White-collar workers	3	5	13	20	24
Artisans	7	6	5	5	6
Shopkeepers	4	5	6	8	11
Peasant farmers	35	36	31	12	6
Working classes	47	44	41	47	39
Farm labourers	24	16	12	6	3
Factory workers	19	21	23	31	25
Services	4	6	6	10	11

[a] = owners, contractors, top managers, and leading professional persons.

Source: Sylos Labini 1975 and 1995.

An industrial society

The first period was characterized by tumultuous growth and the transformation of Italy into an industrial society. The effect on the social structure is set out in Table 1.2. We can note the modest movement between the major classes—in fact, the middle classes retain their equal numerical importance to the working classes—however, the significant changes occurred within each class grouping: substantial growth of the salaried urban middle class (white collars) at the expense of the self-employed rural middle class (peasant farmers); and similar growth of the industrial and service working class and the decline of farm labourers. One thing that is apparent from these figures is that the decline of the rural middle class was greater than the growth of the urban middle class, which means that a substantial number of the former became part of the growing industrial proletariat with an income superior to that earned from the land. This observation draws attention to an absentee from these figures: the size of the underclass (casual labourers and *lumpen*). Estimations in the late 1960s put the former at 3.7 million (1.1 in the North; 2.6 in the South), to be found in such categories as artisans, subcontractors, building workers, and agricultural labourers and the latter at 1.5 million (0.5 in the countryside and 1.0 in the towns, overwhelmingly in the South) (Sylos Labini 1975, 74). This suggests that precarious employment in 1970 affected up to a quarter of the workforce.

As stated, these movements had different significance in different areas. Thus, in synthesis, the importance of the bourgeoisie increased more in the North than in the South. The decline in importance of the peasantry benefited the private industrial middle class in the North, but, in the South, it benefited the middle classes in the public sector. This has been taken as an indicator of the gap between development and underdevelopment (Rusconi and Scamuzzi 1981, 36). Indeed, the rural exodus changed the social structure of the rural population in the South irrevocably. It was no longer divided between the small élite of landowners and a mass of peasants and the poor.

This said, the importance of these changes were as much political as economic. Many observers have pointed to the survival, indeed the increase, of small shopkeepers and artisans, two 'traditional' strata, in contrast to the decline of the peasantry. It was due to direct political intervention: commercial activities were subject to law and regulation (licences) which meant that they were in the hands of politicians from whom the recipients could benefit as 'clients'; their support became all the more important to DC politicians to offset the decline of the peasantry. Not for nothing had Schumpeter called shopkeepers and artisans 'Capitalism's protective strata'.

Similarly, the rise in white-collar workers, particularly in public employment in the South, was also the result of political factors: a political response to resolve the problem of 'intellectual' unemployment. Recruitment of bureaucrats, in fact, was widely effected using 'patronage' criteria (i.e. the job for the vote) with the object of securing political consensus rather than administrative efficiency (Pichierri 1973, 97–8). All of which illustrates that even in the era of the long economic boom when market factors could be considered the supreme adjudicator of changes in the social structure, politics played a significant role. Indeed, Rusconi and Scamuzzi (1981, 28) have claimed that it was a period in which 'politics became a full-time profession and was of crucial importance for the social organization thanks to the resources it controlled and distributed'. In this connection, it is worth recalling that this was the very moment that Sylos Labini (1975) denounced 'the ubiquity of the petty bourgeoisie' and its capacity to condition Italian politics through its control of party organization and public institutions. In fact, he believed that it was one of the causes of the fragmentation of the party system while Pizzorno (1980, 82) pointed out that almost all the government crises of the 1950s were caused by one of the small parties (PDSI, PLI, PRI) in coalition with the DC: all were middle-class parties.

A second observation is pertinent for the period and that is the important process of homogenization which the growth of a mass industrial society brought in its wake. It interested large sections of the working class from the point of view of professional skills with the disappearance of the old craft skills, with the progressive spread of mass production techniques and a concomitant strong egalitarian sense. However, this occurred in the big factories—it was no coincidence that Fiat was the symbol of the age—and was restricted to a limited geographical area (the northern industrial triangle). Thus, although it is true that the great migration was responsible for a renewal of the Italian working class, an increase in its contractual power, a qualitative rise in its goals, and a profound cultural change which had effects on political behaviour (for example, the 1974 Divorce Referendum; Pichierri 1973), none the less, we would stress that its contribution to the social modernization of the country was restricted not only because of its geographical limits but also because of its brevity. Traditional society, above all in the south, although transformed by mass consumption (TV, cars, domestic appliances, mass-produced clothing) was only superficially touched and many traditional 'residues' (religious and magical folklore) persisted as a form of defence. There was a form of adaptation which has been defined as 'modernization without development'. Hence, if it can be claimed that Italy was effectively brought into the community of western nations as an industrial society in the 1960s, 'the inheritance of the past [was] massively resistant' (Bailey 1992, 10).

A post-industrial society

The 1970s energy crisis constituted a watershed in European industrialization. It not only marked the effective end of the *trente glorieuses* but also of the extension of industrialization. Indeed, in all western european countries it opened an era of relative deindustrialization and Italy was not spared, although it did not suffer to the same extent as some northern European countries (UK, Belgium, Luxembourg). Hence, it is not surprising that in the second phase (1970s–1990s), there was, in addition to a continued decline in the rural sector, a decline in the industrial sector workforce, offset in large degree by the rapid growth of the services sector. In terms of social stratification these movements translated, broadly speaking, into a continued expansion of the middle classes and a first contraction of the working class.

Once again, the significant elements are to be sought inside the major social groupings. In the composition of the middle classes, it was the urban sector, and above all the white collars, which continued to expand, but there was also (specific to Italy among industrial countries) a modest rise in the traditional petty bourgeoisie (shopkeepers and artisans). The rural middle class continued to decline as peasant farmers left the land, or more often became part-time farmers with jobs in small industry or the services as their main employment.

Among the blue collars, it was the industrial workers in the heavy industries (steel, engineering, shipbuilding, petrochemicals), many of which closed, that were responsible for the contraction in the working class for the first time since the beginning of the century. In the industrial restructuring of the early 1980s, for example, Fiat shed almost half its workforce (Ginsborg 1998, 107). This loss was not offset by the marginal increase of workers in the services. Most traditional Italian heavy industry was state-owned and it was here that deindustrialization was most strongly felt. It hit certain areas of the industrial triangle (Genoa and to a lesser extent Turin) but also, paradoxically, of the South (Naples, Taranto), particularly hard.

These developments followed the scenario already described for western Europe, that is of the passage from an industrial to a post-industrial society and in which the workforce in the service sector prevails over the industrial. They raise major questions about the nature of the contemporary social structure in West European societies. However, before discussing these and their implications, we need to examine the specificity of Italy in this period because it is somewhat masked by Sylos Labini's figures.

The major novelty of the 1970s was the 'explosion' of the 'Third Italy' (north-east and centre). Indeed, the economic success of the 'high-technology cottage industry' of this area enabled Italy to come through the economic crises of 1970s and 1980s relatively unscathed (at least, in relation to the UK). In point of fact, high-technology cottage industry organized in industrial districts was not only able to achieve the economies of scale of big firms for certain products, but a product flexibility unknown to the big factory. A Bolognese entrepreneur boasted: 'We are very flexible. I managed companies in the USA, in France, in Caracas, in Mexico. But my companies in Emilia-Romagna can change a system of production, of network sales, in minutes' (quoted in Richards 1995, 76). The result was to produce a novel mode of production (*modello NEC industrializzazione diffusa*) that 'does in a decentralised way what large companies like the Thyssen speciality steel division do within the framework of huge organizations: create new demand by filling needs that potential customers have only begun to suspect was there' (Sabel 1982, 223). It was a mode of industrial production that has dominated the Italian economy for more than twenty years and was responsible for the 1980s boom, so that if Fiat was the symbol of the industrial society era, Benetton can claim to be that of post-industrial society.

However, what is important for the discussion of the social

structure is that this development has tended to further fragment an already heterogeneous Italian working class. The relative decline of the core industrial proletariat (traditional big factory workers) and the relative expansion of the peripheral proletariat (small firm workers) has meant that the balance has tipped strongly in favour of the latter. In addition, there has been a multiplication of new tasks in the service sector which has increased its numbers but not as fast as to offset the reduction in industry.

All this has meant a significant decline in the social and political influence of the traditional working class. Ginsborg (1998, 106) has remarked on the diminished role of the factory as centres of workers' mobilization and political initiative. This diminished influence can be seen most clearly in the loss of membership (down from some 12 million in 1970s to 7–8 million in 1990s) and prestige of the organized labour movement after its peak in the mid-1970s. As is well known, artisans and 'home workers' are notoriously difficult to organize because of their (often family) links with their employers and the climate of collaboration that usually exists in the small workshop ('at Benetton, if a worker wishes to speak to Luciano he goes to Luciano and speaks to Luciano whose door is always open. It's all very simple and direct', quoted in *Stella*, 1996, 80). Indeed, to offset membership decline and poor recruitment among young factory and service workers, the unions have had to rely increasingly on pensioners (about 2 million members in 1990). Hence, the claim of organized labour to represent the interests of all workers was not only undermined by this development but also by the growth of autonomous unions (*Comitati di base:* COBAS) amongst new groups of technicians and professionals (above all in the public sector, transport, schools, and health services) whose periodic wildcat strikes in support of particularistic and corporatist interests at the expense of the general public turned public opinion against unions and unionism in general. The result is that since the mid-1980s the organized labour movement was no longer a major social and political factor.

Similar developments to those of the working class occurred in that already fragmented grouping that is the middle class. In addition to the growth of the small artisan-businessman, there was a rapid expansion of the urban middle class. It poses the question as to whether there was growth in the professional and managerial classes, often called the service class, that was characteristic of Italy's West

European neighbours. It comprises a vast array of new occupations based on so-called human capital, as opposed to financial capital, and linked to the new knowledge-based activities (information technology, telecommunications, finance, public relations, and show-business).

Mario Deaglio (1991) has dubbed this group the 'new bourgeoisie'; they are professionals, administrators, managers, and consultants, whose position involves the application of specialized knowledge within the framework of bureaucratic organizations. The human capital is formed of a combination of specialized training and organized work experience which allows its cultivators to work on commission or part time (freelance) without prior financial capital.

The answer to our question would appear to be largely negative in the sense that the high-tech sectors in which these new social figures (like financial consultants, for example) were emerging tended to be underdeveloped in Italy, except in the major cities like Milan and Rome. The greater part of the Italian middle class remained in the traditional sectors (self-employed: liberal professions and shopkeepers; public service: bureaucrats and teachers, etc.). The conclusion is that, despite elements of modernization, the heterogeneity of the middle classes remains. Indeed, as Davico (in Ginsborg 1994, 235) has observed, it was all the more apparent because of the lack of any clear class identity: not only did they not have any common interests but the different groups often mobilized in the name of opposing corporativisms (for example, the COBAS strikes, professional association campaigns, etc.)

The larger question raised by this discussion is whether it is appropriate to talk of classes in post-industrial society. Mendras (1997, 212) has suggested that the triumph of the middle classes in western Europe has undermined the classic industrial society pyramidal schema of classes with the bourgeoisie at the summit and the proletariat at the base. As he has argued, if everybody is middle-class, nobody is; if bourgeoisie and proletariat have lost their character and class consciousness, logically there can be no middle class between them: 'in triumphing the middle class have shattered the class system and condemned themselves' (1997, 232). It is not that European society has suddenly become egalitarian—indeed, in some ways inequality has increased—but rather it (and Italian society) is based more on factors like income and lifestyles than on relations of production and property. Hence, it is more appropriate to talk in terms of strata and status groups. He proposes replacing the traditional image of the social pyramid with that of a pear-shaped strabiloid having a much larger top than tail (see his illustration, p. 231), that is the wealthy are few and very rich, the mass comfortable, and the poor significant (12 per cent below the international standard poverty line: Negrei in Ginsborg 1994, 239–41).

It is true that the traditional distinction between manual and non-manual work remains and can still be seen in types of income (wages or salary), working conditions (shop floor or office), educational attainment (secondary or higher education), consumption pattern and lifestyles. However, the determinants of wealth and lifestyles, not to say major conflicts, now cut across traditional class boundaries, and so the distinction is losing its social prestige. Thus, if it remained broadly true that the average blue-collar wages were generally lower than white-collar salaries (not always the case), it did not mean that white-collar families were automatically richer than blue-collar ones. Indeed, the advent of the two-income (and sometimes more in the Third Italy) family has raised some blue-collar family incomes above that of white-collar ones. In consequence, we now have a situation where there are 'rich' blue-collar and 'poor' white-collar families (much depending on the individual families place in the life cycle), and their lifestyles are often not so different thanks to the social models broadcast by the media.

In this connection, there has been a high level of mobility (if short-range, between contiguous class strata) in the post-war years, largely the result of the great migration. In fact, an inquiry carried out in the mid-1980s indicated that 62 per cent of Italians aged 18–65 years had a different class position to that of their parents (Barbagli *et al.* 1988, 10). Half of those of working class and a quarter of those of farm labourer origin were now either members of the urban middle class or the upper bourgeoisie. Further, there has been a growth in recent years of the number of 'cross-class couples'; their values and lifestyles tend to be nearer the white than the blue collars, 'creating', according to Barbagli and colleagues (1988, 12), 'a stratum between the blue-collar and white-collar classes without a clear social identity or a strong class loyalty'.

At this juncture, we can note that two of the main conflicts of the past two decades have crossed traditional class boundaries: first, between self-employed and employees. There is no longer a distinction between white and blue collars, as was largely the case in industrial society, with the growth of the salaried middle classes, on the one hand, and the virtual freelance situation of many technicians and casual labourers, on the other. The conflict exploded over tax evasion and social security contributions. While employees are subject to tax deduction at source (in their pay packets or salary slip), the self-employed are personally responsible for declaring their incomes. The former complain that they, as employees, pay 85 per cent of health care and demand greater fiscal equity through more stringent tax assessments. Naturally, the self-employed react to the threat of higher assessments (often obtaining frequent remissions), accusing the employees of tax evasion also and moonlighting. They also attack the job security and reproductive nature of much white-collar employment.

Secondly, job security has also crossed traditional class boundaries in the last twenty years. It used to be a distinction between white-collar (above all, the public service) employment and that of blue-collar workers, who were always subject to sackings and layoffs. Indeed, this was no longer the case, for white-collar workers (even those in the public service) were now subject to redundancy and early retirements because of privatizations and new technologies. A bank clerk asserted in 1996: 'A person like me, who has worked at the counter for years, feels humiliated when he realizes that his work is almost superfluous. A transaction across the counter costs a little more than one dollar to the bank, 35 cents if carried out by phone and 27 cents with a credit card. Faced with these figures, how can you not be worried?' (quoted in Ginsborg 1998, 102). Hence, what was a problem which divided the working class between core proletariat (skilled workers in big plants) and marginal proletariat (casual workers in small units and unemployed) has now become a problem affecting all but a tiny élite of the so-called economically and socially fortunate. Basgnasco (in Ginsborg 1994, 229) presents the conflict in terms of the 'included' (*chi e dentro*) and the 'excluded' (*chi resta fuori*): on the one hand there was a 'middle stratum' which extended its boundaries to include a whole host of new occupations, including working-class. In fact, all those who in the boom years had a secure job and a stable family, had bought their home, and saved in various ways, buying Treasury Bonds (BOT) were 'included'. They were able to overcome the difficulties of recession and give their children a good start in life. On the other hand, there were those who had precarious employment, or a job in the 'black economy', who had not qualified for a decent pension, who had reached a certain age, who had no qualifications, or had lost their jobs through industrial restructuring; in short those who had not managed to climb aboard the 'growth train' at the right moment were 'excluded'. Among the latter must also be counted the foreign immigrants (*extracomunitari*) who have arrived in numbers since 1980 (*circa* a million in 1990), mainly from North Africa and East Europe). There is a case for describing the excluded as an underclass because they were not fully integrated into society. In any event, as regards native Italians there have always been family solidarity and structures to limit the severest social consequences.

If it is true, as Mendras has argued for Europe, that the major social classes were no longer the basic social structure of Italian society, this does not mean that we were in the presence of a classless society; far from it. It merely means that other cleavages such as gender and place in the life cycle (youth, working, third age) were tending to take the place of class. In the mean time, a national population's system of values and lifestyles remain oriented by older cultural models. In Italy, as was argued earlier, the class values of industrial society never became hegemonic and class identity was largely subordinate to regional identity: the writer Goffredo Parise was wont to say that he was a Veneto first of all and only then an Italian. In these circumstances, it is hardly surprising that in the passage to a post-industrial society the latter should come to the fore (in the revival of regional movements) always mediated by a transnational media mass culture: industrialism and working-class solidarity in the industrial triangle; localism and a certain familism in the Third Italy; clientelism and organized crime in the South.

The social impact of '68

The students' revolt which shook the western world in the late 1960s had its counterpart in Italy. Indeed, in Italy it gave rise to a series of social movements (students, workers, women, youth, etc.) and a level of collective action and conflicts ('Hot Autumn' of 1969, revolt of

1977) not matched elsewhere. Moreover, it lasted longer (for a decade whereas the French May 1968 was over in three months) and was more extensive (it spread to all areas of Italian society). Certainly, it can be seen as a watershed between industrial and post-industrial societies, if only because the consequences (e.g. the rise in labour costs and workers' control of shop floor in big factories) had a profound effect on the Italian economy (productive decentralization, industrial restructuring, etc.) and politics (crises and terrorism). Furthermore, despite an ideology which was iconoclastically anti-modernist (anti-capitalist and third world), one of its lasting legacies was paradoxically a consolidation of modernist values (individuality and personal needs) and the growth of civil society (role of social movements). This assessment is confirmed by the effect of parallel movements in other western countries since it was as much a western as a purely Italian event. For example, the students' movement can be seen as a continuation and radicalization of the 'beat–hippie' movement of the early 1960s. For, as Umberto Eco remarked in the 1980s: 'Even though all visible traces of 1968 are gone, it has profoundly changed the way all of us, at least in Europe, behave and relate to one another. Relations between bosses and workers, teachers and students, even parents and children have opened up. They'll never be the same again.' (Lumley 1990a, 2).

This is not the place to recount the events of the decade 1968–77 (Ginsborg 1990a; Lumley 1990a). However, some observations are in order. First, they illustrate a famous remark of Tocqueville: the student revolt arose not because of lack of reform, but as a consequence of an attempted reform, namely the raising of the compulsory school-leaving age to fourteen years in 1962 and the abolishing of university entrance exams. This opened up new possibilities for thousands of middle- and working-class children. Unfortunately, it coincided with the disappearance of every rational and controllable connection between developments in the economy, labour market, and educational system (Rusconi and Scamuzzi 1981, 103). Hence, the student revolt rejected the educational system and its inadequacies not in itself, but as geared to the needs of the economy which explains much of its radicalism.

Secondly, the movement was ambiguous and contradictory, radical, iconoclastic and impatient in its critique of authority and behaviour—summed up in its most famous slogan 'Che cosa vogliamo? Tutto. Quando? Subito' (What do we want? Everything. When do we want it? Now)—yet at the same time promoting open discussion and experimenting with new social practices (direct action—sit-ins, squats, and civil disobedience, as well as rent strikes and house occupations). It is claimed that its maximalism and impatience—the belief that the revolution was imminent—were responsible for its relative political failure: the movements were unwilling to work with the traditional institutions for reasonable, attainable goals (not that some reforms like the Workers' Charter of 1971, the Abortion Law and Sexual Discrimination Act, and reduction of voting age to 18 years were not achieved). The participants believed that the destruction of the 'old' existing order would automatically bring forth the 'new' society. Ironically, despite their critique of the historical left parties, the new political groups tended to be sectarian and organized themselves in Leninist forms. Moreover, the maximalism and impatience had a regressive element: 'red' terrorism. In fact, the willingness of many groups to countenance 'revolutionary violence' led some to terrorism. If the revolution was just round the corner but was momentarily delayed, one supreme 'voluntarist' act would bring it about. As Lumley (1990a, 279) remarks of the Red Brigades (BR), it was their 'very radicalness which made them regressive.'

If the new relations of which Eco writes were the main long-term contribution of '68 to European society, its social impact in Italy was to be found in the actions of myriads of groups that made up the great social movements (students, feminists, gays, youths, etc.) that flourished in its wake. Lumley (1990b, 119) states that the social movements' lasting impact lay in their championing and exploring an 'anthropological' concept of culture, which involved the 'acquisition of consciousness and self-consciousness and experience of everyday life'. He further adds, 'the 1970s represent a crucial period ... since traditions were challenged by showing that they were not absolute; they were rather shown to be the products of a particular society at a particular period in time and to have no special claim to superiority.'

What happened was that the people who did not identify with the existing organizations (students, women, homosexuals, etc.) created new meeting places, networks, and media outlets (free radios, magazines, etc.) through which they invented new identities (feminism, gay, environmentalism, etc.) and experienced new ways of living (communes). Although the numbers involved were relatively small and generally middle-class, their activities experimented with and promoted new values, attitudes, and behaviour that were to have an influence out of all proportion to their numbers because the movements not only practised new ways but also spread them. In this situation, it is easy to understand Lumley's (1992*b*, 121) conclusion that the movements were one of the most important agents of cultural change in post-'68 Italy since they generated innovation and undermined the authority of institutions: 'given the failures of the political institutions to bring about reforms in an orderly fashion, it was often the movements that provoked conflicts which opened the door to change'. We can add that Lepore (1995, 242) concurs that the socio-anthropologic dimension of '68 was more important than the political ('the '68 movements' political legacy was practically nil'). The most long-lasting effects were in the sphere of sexual mores which he sees as a reaction to Catholic and Communist morals. However, he disagrees with Lumley in his overall assessment, judging that the cultural changes were already under way. Hence, ''68 reinforced and accelerated, generalising them, processes that at a micro-level were underway for sometime'.

As already noted, one of the aspects of '68 was red terrorism, but it was not the only form: there was also 'black' (i.e. fascist) terrorism. Indeed, the starting point of post-war terrorism was the bomb massacre in a Milan bank in December 1969 which was perpetrated by neo-fascists, despite the original police arrest of anarchists; this caused considerable public confusion and suspicion of the authorities. Whereas red terrorism was undertaken with the aim of activating the revolutionary potential of the working class betrayed by the PCI, black terrorism, which could count on the protection and connivance of the State authorities, was intended to block the leftward shift of the social and political balance of society promoted by the Hot Autumn, through a 'strategy of tension'. It was an attempt to convince public opinion that the victory of the left would lead to chaos and therefore was intended to provoke a demand for a 'return to law and order' (Rusconi and Scamuzzi 1981, 112). Fortunately, public opinion was not provoked.

The red terrorism was aimed at mobilizing the working class for revolution by striking at the heart of the so-called 'imperialist capitalist state' by kidnapping and assassinating state personnel (judges, policemen, public sector managers, party officials) of which the most spectacular was the kidnapping and murder of former DC Prime Minister, Aldo Moro, in spring 1978. However, what the red terrorists seem to have overlooked was that by going underground, far from promoting the construction of a mass movement by changing popular consciousness, they cut themselves off both from the people and from the real world. In fact, although led by a small nucleus of middle-class activists (of left party or extra-parliamentary origins), red terrorism had its social roots in the marginal and youth strata of the large city suburbs (Rome, Milan, Genoa, Turin, and Naples). As Rusconi and Scamuzzi (1981, 113) comment: 'The link with common criminals as well as socially marginalised milieu seems [to have been] an essential element in the planning and execution of terrorist acts' (the Cirillo affair in Naples in 1981 was exemplary in this respect). There is little doubt terrorism reaped a tragic harvest (the terrorist murder rate ran at about fifty per year in the late 1970s) and was one of the elements of the *riflusso* (decline) with the youth revolt (Movement of '77) of the collective movements post-'68. Ginsborg (1990*a*, 362) even suggests that the red terrorists 'were also to contribute greatly to the destruction of the whole movement for change in Italian society'. Thanks to an efficient anti-terrorist campaign led by General Dalla Chiesa and a law which promised *pentiti* (persons who turned state's evidence) reduced prison sentences for collaboration with the state authorities, the terrorists became increasingly isolated, and the BR columns were dismantled one by one and the terrorist threat overcome in the early 1980s.

The women's movement

We have already noted that some observers consider changes in the sphere of sexual morals the most lasting legacy of '68; on the other hand, others suggest that the prime legacy, the Women's Movement, was the most influential agent of the cultural revolution (Lumley 1990a, 333). In any event, to assess the impact of feminism requires a brief look at the position of Italian women in the post-war period and this means discussion of the family, considered by many

(Ginsborg 1990a, 1998; Martinelli 1998) the most important social unit in Italy and the epicentre of social relations and daily life.

Although family structures were extremely varied in different parts of the country in the 1950s (nuclear family with strong kinship and neighbourhood ties in the industrial triangle; large extended families in the sharecropping zones of the Third Italy; isolated nuclear families in the rural South, etc. (Ginsborg 1990b, 25–32)) and they carried out a myriad of functions—'major solidarity structure, a fundamental source of social identity, a mixture of welfare agency, job placement, consumption unit, and, at least in certain regions and for some social groups, a productive unit' (Martinelli 1998, 53)—the role of women was confined to the domestic sphere and largely subordinate. In this the influence of the Catholic Church and teaching was often paramount with its view of the family as the basic social unit and with complementary roles for husband (lord and master) and wife (maid and servant). Moreover, we should not forget the puritan morality of the PCI and its patriarchal, not to say machist attitude.

However, in the 1960s, the situation changed with the transformation of the economy. On the one hand, women's presence in the labour market became more subordinate—their exit to have children was interpreted as due to the new affluence, but it was discovered to be due more to an expulsion from the core to the marginal proletariat; that is, home work and casual employment. On the other, there was the growth of female education and the spread of a romantic sentimentalism which began to undermine the traditional conception of marriage. Hence, it is clear that a plurality of causes, which can be subsumed in the word modernity, had an interrelated and converging effect between them on the position of women. Several were of a socio-economic nature (advanced industrialization, urban civilization, increased participation in the labour market); others were of a cultural nature, but connected to the former (decline of traditional religious values, pluralism of ideas, assertion of individual autonomy) (Zanetta 1997, 10).

Certainly, the machist practices of the students' movement—in which, despite its anti-authoritarian stance, women students were assigned subordinate roles (the famous *angelo del ciclostile*: roneo angel)—and later of the unions (politics was considered quite simply a 'male activity'), directed feminist anger and criticism first against male students and then against men in general. The practices of the students' movement demonstrated the limits of the revolution. Since the Left's emancipation approach simply inserted women into male-dominated structures and ignored the inequalities resulting from the sexual division of labour both at work and in the home, it was obviously vital for Italian feminist groups to distance themselves from this tradition. For this, they looked to the American women's movement with its focus on separation and consciousness raising for inspiration (i.e. 'liberation', not 'emancipation').

Hence, it is important to stress that the form of organization of the women's movement was completely different from that of other '68 collective movements which tended in the course of the years to adopt authoritarian neo-Leninist models. The women's movement—the last in time of the 1970s great social movements—started from the American notion that 'the personal is political' and refused all forms of formal organization. On the contrary, it was formed of complex webs of small consciousness-raising groups where mainly middle-class women discussed their problems and experimented with new forms of sociability without men. The emphasis was on the personal, the subjective, the private: women discovering themselves and so control over their own bodies and lives. Hence, the slogan 'l'utero è mio e lo gestisco io' (the womb is mine and I will look after it) leading to demands for free contraception and abortion; and implicitly, a critique of the family and women's traditional role. From here the movement progressed to demands for the elimination of gender discrimination in the social (schools, etc.), economic (labour markets and work), and legal (family code) fields.

It is generally agreed that the struggle to reform the abortion laws as a 'women's right to choose' issue transformed the feminist groups into a mass movement by furnishing a unifying platform. The crucial years were the mid-1970s when the movement combined mass women-only demonstrations (1975–6), with civil disobedience and the collection of signatures for a referendum. The immediate political result was the Abortion Act which eventually appeared in 1978, but which was judged to be not wholly satisfactory by feminists because of the limitations on the women's right to choose. The longer term effect was to establish the movement as a national force with a 'dense network of collectives, *ad hoc* bodies and friendships' (Lumley 1990*a*, 324) whose important impact was social rather than political. Moreover, attempts, not always successful, were made to find alternatives to the nuclear family and to replace family life with communal living. The social dimension was significant because when the other collective movements declined after 1978 (*il riflusso*), the women's movement not only survived but successfully changed its form. It became:

an 'area' with its latent submerged structures. Internal networks replaced national [i.e. centralized] organizations [. . .] incompatible with the local realities of the movement. New professions emerged, especially in the service sector connected with health and the media. Feminists began to supply goods and services for the market they had helped to create. Above all, energies were channelled into professional activities and pragmatically making such changes rather than mobilising around demands for changes in state provision and legislation. Otherwise activists tended to take their feminist politics into other movements which developed in 1980s such as ecology and peace movements. (Lumley 1990a, 333)

In these circumstances, it is hardly surprising that the general assessment of the impact of the women's movement was essentially cultural; in narrow political terms it was a failure. Lumley (1990*a*) claims that it was the most influential cultural agent of the cultural revolution that occurred in Italy in the 1970s because it created a new awareness of the dimension of sexual inequalities. However, there is an opposing line of argument that asserts that the crucial date in changes in the family, and hence the position of women, was 1965, not 1968 (Barbagli 1990). It is an argument similar to Lepore's referred to above, namely that the social movements (including the women's movement) merely accelerated changes that were already under way as a result of the modernization set in motion by socio-economic changes of the late 1950s and 1960s.

None the less, given the severity of the conflict with the deeply entrenched and institutionalized Catholic culture (despite John XXIII's papacy and Vatican II), it is by no means certain that, without the great collective movements (and the women's movement in particular) the new secular, progressive, and libertarian attitudes to gender relations would have spread so fast. Indeed, there is a suggestion that it was precisely because of the radical nature of the conflict that the newer culture was forged, based on a less inhibited conception of sexuality, greater freedom for women, and less authoritarian family relations (Fiumano in Ginsborg 1994, 296). If this were in fact so, we would have expected a steady defection in the women's vote (which represented over 60 per cent of the DC electorate in the 1950s and 1960s) from the Catholic Party in the 1980s. Though the DC lost votes throughout this decade, it is by no means clear that it was a feminist phenomenon. Indeed, it appears that 55 per cent of the electorate of its successor in 1994 (Forza Italia) were women (33 per cent housewives) (Diamanti in Ginsborg 1994, 665). Hence, we may harbour doubts about the social penetration of this feminist-inspired new culture.

One way of verifying the practical impact of the women's movement is to look at the changes in the Italian family in the wake of the country's post-'68 transformation. What we find on examining the trends is a pattern similar to that of northern Europe, only much less pronounced, except for a dramatic drop in the birth-rate (particularly in the north and centre, less in the South), which is currently the lowest in western Europe (1.3 children per woman). The trends are: smaller families (from an average of 3.6 persons in 1961 to 2.8 in 1991); less and later marriages; so more unmarried couples living together; a modest rise in separations and divorce and so remarriages; and finally a modest rise in children born out of wedlock. Moreover, the same regional differences in types of family persist, but much less pronounced, with a convergence to the smaller nuclear family. Recent social surveys suggest that the two-parent, two-child nuclear family is the model which the majority of Italians prefer (Zanetta, 1997, 18).

In any event, the most significant of the changes was undoubtedly the decline in the birth-rate and here changes in women's attitudes was certainly one of the factors. Increased education and prolonged 'adulthood' meant that women often delayed having children until it was too late (the average age of mothers for the first child rose from 25 to 29 years between 1972 and 1990). Maternity was no longer essential for their fulfilment as women; it had to compete with other desires (professional aspirations for the more educated) and constraints (two jobs: home and work). Moreover, children now demanded economic sacrifices because they were expensive as they remained economically dependent longer than in other European countries.

In this connection, we make two comments. First, the lack of effective public facilities—for example, the failure of the family centres (*consultori familiari*) to become effective support centres. Hence, families were forced to rely on their own resources, making use of strong parental ties (Table 1.3): young working mothers depended on

TABLE 1.3 Closeness of family ties in Italy and the UK, late 1980s (%)

	Italy	UK
Adult children living with parents		
sons	60	32
daughters	58	29
Adult children living within 15 minutes of parents	57	32
Adult children who see parents daily	32	11

Source: Ginsborg 1994, 82.

grandparents and relations to care for children. Secondly, a character-istic of the so-called Mediterranean family, what has been called long adolescence or delayed adulthood, means that most young people of both sexes lived at home into their thirties. The reasons would seem as much economic as emotional given the length of studies in Italy, late entry into the labour market, cost of living, and widespread youth unemployment, particularly in the South. Nevertheless, it pre-supposed at the same time a change in intra-family relations in which the young won an autonomy unknown to earlier generations. Cavalli (1996, 38) claims that a significant factor in the change was the child-ren's greater education, which allowed them to negotiate their own space and autonomy with their parents.

The suggestion is that if the nature of the family has changed considerably, its essence as an economic unit has remained—and in moments of recession has been reinforced—while the practical con-dition of women within it has changed less significantly. The concept of equality of husbands' and wives' roles was more honoured in the breach. Wives, working or not, were still responsible for domestic roles which included not only home and child care but also assistance and support for elderly and infirm relations. Indeed, given the lack of public assistance, the low birth-rate and consequent ageing popula-tion, the burden falling on Italian women is set to increase hugely if the current pattern of family care for the elderly persists.

If attachment to the family was one of the traditional character-istics of Italians of all regions because of the security it brought, above all in times of need, it would not appear to have allowed women to enjoy fully the opportunities that the development of industrial society created and to which the women's movement aspired (Ginsborg 1998, 203). This was partly due to the survival among men of their traditional attitude towards women: domesticity and sacrifice; and partly to the desire, in the case of the affluent, and the need, in the case of the deprived, to utilize all resources to prosper or survive respectively. Individual family strategies persisted in the 1990s with the emphasis on their own well-being as they had done in the 1950s amid rapidly changing social conditions. Norberto Bobbio commented recently: 'Commitment, energy, and courage are squandered on the family and little is left for society and the state' (quoted in Ginsborg 1994, 81).

From Southern question to Northern question

Territorial duality has been a characteristic of Italian society since unification. Indeed, despite regional differences, the distinction between a more economically developed North and a more backward South has been fundamental to Italian politics, such that from its discovery in the 1880s, the Southern question (*Questione meridionale*) has been part of the political agenda ever since. However, if a conspicuous gap between North and South still exists today on all recognized socio-economic indicators, it is no longer that which existed at the end of the war when the contrast was between a modernizing industrial and agricultural North and a poverty-stricken and agrarian South whose big cities (Naples and Palermo particularly) were overrun by a teeming urban pleb.

The profound, even dramatic, changes that have occurred in the South in the last five decades resulted from its participation in the country's socio-economic development (e.g. the great migration, economic miracle, consumer revolution, etc.) on the one hand, and the so-called Southern policy of the 1950s (land reform, 'special' public intervention to promote a process of self-generating economic growth, Southern Development Fund), on the other. However, the outcome was paradoxical: what has been called 'modernization without development' (that is, consumption levels of a developed country but the industrial base and civic conditions of an underdeveloped country: Sales 1993, 45) based on a so-called administrative economy. Moreover, this kind of development has ended by provoking the hostility of the north (Northern Leagues).

To understand how this situation came about, we need to note that the various phases of the special public intervention were compatible with Northern economic development. Thus, the first phase of partial land reform and infrastructure had the twin effects of stabilizing revolt in the southern countryside in terms of political support for the government parties (DC, PLI) without tying the peasants to the land as well as not creating southern industrial competition for Northern firms. In addition, southern migrants ensured an abundant supply of low-cost labour. Public infrastructure projects also benefited the North in the form of demand for its industrial products.

Moreover, in the later 1950s with the miracle under way and migration threatening to drain the south, northern industry consented to support the second phase of southern policy: stimulating industrialization by more direct methods (financial incentives). However, the initial investment was state-controlled and capital-intensive: heavy industry (steel and petrochemicals) which ill-fitted the modernization of local industry. Unfortunately, political or rather electoral considerations determined locations, which led to dispersion of plants (*cattedrale nel deserto*), vulnerable to rapid economic change. It was only at the end 1960s that Northern industry decided on labour-intensive investment in consumer products (Fiat, Alfa Sud). Hence, in 1970 the economic gap between North and South began to close and it could be thought that the special public intervention promoted by the Southern Development Fund was bearing fruit.

Unfortunately, the economic crises of the 1970s, and specifically the first energy crisis of 1974–5, were to sound its death knell. National economic policy took no account of the needs of nascent Southern industrialization: as a result of a compromise between the government and Northern industry, resources were made available to restructure Northern industry to secure competitivity. Industrial investment in the South was abandoned and was replaced by family income support and public works which provided Northern industry with an expanded outlet market in the South without competition. This change in Southern policy, which ensured that the income gap did not widen, even if the industrial gap did was, according to Sales (1993) very important because it led to the creation of the so-called administrative economy. Since the State Treasury was the only source of finance, access to its distribution gave control, hence power.

In this connection, two observations come to mind: first, the expansion of the market through state transfers meant a sharp rise in public expenditure which could be financed while the economy prospered but was vulnerable to a sharp recession; secondly, the 1970s saw a number of reforms introduced, specifically the decentralization of powers and competences, to local authorities (regions, provinces, communes). The latter became important; indeed it was to form the basis of the administrative economy. Sales (1993, 59) argues that the combination of public expenditure as the only economic resource, and its control by politicians, led to the formation of a 'new class' in the South comparable to that of Djilas in Eastern Europe. In a first phase, its role was one of mediation; that is, the patron–client ('clientelism') distribution of jobs, disability pensions, social security payments, buildings permits etc. But it rapidly became one of political entrepreneurship; that is, procuring profitable 'opportunities' through or by emergencies, special legislation, etc. for 'protected' companies (public works, privatization of public services like waste disposal (Ciancullo and Fontana 1995), and the new professions (planners, consultants, etc).

During the second phase (i.e. in the 1980s) the Southern question became increasingly identified with the 'criminal question' and organized crime (Mafia, Camorra, 'ndrangheta). The public authorities' traditional tolerance of all forms of illegality in the big Southern cities (because of the urban pleb's dire need to survive without any apparent resources) turned itself into something very different: the traditional uneasy relationship between politicians and organized crime (votes for protection) expanded into a joint politico-criminal control of the administrative economy. Sales (1993, 87) observed,

In a society with a weak industrial base, in an economy almost exclusively dominated by politics, when the flow of funds to support consumption is the only form of public intervention, organized crime becomes one of the instruments of regulation and distribution [. . .] A non-productive economy and political control of the economy (through party domination of State institutions) are the very factors that favour the entrepreneurial and institutional expansion of criminal power [. . .] It was enough for the Mafia to control certain administrative and political positions to control a consist-ent part of the Southern economy.

In these circumstances, the Italian state was unable to defeat organ-ized crime precisely because the very persons involved in the system were its own representatives (local councillors and administrators).

At this point, we must return to the first observation because it is the basis of the so-called Northern question (*Questione setten-trionale*). The argument here is quite simply that the compatibility (Sales 1993, 71) of the relationship between the economies of north and south broke down in the 1980s. We noted the vulnerability of the policy of state transfers to recession and this duly arrived at the beginning of the 1990s. Northern industrial interests decided that the burden of the supporting the south had become too great, the more so since it no longer brought any benefit. They tended to the view that it was an unequal struggle: throwing good money after bad, if the Southern question had no solution.

However, the relations between north and south (generically speaking) had already worsened during the 1980s boom. As noted above, post-industrial development had led to the rise of new service professionals in the metropolitan areas (Milan, Turin, Genoa). They, together with the small businessmen of the north-east and centre, began to become frustrated and angry at government incompetence and the inefficiency and poor quality of public services (from which many had previously profited through tax evasion, ignoring labour regulations, etc.) in a situation in which world markets were now more important than those in the south. There was a general feeling that the state itself was the real obstacle to continued Northern growth as government policies were believed to favour the south. This was galling to an area that was used to dominating Italian politics.

The feeling was reinforced by a number of factors: first, the gov-ernment was increasingly southern in composition as was the government parties' support during the 1980s; secondly, and more importantly, the resources being channelled to the south as part of the 'special' public intervention—50 thousand billion lire (£20 billion) for the 1980 Irpinia earthquake alone—far from promot-ing self-generating growth did not prevent unemployment from almost doubling in the mid-1980s (Reyneri (1997, 69)). Worse, they stimulated the appetite and the resurgent violence of organized crime in its various regional articulations. The idea spread that the national state (by now identified with the South) was dissipating the taxes of hard-working northerners.

The 'Northern Question', as it was becoming known, was then the sum of hostility and unease of vast strata of Northerners to what they saw as the inability of the state to guarantee identity, support growth, and secure social regulation at a time when the economy and society were growing more dependent on it. Indeed, the state was increasingly viewed as a shackle on the North in contrast to its decisively supportive role in the South (Diamanti 1996, 60).

Events from the late 1980s brought matters to a head. First, regional leagues started mobilizing discontent on the basis of a residual anti-Southernism ('Come on Etna, do your duty!'); later they identified state inefficiency with the South (*Roma ladrona*: Rome thief): the contrast was between the hard-working, productive North and the lazy, parasitic South. Secondly, the fall of the Berlin Wall meant that a major reason for supporting the DC and minor government parties—anti-communism—lost its justification. Thirdly, the single European market, due in 1992, drew attention to the burgeoning public debt. In the 1980s, the public expenditure deficit was running at 10 per cent of GDP and the public debt consequently doubled in the decade from 60 per cent to 120 per cent in 1992. Northern industrialists suddenly awoke to the fact that Italy might be excluded from Europe on economic grounds.

This was brought home to public opinion by the Maastricht Treaty convergence criteria for the single currency; they meant not only that Italy could no longer resolve its competitivity problems by devaluation, but also that it had to put its public finances in order. Increased taxation was the only answer; it was to hit the Italian productive strata very hard in the 1990s recession. Indeed, the Amato government introduced one of the most substantial austerity packages in Italian history in 1992. The result: on the one hand widespread support in the North (almost 20 per cent) for an explicitly anti-southern party (Northern League); on the other, the termination of the special public intervention in the South.

Conclusion

The preceding pages have discussed the transformation of Italian society following the European pattern of modernization, from an industrializing society in the 1940s to a modern post-industrial society, despite important regional disparities in the 1990s. Implicit in this discussion, although not always apparent, was the contrast between a dynamic society and a static polity, between private initiative and resilience, and public incompetence and inflexibility.

The question posed, as the so-called transition to a Second Republic falters inconclusively, is how long can politics be left behind? The adequacy of the polity is all the more pressing on the threshold of the new millennium, now that the great narratives of progress, emancipation, and liberation that sustained the development and modernization of European (and so Italian) society over the last two centuries have dissolved.

2

Evolution of the economy

Vera Zamagni

Introduction

Italy ended the Second World War with modest overall losses in its industrial capacity, which actually resulted in a greatly enlarged engineering sector. This was the sector destined to become the cutting-edge of the great industrial expansion in the following half century. What Italy really needed, however, was a reorganization of political life after dictatorship that would enable it to take part in the 'golden age' that the *pax americana* was about to bring to the western world. Although far from easy, this turned out to be possible in the end, because of the pro-Western European option that prevailed. It launched the Italian economy first into the Marshall Plan and then into the 'economic miracle' and the European integration movement. The result of this process was to place Italy firmly in the restricted club of the most advanced nations in the world.

The present chapter will first retrace this spectacular catch-up, sketching its most important episodes; then it will offer some reflections on its peculiarities, grouped under three main headings: the special industrial setting of successful small enterprises; the effects of state behaviour which was intrusive but not domineering; and the belated but irreversible rise of a more assertive civil society, that brings back the timeworn and deeply rooted Italian civic traditions. These three features of the Italian economy have been selected in order to answer the question which has been often voiced outside Italy and sometimes even inside: why has the Italian economy been so successful following a path that is so different from the paradigm established by the USA?

A success story between ups and downs

It is not as simple as it might seem to give an overall evaluation of the expansion of the Italian economy in the last fifty years in terms of per capita GNP and related indicators. The reasons for this stem, on the one hand, from a rather shaky statistical starting base and, on the other hand, from the number of revisions of GNP levels done by the statistics institute Istat in the 1970s and 1980s. The former problem is due to the difficulties of reorganizing the statistical offices after the war, that produced multiple estimates of national income aggregates for the years up to the early 1950s (Zamagni 1986). The later Istat revisions are instead due to Italy's peculiarly fragmented enterprise system (which will be discussed below), which was severely under-valued by the earlier official Istat estimates, based as they were for a long time on samples which did not include enterprises with fewer than twenty employees, precisely the ones showing the most dynamic growth.

It is this lack of a firm statistical basis, not entirely overcome even today,[1] that has long prevented the realization that Italy has been second only to Japan in terms of income growth among today's most advanced large economies over the entire period under consider-ation, as Table 2.1 shows. If it is true that the rate of growth of Italian national income has been very rapid, Italy was by no means a peasant society even at the beginning of the period under consideration. As I have had the opportunity to explain in a recent essay (Zamagni 1998), Italy lost the Second World War because the Italian economy was unsuited for the massive scale of production needed to fight it, and was lacking the raw materials and oil necessary fully to use the cap-acity and the armaments in existence. Moreover, the commitment to

---

[1] At the Historical Research Office of the Bank of Italy a group is presently at work, of which the author of this chapter is part, thoroughly revising the estimate for 1951, as well as 1938 and 1891, which, with the 1911 estimate already published, will be the four benchmark years at the basis of a new estimate of the time series of Italian GNP 1890–2000.

TABLE 2.1 Levels and growth rates of real per capita GDP in G7 countries, 1950–1996

	1950–73	1973–96	Levels 1996 (ppp)[a]
USA	2.4	1.5	100
Japan	8.0	2.5	83
Canada	2.9	2.5	92
UK	2.4	1.6	73
France	4.0	1.5	77
Germany	5.0	1.2	73[b]
Italy	5.0	2.1	73[c]

a USA = 100; ppp – purchasing power parity expressed in US$.
b including East.
c the Italian level has been taken from Eurostat, because Maddison's lower estimate (based on Maddison 1991) is a personal view of the author, not shared by official statistical offices.

Source: Maddison, 1997.

the war by people, enterprises, and even the military personnel was low so that the actual mobilization of the economy for war was very limited, the lowest among all the belligerents. The Italian defeat must not, therefore, be interpreted as the result of a very backward economy, just as the Soviet victory must not be interpreted as the result of a more advanced one. The Soviet Union was an immense country, ready to let 9 million soldiers and 26 million civilians die (as against fewer than half a million in Italy, overall) and on top of this the USSR received substantial aid from the Americans in the years 1943–5.

Italian industrialization had started in the north-west of the country (the well-known 'industrial triangle') at the end of the nineteenth century and had proceeded unabated since then. This is well established (Zamagni 1993). More recent research has shown that other areas of the north-east-centre (NEC) had given birth to small but often quite specialized enterprises already in the 1920s and even in the 1930s. The context, national and international, of the period was, however, not favourable to great leaps forward, because of crises and slow expansion of private consumption. But those firms accumulated technical know-how and market presence that would be of use later.

Some of the small firms expanded temporarily during the Second World War, training workers who were then laid off at the end of the war with enough skills to start their own business. If it is true that in

1951 a considerable amount of the Italian workforce was still working in agriculture (37.1 per cent, see Table 2.2), it was only the south of the country which could be considered a peasant society. Elsewhere there was enough entrepreneurial talents and organizational capabilities to meet the new challenges that emerged during reconstruction (Rossi and Toniolo 1996).

Reconstruction (1946–1952)

The options that were embraced by the country during reconstruction were strategic and formed the solid stepping stone on which the subsequent expansion could be based. There were four: (1) a modernizing-industrializing approach that left little room for investment in agriculture and concentrated on industry and infrastructure; (2) a western, pro-European approach, that pushed Italy to be present in every negotiation leading to every new institution in Europe, rooting the country deeply in the integration process that proved highly successful; (3) a selective adoption of American technology and managerial values; (4) a surprising continuity in the institutional setting and economic leadership.

To give more detail on the four above-mentioned aspects, let me start with the industrial push. The four-year long-term plan prepared for the European Recovery Program (ERP) envisaged a modest increase in farm output (15 per cent), but a 40 per cent increase in industrial output (that had already recovered its pre-war level in 1948) over the span of the four years of the plan. The actual results were even more clear-cut: the increase in agricultural output reached only 5 percent, while industrial output grew by 49 per cent. As much as 60 per cent of the ERP counterpart funds were used for industry

TABLE 2.2 Distribution of the workforce, 1911–1990

	Agriculture	Industry	Services	Public administration	Total
1911	57.6	27.7	9.8	4.9	100
1951	37.1	30.6	22.9	9.4	100
1971	18.9	38.1	28.5	14.5	100
1990	9.5	29.8	42.6	18.1	100

Source: Rossi, Sorgato, and Toniolo, 1993, table 6.

and infrastructures, while agriculture only received 29 per cent. Heavy industry was favoured against light industry, with engineering, metallurgy, energy (electricity/oil) and chemicals absorbing the lion's share of the funds. To the industrialists and the policy makers of the time the long-term vision of an Italy having to follow the American path of development into mass production was not absent. The limits came from the previous artisanal tradition of the country and the incredibly restricted domestic consumption markets. One has to keep in mind that, for reasons connected to the generally poor agriculture (with the exception of the Po valley) and the two world wars, the Italian population had increased its levels of private per capita consumption over the whole period from unification (1861) to the beginning of the 1950s by only one-third. But it was clear to many (though not to all) industrial and political leaders of the reconstruction years that things were going to change and they tried to prepare conditions adequate to the change in this new international and national context.

As for the international place of the country, in spite of the presence of a strong left, there was little discussion about the option of remaining in the capitalist world, an option which was made irreversible by the results of the 18 April 1948 elections. What, instead, is of more interest is the active pro-European stance taken by the Italian government that brought Italy into the first customs union negotiations (Fritalux–Finibel, see Fauri 1995) and then into the European Coal and Steel Community (ECSC), much to the surprise of many, because Italy was very distant from the Ruhr and had always had a very marginal metal industry. The way Italian diplomacy handled the ECSC has been studied at length and its success in inserting Italy in the first European agreement that bound six countries to give up some sovereignty to a common supranational institution is undisputed. This was for Italy the beginning of a process that turned the country into a major producer of steel, second only to Germany, in spite of the major problems caused by the inability to control the efficiency of the gigantic steel plants built by the public holding company. These brought about the privatization of the entire sector after disastrous losses. The ECSC was also the first stage of Italy's active role in the process of European integration, which kept the country firmly rooted in a project of modernization, in spite of domestic political developments which might otherwise have slowed down if not temporarily reversed the economic transformation of the country.

Coming to the interesting topic of 'Americanization' (Zamagni 1992 and 1995), it is certainly no surprise that the Italian approach was selective, and we will see in the following sections of this chapter how selective it was, but it is important to note here that the fundamental message of the American way of doing business—to increase supply for a market that would certainly grow or would be 'forced' to grow with appropriate marketing techniques—was caught and many industrialists started equipping themselves for this prospective mass market. The case of Fiat is well known (Fauri 1996), as well as those of the electricity firms (which before nationalization enlarged capacity in thermoelectricity, with American technology) and of the oil refineries and new petrochemicals plants. The public steel holding company Finsider, after being accepted into the ECSC, made a technological agreement with the American corporation ARAMCO to design the new integrated steel mills. But smaller firms too in many other sectors and especially in engineering studied American production rationalization, managerial organization, and industrial relations methods.

Finally, an element that strongly supported the Italian drive during reconstruction and the economic miracle was the availability of economic leaders trained during fascism who were placed in key economic positions. In fact, among the major players of Italy's economic recovery, only Luigi Einaudi had been one of the leading Italian economists before fascism.[2] All others were people who had gained their experience during the fascist years, often in key operative positions. Among the many, one might mention Menichella,[3] Mattioli,[4]

[2] Luigi Einaudi became Governor of the Bank of Italy in 1945–46, Minister of the Budget in 1947 with De Gasperi's first government without the left, President of the Republic 1948–55. He was responsible for the successful stabilization of the lira in the summer of 1947 in connection with entry in the IMF and the preparation of the Marshall Plan.

[3] Donato Menichella started his career at the Bank of Italy in 1921; later he collaborated on the creation of IRI in 1933, of which he became director general; he was governor of the Bank of Italy 1948–60.

[4] Raffaele Mattioli started as a professor of economics at the Bocconi University; in 1925 he was appointed to Comit, which he helped to overcome the effects of the 1929 crisis, becoming managing director after Toeplitz, a position which he held uninterruptedly up to 1960.

Sinigaglia,[5] Saraceno,[6] Giordani, Osio, Cenzato, Reiss Romoli, Adriano Olivetti, Valletta.[7] This continuity of the economic leadership was favoured by the mild political attitude towards the purge of fascist collaborators and by the continuity of institutions. Not only did the Bank of Italy and the major Italian corporations not undergo major changes, but the public corporations which had been founded under the fascist regime remained in place and even grew more important. One example is IRI (*Istituto per la ricostruzione industriale*, born in 1933 as a result of a major bailing-out operation of the three largest universal banks Comit, Credit, and Banco di Roma), another is AGIP and then come the many public banks, like Banca Nazionale del Lavoro and IMI (*Istituto mobiliare italiano*, 1931). AGIP, founded in 1926, should have been liquidated under American pressure, but it was instead enlarged and built up by Enrico Mattei into a new public holding, ENI (*Ente nazionale idrocarburi*, 1953) which became a large oil and chemical company (in sixth position in the world today).

The already numerous public banks were increased in number with the foundation of Mediobanca in 1946 and of the Mediocrediti in the late 1940s to early 1950s (in the Italian banking sector public ownership reached about 80 per cent). Mediobanca especially became a strategic institution, because it placed itself at the centre of the financial businesses of the major Italian public and private corporations. It has been led for fifty years[8] by Enrico Cuccia,[9] who was the son-in-law of the most famous financial manager of the 1920s–1930s,

---

[5] Oscar Sinigaglia graduated in engineering and started as a steel entrepreneur at the beginning of the century. After selling his firm, he became a high-level steel manager and initially supported fascism, with which, however, he had a clash in 1935 over strategies for the steel sector. Emarginated by fascism, much to his regret, he was called back in 1945 to lead the steel holding of IRI Finsider and was a protagonist of the integrated steel mills plan and of the ECSC negotiations.

[6] Pasquale Saraceno, professor of business administration, worked first in Comit; he was later appointed to lead the research team of IRI in the 1930s; after the war, he was responsible for drawing up the Italian plans for ERP, he founded and led SVIMEZ, which was the think-tank producing plans for intervention into the South, and was active in many other research teams that drew out public projects, including the so-called Vanoni plan.

[7] Vittorio Valletta, a graduate of the High School of Commerce of Turin, was appointed in the 1920s general manager of Fiat by the founder, Giovanni Agnelli, whom he replaced after his death in 1946 as president of Fiat.

[8] Some still say it is led today, after Cuccia, in his nineties, has become honorary president!

[9] Enrico Cuccia started his career in Comit in 1938.

Alberto Beneduce, the inventor of the Italian public long- term financial institutions and the founder of IMI and IRI, of which he was president in the earlier years 1933–9. This continuity of economic leaders led to rapid operative planning and implementation of plans, although it might not have been so positive over the long run.

There are obviously other aspects of the period of reconstruction that would merit discussion, like the agrarian reform of 1949 and the foundation of a special government agency for development of the South—Casmez (*Cassa per il Mezzogiorno*)—but a short chapter cannot but be selective.

The economic miracle (1953–1963)

After the major strategic decisions taken during reconstruction, this is a period obsessed with enlarging capacity. There was a scramble to produce and to conquer foreign markets and the results are truly amazing: steel production trebled, automobiles increased ten times, oil refineries quadrupled their output, electricity doubled its output and many new products like refrigerators, typewriters, plastic materials, motorbikes (the Vespa) were a great success in the domestic market and abroad. It has been stressed many times that the cost of labour was comparatively low in Italy, as a result of wage compression during fascism and of the weakness of the trade unions in this period, and that this is an element in the success of the Italian economic miracle. While the fact is undeniable, it is hardly a peculiar feature of Italy at the time (it was in general a period of stability in the national and international economies), nor the really decisive factor. Italy was not a country, with a few exceptions, of large corporations, where cheap labour is a strategic asset. It was rather the widespread entrepreneurship, which strengthened or started anew small and medium-size entreprises, that must be considered decisive for the future development of the Italian economy. During this period, however, Americanization was the most pervasive slogan and the one that has attracted more attention by commentators. A small number of firms tried hard to become big by Fordist practices, introducing conveyor belts and complementing the limited supply of northern workers with a southern inflow. Internal migration from the South to the North, that had started already in the 1930s, became in the 1950s and 1960s very intense.

The distributive struggle (1964–1974)

The year 1963 marked the end of this initial 'miraculous' phase. It was the year of the first round of serious strikes and wage increases, of inflationary price rises and a loss of competitiveness of Italian exports, which had a negative, though temporary, repercussion on the balance of payments. For the time being, both the inflationary pressures and the international competitiveness were easily recovered, and the growth rate of the economy was only marginally curbed, but this was the first sign of the struggle over the distribution of the results of the economic miracle that would explode in the famous 'Hot Autumn' of 1969. Although the burst of worker and student discontent at the end of the 1960s was a European phenomenon, in Italy both the employers and the state were particularly unprepared to smooth the protest with the energy and the skill needed, while the Italian trade unions flirted for too long with the idea of being able to impose successfully whatever bargain they could reach, without any thought of compatibility with the existing state of the Italian economy. It must not be forgotten that the charismatic leader of the CGIL Luciano Lama went on speaking of the wage as an 'independent variable' for most of the 1970s. The concessions won by trade unions in this context were very substantial. A new workers' statute was passed in May 1970; the Italian social security system was largely improved, with a substantial increase in pensions and in health benefits, leading to the setting up of a comprehensive national health service in 1978. The fact is that the increase in public expenditure was not met by a corresponding increase in taxation, considered politically unfeasible, given the circumstances. A taxation reform was envisaged, but only enacted in 1974, producing the first results in 1976. It was this distributive struggle that marked the beginning on one side of state budget deficits and on the other side of inflation (see Table 2.3), two evils that were reinforced by the subsequent international period of turmoil connected with the oil crises and the demise of the fixed exchange rate regime.

How instability was faced (1975–1983)

If budget deficits and inflation were unleashed by the effects of the the 1969 'Hot Autumn', the point of no return of this use of expansionary monetary and fiscal policies to soften the domestic distributive struggle was determined by the great shock produced by the two oil crises, coupled with the opportunity to let the exchange rate go down, which was offered by the demise of the Bretton Woods fixed exchange rate regime. As can be seen in Table 2.3, inflation soared up to 1980, while budget deficits appeared first in 1971, then doubled in 1972, increasing slightly thereafter (with a peak in the dramatic year 1975), but accelerating after 1981 and producing a doubling of public debt from 33 per cent of GDP in the late 1960s to 69 per cent in 1983. The opposite trend after 1980 of declining inflation and rising budget deficits is due to an important event that had taken place in 1979, namely, the creation of the European Monetary System (EMS), which Italy wanted to enter, an event that persuaded the Italian political authorities to put a brake on inflation. At that point, the budget deficits and the wage increases could no longer be paid for almost entirely by printing money. The state had to borrow from the public, which reacted back on the budget deficit, further enlarging it through increased interest payments.

TABLE 2.3 Annual economic indicators, 1969–1983 (%)

	GDP growth	Cost of living growth	Exports growth	Unemployment rate	Current budget deficit on GDP
1969	6.0	2.1	11.9	5.2	0.1
1970	5.6	5.3	6.4	4.9	0.3
1971	1.8	5.0	7.0	4.9	−2.0
1972	2.8	5.7	14.0	6.3	−4.2
1973	6.9	10.8	2.0	6.2	−4.0
1974	5.2	18.7	7.3	5.3	−3.6
1975	−2.5	17.1	2.3	5.8	−7.1
1976	6.5	16.4	12.2	6.6	−5.0
1977	3.4	17.1	8.0	7.0	−3.9
1978	3.6	12.5	11.2	7.1	−5.8
1979	5.8	14.5	8.1	7.6	−5.0
1980	4.1	21.3	−8.5	7.5	−4.4
1981	0.6	17.9	4.3	7.8	−6.9
1982	0.2	16.3	0.4	8.4	−7.0
1983	1.0	14.8	3.5	8.8	−6.8

Source: Maddison, 1991 and Ministero del Tesoro, 1988.

This mechanism, that, in the presence of uncurbed current budget deficits,[10] disinflated the Italian economy at the cost of enlarging public debt, was institutionalized through the 'Treasury–Bank of Italy divorce'. This took the form of a bill passed in the summer of 1981, allowing the Bank of Italy to decide on the amount of government paper to be directly financed by money printing.[11]

The virulence of inflation was only partly due to government budget deficits; in large part it was the result of a wage–price accelerating spiral produced by the 1975 agreement between Confindustria (led by Gianni Agnelli) and trade unions on an upwards-sliding wage scale (the 'escalator') that automatically adjusted wages to price increases every three months.[12] This was perhaps the worst possible result of the wage-as-an-independent-variable theory and it was all the more foolish because it was reached in the worst crisis year of all the post-Second World War period. At the same time, the fact that it was precisely the most prominent of the Italian industrialists who negotiated such a disruptive measure goes a long way to explain what was the mood of the time.

In the midst of such high instability, the growth of the Italian national income became more volatile and decreased on average, but not as much as in most other developed countries. This was mostly due not to large industry, which suffered enormously and discharged a lot of labour, but to the resilience of the small and medium-size Italian firms, which had a leap forward and gained new export markets. The peculiarity of this Italian experience is so great that it is worth devoting the second section of this chapter to looking at it more closely.

The unbalanced recovery (1984–1992)

After the second oil crisis had left the international stage, the Italian economy staged a strong recovery. These were the years in which

[10] It must be kept in mind that the total deficit was larger, if we include that on capital account, and makes the initial figures before 1971 less positive.

[11] This was the first step in the autonomization of the Bank of Italy, that was completed only at the beginning of the 1990s, when the Bank of Italy was charged with fixing the discount rate autonomously.

[12] The escalator was abolished by government decree in 1984, as part of the measures to disinflate the Italian economy. This abolition was confirmed in 1985 in connection with a referendum that caused a memorable political and social battle, leading to a definitive curbing of the trade unions' power.

large Italian corporations regained a healthy performance, while the expansion of smaller firms continued unabated and exports grew at an average rate of 5 per cent per year. But the state finances continued to deteriorate. Successive governments were paralysed when faced with the need to put a break on public spending and debt mounted to 108 per cent of GDP in 1992. The reasons for this are entirely political (see Pasquino's Chapter 3 below), because from an economic point of view there was plenty of room in the expansionary years to redress public finances. Inflation too, which had gone down to 5–6 per cent, was still above the European average, and this caused much speculation against the lira in the summer of 1992, forcing Italy out of the EMS. This, together with the beginning of 'Clean Hands' in March of the same year and the signing of the Maastricht Treaty, marks the beginning of a great shake-up of Italian society and politics, which had a considerable impact on the economy as well.

Europe (1993–1998)

This latest period started with a year of economic crisis, shared by Italy with the continental European countries, but not with the Anglo-Saxon world (see Table 2.4), while the Japanese economy was stagnant. A very weak recovery followed, in spite of the boom in Italian exports due to the devaluation of the lira following the exit from the EMS in 1992. On average over these last years, the Italian performance was only better than the dramatically negative Japanese one, although the difference with the other continental European

TABLE 2.4 Annual GDP growth rates, 1993–1998 in the G7 countries

	1993	1994	1995	1996	1997	1998[a]	Average
USA	2.3	3.5	2.3	3.4	3.9	3.5	3.1
Japan	0.3	0.6	1.5	3.9	0.8	−2.5	0.7
Canada	2.5	3.9	2.2	1.2	3.7	2.3	2.6
UK	2.1	4.3	2.7	2.2	3.4	2.3	3.1
France	−1.3	2.8	2.1	1.6	2.3	3.1	1.7
Germany	−1.2	2.7	1.2	1.3	2.2	2.6	1.4
Italy	−1.2	2.2	2.9	0.7	1.5	1.4	1.3

[a] The 1998 figures are forecasts, with the exception of Italy.

Source: Banca d'Italia, Bollettino economico, Oct. 1998.

countries is marginal, while the success of the Anglo-Saxon countries is startling, given their previously unsatisfactory long-run perform-ance.[13] What are the reasons for this worsening of the relative position of Italy in the club of the most advanced countries? There is little doubt that the political turmoil of these years, coupled with the joint efforts to curb inflation and public deficit for the purpose of being admitted into the common European currency area on its inception in 1999 imposed, especially in the years 1996–8, strongly restrictive monetary and fiscal policies never experienced by the country in the whole period after the Second World War.

The planned targets were indeed reached: price rises came down to 1.7–1.8 per cent; budget deficits decreased from around 10 per cent of GDP to 6.7 in 1996, 2.7 in 1997 and 1998; interest rates realigned with those of the Euro countries and Italy went back into the EMS in November 1996. Italy therefore met the Maastricht criteria (with the exception of public debt, which is very slowly declining) and was admitted into the Euro group. Seen from this angle, the performance of the Italian economy over the last three years looks even too good. The severe treatment inflicted on it by the Prodi government to gain admission to the Euro could be considered highly successful simply because it has not produced major dislocation. Whether this explan-ation based on short-term considerations is sufficient to explain the Italian lag and whether there are not other structural shortcomings of the Italian economy that will continue to hamper a stronger recovery in the years ahead are, however, debatable questions that must be placed within the larger framework of the apparent lag of the continental European economy with regard to the Anglo-Saxon countries. It must be noticed too that this period has also seen Italy's belated joining in the European trend of privatization of public entreprises, something that had never taken off before, because of the opposition of the pre-Clean Hands ruling parties. Privatization is proving difficult in a country with a lack of tradition of public companies, but the presence of a number of authorities supervising various key sectors should encourage the enlargement of a healthy private sector.

---

[13] A comparison with Table 2.1 is instructive. It can be seen that over the entire period after 1973 to present, Japan and Italy have still a slightly better economic per-formance than the other five countries of the G7 (which have shown a realignment of their performance), but that the gap is going soon to disappear, if the recent trend lasts.

A 'niche' capitalism

Italy tried very hard in the 1950s and 1960s to adopt the American model of the corporation, but the success has been very limited. Only a few firms succeeded in not only getting bigger, but also in adopting the American methods of managerial organization adequate to their new size. The best examples are Fiat and ENI, the newly born (1953) Italian state oil company. In most cases, however, after expanding, the new corporations encountered difficult problems of wholly inadequate management, which they solved either by being bailed out by the state (which increased the number of public entreprises) or by foreign absorption. The most emblematic cases here are to be found in the chemical industry, where the Italian pioneer Montecatini (born in 1888) proved incapable of mastering the capacity enlargement it had projected, fell short of liquidity, and merged with Edison becoming Montedison, but in 1968 was in such dire straits that the state had to intervene. That intervention was unfortunately so ill-conceived, that in the end, after many unforeseen developments, Montedison ceased to be a chemical company and very little chemical activity was left in Italian hands.

Among the reasons considered responsible for the limited success of the American model of corporation in Italy, finance and trade union behaviour are the most convincing. To take finance first, the demise of the universal banking system that Alberto Beneduce wanted with the 1936 banking bill and its replacement with a system of public long-term banks did not prove entirely satisfactory. Only one of these public institutions—namely Mediobanca, led by Enrico Cuccia—proved willing and able to support large corporate finance, while the others were not dynamic partners in the relationship between banks and industry; at the same time, the stock exchange remained small and undeveloped and the commercial short term banks were fragmented and local. All this led to a supply of credit directed mainly to small and medium-size enterprises, which needed smaller amounts of capital and did not require high expertise in the banks' officials. In turn this worked against projects that needed large amounts of capital.

As for trade unions' behaviour, their high and persistent level of militancy in large corporations suggested to companies that they remain small and even decentralize. It is quite common in Italy to have entrepreneurs who own several small autonomous companies, easier to manage under many accounts (finance, taxation, industrial relations), rather than fusing them into a bigger one. But it is even more common for entrepreneurs to encourage some of their employees to set up their own autonomous companies whenever they need to have a spare part produced, rather than producing it themselves. The strong crafts tradition that the country carries from its past, together with the diffusion, especially in the North and Centre, of excellent technical and vocational schools, makes possible the widespread self-employment implied by the mechanism just explained. So it was that small companies remained alive during the decades of the 'Americanization' and were ready to become a possible alternative in due time.

Something had to happen on the technological side and on the side of markets to make small enterprises the winning card of the Italian economy. When the instability of the 1970s made markets volatile and unstandardized, they required flexibility and customization of production, while at the same time the electronics revolution became sufficiently widespread to allow the breakup of plants without loss in efficiency. The golden age of the Italian small company had come. Since then, the small and medium-size entreprises (SME) system has proliferated in Italy, as can be seen in Table 2.5, where the six major advanced countries are compared. It can be seen that today Germany, France, and the UK have a size structure of firms more similar to the USA, although they certainly have a much smaller number of colossal entreprises than the USA. Italy stands out as the country having a

TABLE 2.5 Share of the labour force in industry by size of firm in the early 1990s (%)

No. of employees	Italy[a]	Germany[b]	France[b]	UK[c]	USA[a]	Japan[a]
1–9	23.3	7.4	8.1	7.2	3.0	5.0
10–250	48.1	30.1	38.9	37.3	33.6	69.1
> 250	28.6	62.5	53.0	55.5	63.4	25.9
Overall	100.0	100.0	100.0	100.0	100.0	100.0

[a] 1991.   [b] 1992.   [c] 1993.

Source: Eurostat, Enterprises in Europe, Brussels, 1996.

disproportionate number of tiny enterprises of artisanal type (the first category 1–9), while it shares with Japan (unexpectedly!) a good stock of SME. If we carry out a detailed analysis of the Italian industrial censuses 1951–91, it is possible to see that the size of firms has *declined* over time in relative terms, more rapidly since the 1970s. In fact, in that span of time, firms with more than 499 employees have passed fom 25.1 per cent of employment to 13 per cent, in favour especially of firms with 10–19 employees (from 5.4 to 15.3 per cent of employment) and firms with 20–49 employees (from 8.7 to 16.3 per cent). If we add to this 'official' picture domestic work, which is quite widespread in Italy especially as a complementary activity, and the 'unofficial' small firms of the black economy, also quite widespread in Italy, we can readily conclude that the fragmentation of the workforce in Italy does not have a parallel in any advanced economy of the world. It is not uncommon to find among the Italian SME world leaders in some niche product, be it a bolt or a machine, tiles or spectacles frames, gears or bycicle saddles, sky boots or medical equipment, so that the most appropriate definition of the strength of Italian capitalism is that of *large-scale niche capitalism.*

The reasons that have led the SME to prosper guide us to the heart of the Italian economy. It is now widely known that the most important reason for the strength shown by SME is the formation of 'industrial districts'. Local systems of SME specialized in particular products or families of products, where a common 'industrial atmosphere' allows the spread of know-how and of innovation, the formation of a specialized workforce, the presence of all the needed services and complementary firms, and the use of subcontracting and domestic work. The district offers to national and international buyers the most diversified, complete supply of the various brands of a specific product. A widespread sense of community based on family and neighbourhood ties provides enough *trust* to keep costs of transaction low, in spite of the fragmentation of firms.[14] Coordination is mostly informal, through personal relations, although recently some industrial districts have developed more formal coordination. It is not so easy to capture statistically the extent of the diffusion of the

---

[14] Fragmented firms need to resort to the 'market' for acquisition of factors of production to a much larger extent than integrated firms that produce many needed inputs internally. They are therefore much more sensitive to transaction costs.

industrial districts, because it is not possible to define an industrial district unequivocally. A complicated procedure (Sforzi 1990) has been invented to identify in Istat's censuses local systems of SME with a strong predominance of employment in one specific industrial branch.[15] According to this procedure, in 1991 there were 199 such districts with 2.2 million people employed, equal to 42.5 per cent of total manufacturing employment. Using a slightly different definition, it is possible to establish that employment in the industrial districts had multiplied by a factor of 5 between 1951 and 1991, while total manufacturing employment has only increased 50 per cent!

What strikes foreigners most about the Italian SME is their export orientation. In 1992 Italian manufacturing firms exported on average 23.2 per cent of their turnover. An inspection of this export share by size of firms shows that smaller firms (up to 99 employees) have a slightly lower than average performance,[16] while the 100–199 category is the best performer with 25.6 per cent, followed by the more than 500 category with 24.9 and the 200–499 category with 23.5. But the industrial districts often have a much higher export share. To the national or international buyer industrial districts appear like an enormous but very localized exhibition place, where hundreds or thousands (depending on the type of products) of different models and brands of products can be found to meet all conceivable different needs and tastes. This has been termed the 'exhibition effect' of the industrial districts. Some of them also have common trading organizations or people who are in charge of the contacts with foreign markets, but increasingly medium-size firms develop their own network of foreign contacts or branches.

It is of no less interest to analyse the specializations of these industrial districts and their localization in the country. An aggregate picture is available in Table 2.6. It can be seen that the Italian fashion trade has the lion's share of the employment of the Italian industrial

---

[15] This procedure underestimates the real extent of the phenomenon. For instance, the well-known 'packaging valley' located in Bologna (Emilia-Romagna), where around 300 engineering firms specialized in packaging machines produce most of the Italian output in the branch, export more than two-thirds of their products, and share world markets only with the Germans, is not included because Bologna is a city with many other firms as well and therefore packaging machinery is not so 'dominant' in total employment as the definition imposes.

[16] Firms with 20–49 employees had an export share of 18% and firms with 50–99 employees 22.4%.

TABLE 2.6 Industrial districts by sectors and regions, 1991

	Textiles and clothing	Leather and shoes	Furniture and household decoration	Engineering	Foodstuffs and beverages	Jewels, toys, sport	Others	Total
Piedmont	5		3	5	2		1	16
Lombardy	19		3	12	3		5	42
Liguria					1			1
Trentino	1		1	2				4
Veneto	15	3	10	5		1		34
Friuli			2	1				3
Emilia-Romagna	4	1	5	6	7		1	24
Tuscany	6	4	4	1	1	1	2	19
Umbria	2		2				1	5
The Marches	11	14	6		1	2		34
Latium			1				1	2
Abruzzo	3	2	1					6
Campania	1	2	1					4
Apulia	2	1						3
Calabria					2			2
North–West	24		6	17	6		6	59
North–East	20	4	18	14	7	1	1	65
Centre	19	18	13	1	2	3	4	60
South	6	5	2		2			15
ITALY	69	27	39	32	17	4	11	199

Source: Istat, 1991 Industrial Census.

districts, but engineering districts are also present, as well as districts producing kindred products, like the famous tiles district of Sassuolo in Emilia-Romagna or the Mirandola district for medical material, again in Emilia-Romagna. With reference to the localization of districts, the north-east-centre (NEC) of the country has based its post-war industrialization on this form of industry, while the north-west, also known as the 'industrial triangle', although it does host some districts, was already industrialized before. It first followed the logic of the British industrial revolution (textiles) and then headed the process of Americanization (steel, cars, electricity, chemicals).

It is for this reason that the boom of SME in Italy is identified with the 'Third Italy', as Bagnasco (1977) has termed the NEC area. It is an area where banks are more local and small and where capital accumulation has been on a small scale owing to the prevailing sharecropping arrangements in agriculture. Sharecropping also provided the model for the family as a productive enterprise and for the family-sized entreprise, as well as the attachment to the place of origin.[17] In the regions of NEC the most widespread traditions of solidarity and co-operation, whether of Catholic, republican, or socialist inspiration, are to be found, those 'civic' traditions so much stressed by Putnam (1993). The way these regions of 'Third Italy' have caught up with the industrial triangle has been spectacular, in particular in the case of Veneto and Marche, as can be seen in Table 2.7. It is a region of the NEC, Emilia-Romagna, which is now on top of the list, having surpassed Lombardy, which has for long been the wealthiest of the Italian regions.

As for the South, Table 2.7 shows that only one of those regions has registered a remarkable success, namely the Abruzzo, which has come to share some of the features of NEC industrialization, while the other regions have barely kept their relative position. This of course means that there has been remarkable growth there too. In fact, the South has kept pace with the rates of growth in the rest of the country, and it is no longer today a generally poor area, having the same average per capita income as Spain. But so far growth has been mostly exogenously induced, by means of a public intervention that has been

---

[17] The landless day labourers on the capitalist farms of the Po valley went easily where there was work, while the sharecroppers, having a farmhouse, an orchard, and animals to tend, were non-migratory and tried to complement farm work with other types of work, especially domestic, rather than moving elsewhere.

TABLE 2.7 Per capita income in the Italian regions, 1951–1997 (Italy = 100)

	1951	1970	1980	1997
Piedmont	153	124	118	116
Lombardy	159	135	131	129
Liguria	154	119	112	118
Trentino	113	106	119	128
Veneto	88	107	110	123
Friuli	117	103	114	125
Emilia-Romagna	105	115	131	130
Tuscany	99	110	110	109
Umbria	80	90	101	96
The Marches	75	92	108	108
Latium	104	108	102	112
Abruzzo	62	73	84	89
Campania	71	70	66	62
Apulia	64	74	71	67
Basilicata	53	63	68	65
Calabria	53	58	57	57
Sicily	62	66	66	63
Sardenia	80	79	72	75
ITALY	100	100	100	100

Source: SVIMEZ 1961 and 1998.

vastly criticized and has not succeeded in freeing the area from dependence on outside resources and decisions. It is only recently, under the pressure of cutting down public spending and in presence of a strong demand for decentralization, that the local forces in the South too have been trying to organize themselves and become more assertive and creative both at the level of local government and at that of entrepreneurial groups. The significance of this new development will be better appreciated if we consider the following argument.

Between a paternalistic state and a rising civil society

A theme of the previous section was that the typical feature of Italian capitalism is the completely autonomous and self sufficient SME, which has produced the peculiar organizational innovation of the industrial district (Best 1990). A discussion of the role of the state in Italian industrialization cannot, however, be avoided nor an account of the major changes taking place at present.

Republican Italy inherited from fascism a much enlargened and pervasive state intervention in the economy. As already argued, it is somewhat surprising that the new republic did not cut this state presence during reconstruction, but rather increased it. This might not be considered a special feature of Italy, in view of the extensive nationalizations that took place in France as well as in Great Britain and in other European countries in the late forties. Italy, however, continued to add public entreprises up to the 1970s, although, after the formation of EFIM in 1962 to promote mechanical engineering and the nationalization of electricity in 1963 (with the creation of ENEL), this was the result only of repeated bailing-out operations.[18] These brought under state control even ice cream and cake manu-facturers (Motta and Alemagna). The enlargement of the public sec-tor was supported by the left, which saw the public entreprises as being more favourable to improved workers' conditions, but in cer-tain cases like the nationalization of electricity it was sponsored even by the *radicali*, who considered it the most effective way of getting rid of private monopolists.

The state involvement in the Italian economy was not limited to the administration of public entreprises. Through the public invest-ment banks and a wide array of soft loan schemes, as well as through legislation, the state was able to influence much of the private sector as well. The persistence of a highly fragmented distributive structure of small independent shops—another anomaly of Italy—is for instance due to legislation that, up to the late 1980s, prevented the material building of large super- and hyper-markets. Finally, the special agency set up in 1951 to help the South—the Casmez—became not only another important instrument of state intervention, but shaped the model of southern development up to the late 1980s. It is precisely this omnipresence of the Italian state that has led to the definition 'paternalistic state', a state that is ready to pay attention to all needs and give something to everybody, creating dependence

---

[18] In 1971 IRI, ENI, EFIM, and IMI together founded GEPI (Società per la gestione di partecipazioni industriali) with the explicit aim of redressing bailed-out companies and reprivatizing them, to stop the unplanned increase of the public enterprise sector and avoid continuous interference with the industrial projects of the state holdings.

because of its inability (or unwillingness?) to help businesses to stand on their own.

There is a great amount of literature on the achievements and shortcomings of these public policies (Amatori 1997) and we cannot possibly review it here. Anyway it would be more interesting to offer some interpretation. Public entrepreses were generally run with expansion as a target; sometimes this was pursued beyond reasonableness, as in the case of steel and chemicals. Some enterprises were administered by capable people and prospered; others, run by less adequate managers, failed. These, which could not be privatized, often continued to operate. They covered their losses by drawing on public money.

At this level the Italian state experience with public enterprises cannot be dismissed as an obvious failure as in Great Britain, nor can it be praised as a success as in France. Corruption is another topic which is usually much discussed in connection with public enterprises, but widespread corruption is linked rather to the general political situation of the country than to the existence of public entreprises *per se.*

The kind of argument I want to develop here starts from a different viewpoint and takes a global view of the implications of state-run enterprises on the structure of the Italian economy. As it happened, while the share of public enterprises in the Italian economy never reached the French or Austrian peaks and was only slightly above the British or German share, because of the peculiar size structure of Italian firms, the state came to control a disproportionate amount of Italian big business in the most highly advanced sectors of production. It has been shown that the best state enterprises did try to adopt sound managerial practices and to spread management education following American models. But the continuous political interference into the plans of the managers, the nationalistic approach of the public companies that refrained from any involvement abroad (with the exception of ENI), their inconsistent research efforts, the lack of domestic alliances with private companies to strengthen competitive positions in certain branches—all these things together produced a rigid and semi-bureaucratic model of the large corporation in Italy. There was no osmosis between public and private firms; there was no room for private entrepreneurs to enlarge their business in the most advanced sectors, beyond the few which had traditionally been left in their hands. This was another powerful motive that pushed private entrepreneurs to confine themselves to small size and not to challenge the existing balance, which finally started to fall apart only after privatizations got under way.

But there is another aspect of state behaviour that I consider important. Perhaps because of the piecemeal acquisition of enterprises, or because nobody clearly saw their strategic role, in face of the predominance of small business, or as a result of the typically Italian lack of tradition in operating on a large scale, the Italian state gave up very early (after the reconstruction period and the Vanoni Plan) any effort to play the role of leader in projecting Italian economic development. In an economy where most big businesses are in private hands, this is not important, but in an economy where most of the large corporations are state-managed, it is certainly a handicap. We can measure here the difference between Italy and France. Also, it is precisely this consideration that leads us to refrain from considering the Italian case as a case of state-led growth, in spite of the large presence of the state in the economy.

In offering a brief evaluation of the results of state intervention into the vexed 'Southern question', one must certainly start by recalling the extreme state of poverty and backwardness of the area at the end of the Second World War. This made the creation of a special developmental agency almost inevitable, prompting it to undertake public works for the agricultural sector and for infrastructure. Then came the strong demand of unskilled labour on the part of the industrial triangle in the 1950s and 1960s at the time of the Americanization of Italian industry which attracted for the first time a lot of Southern immigrants. Conditions in the South started improving.

With the overcrowding of the Northern towns and the persistent lack of local industrialization in the South, the idea was conceived in the 1960s of using public entreprises and the large northern and foreign private entreprises to industrialize the South with public support. In this way, a number of plants, some of them quite large and advanced, were located in the South by firms which invariably had their main decision centres, complementary plants, and markets outside the area.[19] Industrial employment in the South was for the first

---

[19] These plants were labelled 'cathedrals in the desert', to underline their isolation in the southern context.

time boosted, but very little local mobilization of resources was produced. Forward and backward linkages were never established and even skills were generally not built up, as a consequence of the Fordist model of plants which were generally built there.

Could the intervention have been planned differently? Although it is clearly a theoretical question, one might ask if the answer could be instructive. I think that in the context of the early 1960s, when Italy and Europe at large were still busy trying to adopt the American Fordist model, not much else could be conceived. Things went wrong later, starting in the late 1960s to early 1970s. When the American model went into crisis, not only did the Italian state prove incapable of switching to a different approach, but the South suffered the worst consequences of the belated realization of the crisis. In the 1970s additional capacity was added in steel (the dramatic doubling of Taranto's capacity, which led to the failure not only of that plant, but of the IRI steel holding Finsider itself), in chemicals (in Sardinia, Sicily, and Calabria a number of plants costing many hundred billion lire were never put in operation!) and in cars (the Pomigliano d'Arco Alfa Romeo plant, called Alfasud, which was a disaster, dragging the entire Alfa Romeo company into failure). From that time on, Casmez policies were in disarray; the organization was replaced by another agency in 1986 without any strategic new drive. This experiment was finally liquidated in 1993 by a referendum that abolished the ministry for the *Mezzogiorno* and its agency. Official developmental policies relied on the European Union structural funds, which the Italian Southern regions had never been accustomed to using efficiently.[20]

Meantime, since the southern situation was far from settled, it was from the lavish Italian welfare system that most of the public support for southern incomes came. While production kept the southern regions, with the exception of the Abruzzo, barely in line with the positions achieved in the 1960s and 1970s, consumption was vastly supported by welfare transfer payments, bringing the South about 10 percentage points nearer to the average for the country compared to the production levels depicted in Table 2.7. Also, it must be noticed

---

[20] Small institutions aimed at creating new jobs or replacing workers laid off by the Fordist plants burgeoned here and there in the South, up to the creation of a coordinating agency called Sviluppo Italia at the beginning of 1999. This was to be in no way a replica of Casmez, but a lean instrument of support to the creation of jobs in the *private* sector in the South.

that in recent years a more successful enterprising activity is arising in the South, although it is still exceptional to have some internationally known company quoted on the New York stock exchange, like Natuzzi which produces sofas. Local firms are mostly hidden in the black economy and it is not clear whether they could remain competitive if they moved into the legal economy paying taxes and standard wages.

A rapid reference to the Italian welfare state is inevitable at this point. On the whole Italy has followed the well-known European pattern, except in one important feature: pensions. Not only has the average Italian retirement treatment been one of the most lavish, but the number of people enjoying privileges has been enormous. For instance, republican Italy inherited from fascism a system of special treatment for civil servants, who got larger pensions and could retire earlier. Rather than scrapping such privileges, the republican governments successively stepped them up, to the point that a female civil servant could retire after only fifteen years of work. But artisans, farmers, and shopkeepers all payed too little. Anticipated retirement too was increasingly used to help large corporations restructure and lay off workers. Invalidity pensions were used to meet poverty in the South. All this exploded into excessive public spending that is proving very difficult to control, in spite of the repeated efforts at reform.

From this rapid survey of the Italian state's welfare policies it is possible to draw a couple of important conclusions. The 'paternalistic' state, that probably had its roots in the good will of the early politicians who wished to redress the Italian situation after the end of the Second World War and also sought to end certain Fascist and pre-Fascist traditions, strengthened parties (and trade unions), making them authoritative intermediaries of demands coming from groups of citizens or even individuals, whose improvement, or simply survival, depended upon them. This was at the same time the source of corruption (parties wanted increasingly to be 'paid' for the favours they dispensed) and the cause of their sticking together and refusing any change that would inevitably put an end to the primacy of parties over society. Obviously, as has been noticed above, this was also the cause of the weakness of civil society, entrepreneurs included.

It was only when the excess of corruption percolated down into the smaller firms and threatened the very roots of Italian prosperity and the Italo-European partnership that the parties' grip was at first loosened and then largely eliminated. At that point a long transition started for the Italian society and economy which set out towards a new equilibrium. The impact of this long march in the economic field is quite clear and is leading to a remarkable transformation of the Italian economy.

First of all the Italian state is finally slimming down and losing its 'paternalistic' connotation. Privatizations in banks have pushed them to merge, increase profitability and get ready for the European adventure. The process is far from complete, but immobility has been abandoned. Strangely enough, the banks that have done better are not the ones like Comit and Mediobanca which were on top before (although Cuccia will fight to the end) but rather the Credito Italiano and San Paolo-Imi. Even the local non-profit banks (*Casse di risparmio*, Banche del Monte, which are the offspring of the old pawn banks) have benefited from the splitting of their charity side, turned into foundations, from their commercial side, which has become an ordinary joint stock company, increasing profitability and size.

Privatizations of public entreprises have freed management from unofficial contributions to political parties (the *tangenti*), but also from *oneri impropri* (improper burdens, namely demands from the political class to keep more labour than needed, to localize plants in underdeveloped places, to refrain from competing, to bail out failed companies). This has resulted in an immediate improvement of profitability. But perhaps it is not the most important result. Slowly the stock exchange is becoming less feeble and sleepy, while people have shown an incredibly strong interest in the shares of the newly privatized companies, which have been sold out quickly, forming a few public companies. These will still have an uneasy life in Italy for some time, because of lack of traditions and institutional investors like the pension funds, but it cannot be denied that the dynamism of the private sector has been enhanced. The withdrawal of the state from administration of banks and enterprises has been accompanied by the creation of a number of authorities (on the stock exchange, energy, telecommunications, anti-trust), that are shaping a new type of state as regulator and arbitrator.

But the state is due to slim down in the welfare sector too. The bureaucratic provision of welfare is giving way to production of welfare services by social co-operatives and non-profit organizations, which are growing stronger and enlarging their fields of activity. The co-operative movement, which had been strong in Italy, but somewhat hampered by its tight links with the old political parties, is now finding a new entrepreneurial drive and is progressively lowering the walls that had traditionally separated the *white* co-operatives of Catholic inspiration from the *red* co-operatives linked with the Socialist and Communist parties and from the *green* co-operatives of republican origin (Mazzini).

The second major impact of the Italian peaceful political revolution on the economy has been a new accountability of people and institutions. Typically, in the public sector it was difficult, if not utterly impossible, to find out who was responsible for what; this wasted time and produced ineffective results and discontent. A reform of public administration, the autonomization of schools, universities, banking foundations, the privatization of public entreprises are now decentralizing decision centres and civil society is enjoying a new vigour.

One final word on federalism. The ancient Italian tradition of city-states and local powers had been suffocated by the centralized French-style form of government chosen at the unification of the country. Centralism had culminated under fascism, but the republic was slow in breaking it. In the new 1948 Constitution, regional governments were contemplated, but their institution was deferred to 1970, while they as well as the municipal governments did not have freedom to tax. The 1993 referendums abolishing a number of central ministries, and the new electoral law giving more authority to city mayors, together with pressure coming from Bossi's Lega movement, persuaded the new governments to start a process of effective decentralization of economic policies in many fields. This, again, increased the accountability and vigour of civil society.

At this point, it is hardly a surprise to see the loss of authority on the part of parties in general, not only of those which have 'misbehaved'. As Italian society understands that resources are given back to the people and economic leverage is no longer so largely in the hands of the state, parties as intermediaries become superfluous and politics, beside economics, must be reorganized according to an entirely different approach, that of bottom-up representation of the will of the people.

3

Political development

Gianfranco Pasquino

Italy's political development from 1945 to 1999 can be appropriately divided into three different phases: 1945–79; 1980–92; 1993–99. These phases do not coincide with the different alignments of the various Italian coalitional governments, that is: centrist coalitions (1947–62); centre-left coalitions (1963–76); national solidarity (1976–9); *pentapartito* (1980–92); centre-right vs. centre-left (1994–present), that have been traditionally utilized. None the less, I believe that a different criterion, referring to the nature and dynamics of democratic life, is overriding and can be precisely and profitably used.

From 1947 on there was a belief among the Christian Democrats (Democrazia cristiana, DC) that Italian democracy could be expanded under their continued and enlightened leadership. This belief, precisely embodied by their towering leader Alcide De Gasperi, and carried on by Aldo Moro, shaped the very strategy of the DC that aimed at being a centrist party looking to the left. Realistically, the Christian Democrats pursued the strategy of the expansion of democracy, first by obliging the Socialists to come to terms with the success of the centrist coalitions in producing or at least in permitting, an 'economic miracle' and then by accepting the long-standing challenge of the Communists: 'chi ha più filo tesserà più tela' (he who has more thread will weave more cloth). For a long period the Christian Democrats did not lose control of the democratic process and of the governments presiding over it. The kidnapping and the tragic murder of their leader Aldo Moro by the Red Brigades in March–May 1978 put an end to this thirty-year strategy. Henceforth, as Moro had predicted, the destiny of the Christian Democrats was no longer in their hands. Secondly the majority of the party decided to abandon the search for a new path to be followed by the Italian political system.

In the eighties the Christian Democrats had for the first time to yield the office of prime minister first to the Republican Giovanni Spadolini and then to the Socialist Bettino Craxi. Afterwards, they also lost the overall political initiative to Craxi himself who, though the leader of a party obtaining only about 10 per cent of the national vote, was extremely influential, most of the time even decisive in the selection, the approval, and the implementation of public policies. Finally, in 1992 they lost so many votes that the cherished and essential quality of their success, that is, the unity of the party, gave way and they were reduced to several splinter groups. The advance of one of the few dominant parties in contemporary democracies capable of keeping power for more than forty years came abruptly to an end, ending along with it the First Republic. Its accomplishments in terms of economic changes and of strengthening democratic behaviour and institutions had been considerable though perhaps inferior to Italian potential, but the demise of the First Republic in the midst of systemic corruption and the suicides of leading figures tended to make analysts forget how much territory had been covered by Italian political parties and societal associations in a complex and often confrontational interaction. No party has yet been able to occupy the pivotal role enjoyed by the DC in the old republic. Indeed, it is easy to predict that there will be no new, stable, functioning Italian republic unless a political alignment comparable in size and strength to the ones constructed and dominated by the Christian Democrats comes into being and reshapes the Italian Constitution and its institutions. It will be the task of this chapter to explore the most important political events of post-war Italy and to highlight the turning-points, the opportunities taken and missed and the problems remaining.

The expansion of Italian democracy

Twenty years of fascism had destroyed the not so limited democracy in terms of competition and participation which the Liberal prime minister Giovanni Giolitti (1900–14) had created. Fascism had erased almost all those political and civic organizations that had sprung up. Having reached a controversial agreement with Mussolini in 1929, the Church alone, along with its several socio-cultural organizations, had survived. One year and a half of the Resistance struggle had given some Italians a renewed sense of dignity and had revived some organizations of civil society, especially in the North. After Italian Liberation in 1945, the most pressing problem was reform of the state and the creation of a viable democratic regime that would embrace all citizens. The monarchy, one of the main obstacles, was immediately removed through a referendum. Another obstacle materialized with the beginning of the Cold War.

Though actively participating in the drafting of the new Constitution, after May 1947, the Italian Communist Party was excluded from all governing coalitions up to 1976 because of its ties with the Communist Party of the Soviet Union (CPSU). Nonetheless, because they had constructed an entrenched and powerful political organization, representing the interests and the aspirations of several sectors of Italian society, the Communists (*Partito comunista italiano*, PCI) continued to govern several important cities, such as Bologna and Florence, as well as Rome and Turin from 1975 to 1985; and regions, like the Red Belt of Emilia-Romagna, Tuscany, the Marches, and Umbria. Because of their discipline and their commitment, they also continued to exercise significant influence on policy at the national level. The fact that they were unable to become a credible alternative to the Christian Democrat-led governments condemned Italian politics to limited, gradual, and finally, inadequate changes.

Several times the Communists had the opportunity to break with the Soviet Union and to become a truly West European left-wing party: in 1956, 1964, and 1968. Following the invasion of Hungary by Soviet troops there was enough dissent within the PCI—even despite the intellectuals—to justify a break with the CPSU. In 1964, following the overthrow of Krushchev, the situation was even more promising because the Communists might have either joined or at least supported the Socialist Party in trying to inject into the centre left as much reformist *élan* as possible. Moreover, the PCI was undergoing its first major succession crisis because its historic and charismatic leader Palmiro Togliatti, who had the closest ties with the CPSU, had died in August. Then, another splendid opportunity was offered to the Italian Communists by the occupation of Czechoslovakia by the troops of the Warsaw Pact in August 1968.

The PCI had supported the Prague Spring in a convinced, brotherly, and firm manner. It could therefore criticize Soviet behaviour and draw definitive conclusions. Later a not so different opportunity was offered first by the Soviet invasion of Afghanistan and creation of a puppet government in 1979 and then by the military coup in Poland in 1981. Even though the view that the coup was directed as much against the Soviet hard-liners as against Solidarity was probably correct, that coup was the final demonstration of what the Communist secretary Enrico Berlinguer had been arguing for some time: there was no longer any *spinta propulsiva* (dynamic thrust) in the Soviet type of Communism. While Stalinism was, in Togliatti's words, a degeneration within the system, the repression of Solidarity was the best evidence of the degeneration of the (Communist) system beyond repair. Still, Italian Communist leaders were unable to bring about a dramatic break with the Communist world fundamentally for fear of a Soviet-financed split of their party. Indeed, when in February 1991 the PCI officially transformed itself into a new party— the Democratic Party of the Left (PDS)—a dangerous split duly took place.

Precisely because it could not have been supported and financed by the no-longer-existing CPSU, the success of the split and the creation of a small though by no means uninfluential party, Communist Refoundation (Rifondazione comunista, RC) showed that the previous fears were seriously grounded. However, the success of RC could also be interpreted as the consequence of a change that had been postponed for too long a time allowing hard-line, or simply conservative, Communists to regroup, reorganize, and convince an electorate that had not been taught the virtues of political democracy and of reformist policies along the Western social democratic model.

Following the exclusion of the Communists from the government and their political unavailability for any coalition as well as the politically and constitutionally dictated isolation of the neo-fascist Movimento Sociale Italiano (MSI) on the extreme right of the Italian political alignment, there could practically be no rotation of parties in the government and no alternation through competing coalitions. From the very beginning the Italian political system was fundamentally blocked. Starting from this point, the Christian Democrats soon realized that they had to go beyond the political and parliamentary representation of purely Catholic and moderate (i.e. conservative) interests and groups. Following their outstanding leader Alcide De Gasperi, the DC pursued the modernization of Italy and, above all, accommodated the pressures coming from some mildly progressive politicians to launch Italian participation in the process of European integration from its very beginning. Though Italian governmental coalitions were all multi-party, necessarily heterogeneous, and frequently litigious, several reforms were produced but usually in the first years of their spell in office and as a response to their electoral commitments. As long as the Socialists remained too close to the Communist Party, the DC included the right-wing Liberal Party in the governing coalitions together with the Republicans and the Social democrats (1947–1960). When the support of some sectors of the industrial working class became indispensable, both for political reasons (in order to enlarge the consensus for the government) and for economic reasons (in order to deepen and accelerate the process of industrialization), the Liberals were dropped and the Socialists became part of the governing coalition in the so-called centre-left experience (1962–72). Conducted from a dominant position, the Christian Democratic strategy was based on a combination of distributing growing resources to its governmental allies and of sharing the burden of executive responsibilities. Retaining the central position in all governments, the DC did not suffer any electoral decline while all its allies were incapable of growing and challenging its role. Outside the governmental area the Communist Party was slowly gaining votes, but it was never considered a credible alternative until 1976. The Communist domestic policy positions were never supported by more than one-third of the voters and their international alignment with the Soviet Union made them completely unacceptable to a large majority of Italian voters.

About thirty years after the enactment of the Italian Constitution,

to broaden the ranks of its supporters. While willing to accept the parliamentary support of the Communists, the Christian Democrats sternly rejected their offer to join the government because they wanted to retain control over all governmental appointments, the source of much of their power. This they did by staffing the two single-party governments of this coalitional phase, known as 'national solidarity'. The mastermind behind all this was Aldo Moro, who thought he could successfully repeat the same strategy used with the Socialists: embrace and suffocate the Communists. And because of his close and reassuring ties with the state apparatus, the armed forces, and the Vatican the wily Giulio Andreotti was the prime minister of both governments.

While Andreotti was essentially interested in the pursuit of his political career and in the strengthening of his own faction, in Moro's political thought the third phase of the Italian political system would see the full legitimation of a reduced Communist Party at last capable of competing with a reformed Christian Democratic Party, though never able to defeat and replace it. To be sure, the Communists saw their electoral strength and their political appeal much reduced after the phase of national solidarity. Nevertheless, Moro could not see the completion of his ambitious strategy because he was kidnapped by Red Brigade terrorists in March 1978 and murdered by them in May. No one among the Christian Democrats was capable of rigorously continuing Moro's strategy of democratic expansion and inclusion of the Communist Party or, for that matter, of devising an alternative strategy. As Moro had predicted, 'the future was no longer in the hands of the DC'.

The blocking of Italian democracy

Too long a junior partner in the national governments with the DC and in local governments with the Communists, the Partito socialista italiano (Italian Socialist Party, PSI) had paid a high electoral price for its pivotal though subordinate role. To be sure, it received important governmental offices and other 'spoils' in exchange for participation and support, but its electoral support, less than 10 per cent of the national vote, was disappointing. The pride and the power of the

Socialists were revived by their newly elected (1976) secretary Bettino Craxi. Skilfully utilizing the pivotal position of the Socialist Party in the Italian political alignment, Craxi challenged both the Christian Democrats and the Communists, respectively at the national and at the local level. In a few years he succeeded first in having a Socialist, Sandro Pertini, elected for the first time to the Italian Presidency (1978). Then, he increased the Socialist vote and acquired full control over the party, crushing any dissent and destroying all internal factions (1981). He also questioned the continued validity of the Italian Constitution and advocated a Grand Reform indispensable in his view not only to modernize the Italian political system, but also to produce the conditions for alternation and governability. Finally, in the wake of a serious electoral defeat of the Christian Democrats in 1983, Craxi became the first Socialist prime minister.

His long term as a prime minister, a record high of 1,060 days (August 1983–April 1987) was full of novelties that substantially reshaped the functioning of the Italian political system. Craxi wanted more than an enhanced role for his party; he wanted personal power and, as we now know, personal wealth. He also inaugurated a new style of politics which set him apart from all that the Christian Democrats and the Communists had done in the past. While the DC had studiously pursued a politics of incessant negotiations with all politically relevant organized groups, Craxi consciously resorted to the politics of confrontation with some of them. The most famous example was his February 1984 decision to reduce the indexation system by decree, defying the opposition of the Communists and their flanking trade union the CGIL. Moreover, Craxi avoided any subsequent compromise and accepted the challenge of a referendum called by the PCI in order to repeal that law. The referendum held in May 1985 saw the unexpected support of Italian voters both for a governmental measure that affected their wages and for the Socialist prime minister. At the same time, it demonstrated the reduced ability of the Communists to mobilize and the numerical and political decline of the organized working class. Moreover, whenever parliament appeared slow in passing some of the government legislation, Craxi resorted to decrees stressing his decision-making style, even giving it a sort of authoritarian imprint much to the irritation of Communists and Christian Democrats alike. Indeed, while the Christian Democrats had always taken into account what they thought would be the reactions of the Communist Party to their decisions, Craxi deliberately tried to show the Communists' irrelevance.

In Craxi's political theory and practice, one should and moreover one could govern not only without consulting the Communist Party, but also, whenever necessary, against its preferences. Whereas the Christian Democrats had asssumed a very low profile on the international scene and had remained a subordinate and passive ally of the United States, Craxi took advantage of a clash with US authorities over Italian national sovereignty in 1985 (the Sigonella case involving the safe conduct given by Italian authorities to alleged Palestinian terrorists) in order to revive Italian national pride, and some lingering anti-Americanism. His Atlantic credentials were, however, impeccable because, also with the aim of embarrassing the Communist Party, Craxi had been in the front line of the not too many Italian (and European) politicians willing to install on Italian territory the Cruise and Pershing missiles. Last, though by no means least, a decree enacted by his government in 1985 must be considered deliberately responsible for allowing his friend Silvio Berlusconi to consolidate his TV media empire with extraordinary consequences on the future of the Italian political system.

Much of Craxi's governmental and political success consisted in taming the Christian Democrats and in isolating the Communists. Luck also played a role because both the Christian Democrats and the Communists underwent a succession crisis. Soon the Christian Democrats accepted the prospect of a long-term alliance with Craxi that would not only isolate the PCI, but also considerably reduce its political power. The price to be paid to Craxi in terms of offices and policies appeared to the ageing DC leadership less high than the cost of challenging and/or bargaining with the PCI. For its part, the PCI was seriously weakened not only by the sudden death of its charismatic leader Enrico Berlinguer (June 1984), but by its very inability to renew its organization and policies. The Communists contributed to Craxi's strategy by making themselves irrelevant, for instance, both in the area of labour policies and in the renewal of the Italian institutions and Constitution. Craxi's policies appeared progressive, even 'liberal', because he wanted to curtail and, possibly, to eliminate the power of the industrial unions. The unions and the Communists appeared conservative because they aimed at maintaining that power in a situation where many Italians thought that the socio-economic system was offering increasing opportunities, whereas the power of labour was keeping and even introducing exaggerated rigidities in the market. It did not matter that many of the opportunities were paid for out of the state budget: the atmosphere of the times was that of 'enrichissez-vous'.

A strange, though not unprecedented, mixture of selected 'gifts' from the state, that is, from public authorities to their privileged groups, and of rugged individualism accompanied by massive tax evasion and fraudulent budgets characterized the eighties and produced a restructuring of the class profile of Italy. Industrial workers increasingly lost their socio-political power and independent small businessmen, consultants, speculators of all kinds acquired opportunities, privileges, status, and political visibility. However, they were not at all inclined to support the Christian Democrats, identified, after all, with a state that had protected public employees and produced too many obstacles to independent activities. They were not even favourably predisposed towards the Socialists whose tradition and political niche as well as some of their policies and even their party label were neither fully appealing nor completely acceptable. The new strata of independent businessmen and autonomous workers were available for mobilization by a shrewd 'political entrepreneur' who could challenge the system from outside without being identified with it.

As to the issue of the reform of the Constitution, the Socialists could again challenge both the Christian Democrats and the Communists for their institutional conservatism. Ideologically and practically, both the Christian Democrats and the Communists were indeed conservative with regard to a Constitution they had substantially written and that had served them well. Moreover, the Communists could and did cite their participation in the drafting of the Italian Constitution as one of their most cherished democratic credentials. In fact, Craxi just talked about the theme of the Grand Reform without referring to any concrete proposal except for the timely abolition of secret voting in Parliament that had become the weapon of dissenting party factions and powerful lobbies. He knew perfectly well that the Italian system, as it was structured, allowed a party the size of the Socialists plenty of room for political manœuvring and that any change that streamlined the functioning of Italian institutions would automatically reduce the power of the Socialists. In any case, neither the DC nor the PCI were in a position to call Craxi's bluff by themselves advocating a Grand Reform and by reaching an agreement that Craxi would immediately deride as 'consociational'.

The collapse of the party system

In spite of many inconveniences, the Italian system of government of the previous decades had permitted and even produced political change. Both the centrist and the centre-left coalitions had formulated and implemented significant policies capable of making the Italian system more European and of modernizing it. The evaluation of the short-lived phase of national solidarity is more controversial from a policy point of view, even though well-meaning attempts to change flourished and a national health system was created. Moreover, the political system seemed to be capable of further evolution, be it the full absorption of the Communist Party in democratic politics or the preparation of alternation in the government.

Contrary to such movement, the phase of the *pentapartito* (1980–92) represented the end of the politics of inclusion and of any hope of alternation. The five parties in power (DC, Liberals, Republicans, Social Democrats, and Socialists) excluded the declining Communist Party and renounced any institutional change that might create the conditions for alternation in the government, at the national as well as at the local level. In fact, negotiations at the level of national party secretaries dealt not just with the creation of the national government and the allocation of ministerial portfolios. In a complex and carefully elaborated exchange, the creation of local governments and the allocation of all local offices (plus, of course, all patronage resources) were decided. The reinvigorating feeling of impunity by the leaders of the *pentapartito* was strengthened both by their ability to reject all judicial requests for authorizing the indictment of parliamentarians and ministers and by their exclusive role in granting licences, contracts, subsidies to small and large entrepreneurs, in fact to anyone who needed something from national and local power holders. While some political corruption had always been present in Italy, a true system of corruption could come into being only when the politicians felt totally confident in their impunity and when the socio-economic operators realized that they had to deal with those politicians and their like for an indefinite period to come. Indeed, the *pentapartito* period might have been indefinitely long had it not been for some unexpected events.

The most unexpected of these events was also the most devastating in its consequences. The fall of the Berlin Wall in the night between 9 and 10 November 1989 affected not just, though immediately and visibly, the Italian Communist Party, but its traditional opponent, the Christian Democrats, and the entire Italian electorate. While ritually reviving their anti-Communist slogans at any electoral campaign and stressing their irreplaceable role as anti-Communist bulwark, the Christian Democrats might have come to underestimate or even to forget how important those factors were in convincing many voters to support their party. In fact, the electoral support the DC enjoyed in the eighties was not the consequence of specific policies. It was largely determined by anti-Communism, by an extensive clientelistic network, and by being considered the political representative of most Catholic associations. Its ageing leadership was certainly neither representative of a changed society nor responsive to a post-materialist electorate ; its policies were not innovative and often only created obstacles for several dynamic sectors of Italian society; moderate voters did not appreciate the subservient attitude the Christian Democrats showed towards the Socialists; last, though by no means least, Northern voters felt somewhat left out by the Christian Democrats.

Still, while the Communist Party under the leadership of Achille Occhetto began its perhaps excessively protracted journey towards the uncharted destination of a new political formation whose only predictable quality was negative, that it was no longer a Communist party, the DC followed its classic bargaining strategy: business as usual. However, the times were very unusual and only an ageing and fundamentally southern leadership could miss the point so completely. In the North millions of voters who had supported the DC and its *pentapartito* allies precisely because they promised to prevent the Communist Party from obtaining governmental power suddenly felt liberated. They still did not like the Communist Party and did not feel in the least attracted by its successors, but they were no longer obliged to support the *pentapartito* parties. Fortunately there was a ready-made alternative vehicle for their political and social dissatisfaction, an organization capable of appealing to the most elementary and, at the same time, most significant of their feelings: their territorial belonging. Those voters were above all Northern voters, and the Northern League, in its several regional components, was there to inherit all the votes that they did not want to cast for the *pentapartito* and never thought of casting for Communist, former Communist, post-Communist candidates.

Much to everybody's surprise, in the national elections of 1992 the Lombard League, as it was then called, polled 3,395,384 votes as compared with 186,255 in 1987 for the Chamber of Deputies and 2,732,461 votes as compared with 298,883 in 1987 for the Senate and elected respectively 55 deputies and 25 senators. Previously it had one incumbent in each chamber. The League was not the cause of the now visible crisis of the Italian socio-political system. It was as much a consequence as a catalyst of the socio-political crisis. Never before, except for a short period between 1947 and 1953, had an outspokenly anti-political movement acquired such a significant electoral success. Then it was the Uomo qualunque (Everyman's) movement, strong only in Rome and in the South and representing a reaction to a democracy in the making. Now a movement emerged in the richest areas of the country, challenging the type of centralized democracy that had been created and exposing its declining ability to respond to a changed electorate. The panel of judges in Milan discovered through an investigation dubbed *Mani pulite* (Clean Hands) that not only could politicians not respond to the demands of the electorate, but that there had been a growing willingness on the politicians' part to resort to outright corruption in order to buttress their electoral power and to facilitate their political careers. Officially, the Pandora's box of Italian political corruption was opened in February 1992. The Milan magistrates had repeatedly asked parliament for the authorization to investigate some of its members, who were involved in a major network of corruption in Milan, as early as 1989. But the *pentapartito* majority voted no.

Undermined by the competing ambitions of Craxi, Andreotti, and Forlani, three top politicians vying for the two top offices (prime minister and president of the Republic) available in the spring of 1992, the *pentapartito* was not yet in shambles. But the results of the April 1992 elections had been rather disappointing and, in any case, the Milan judges were collecting sound evidence through the incrimination of some small (but talkative) fish. They bypassed the need for parliamentary authorization by not pursuing the big fish. It is impossible to describe in any detail the Herculean activities of the panel investigating the Italian system of political corruption. Suffice it to say that by April 1993 almost half the ministers of the government led by Giuliano Amato had to resign because they were served with a judicial notice and almost one-third of the sitting parliamentarians had been indicted. By May 1994 all the secretaries of the *pentapartito* parties had been ousted and were under trial and Bettino Craxi left Italy for Tunisia in order to escape being arrested.

The Italian system of corruption must be defined as political because the politicians constructed it and remained at its centre. However, it would be totally misleading to believe that there was a sharp distinction between something like a clean and pure civil society on one hand, obliged to pay bribes to a dirty world of politicians on the other hand. Italian corruption was 'systemic' because a multitude of actors was involved in it and many of them happily took advantage of it. Obviously, the politicians initiated the corrupt exchange in one way or another. However, it would be preposterous to think that had they wanted to, some major private and public companies such as Fiat, Olivetti, ENI, and (as we now know) Fininvest could not denounce the system, those parties, and those individual politicians who were blackmailing them.

The crux of the matter is that the companies entering into a corrupt exchange established a profitable, working relationship with politicians at the expense of the market and the type of competition other companies, unwilling or unable to look for and have access to the influential politicians, could wage. Moreover, not only did the companies willing to resort to corrupt practices justify their behaviour by stating that in any case they were financing 'democratic' parties suffering a not well explained unfair competition coming from the (no longer existing) Communist Party, but also they were not really wasting their money. In too many instances, those companies were allowed to raise their prices and to get additional benefits that were more than enough to cover the cost of the bribes. All this meant that in the end the entire burden of corruption was carried by the state budget. Indeed, the public debt of the *pentapartito* era skyrocketed and its size had became larger than the Italian Gross National Product. Can one find a better indicator of the size of corruption than the growth of the public debt in a period of economic expansion?

While actively engaged in corrupt practices, the ruling political class had suffered another major blow to its legitimacy, though it underestimated its long-term impact. Neither the Christian Democrats nor the minor parties of the *pentapartito* could be interested in any significant reform of the institutions and the Constitution that would create some uncertainty. While still proclaiming the need for a Grand Reform, Craxi had joined them in defending the institutional status quo that was so conducive to the political status quo, that is, to the 'freezing' of the governmental alliance. That Craxi had become a conservative in the field of institutional reforms was blatantly revealed by his behaviour when a referendum initiative was launched by a few representatives of the political class, highly dissatisfied with the functioning of the political system, and by several representatives of social and cultural organizations. The referendum was called to reform the electoral law. In the first instance the referendum could only repeal a minor clause of the electoral law, June 1991, though it was interpreted and understood as being addressed against the immobilism of the ruling political class. The second time (April 1993) the target of the referendum was no longer a discredited and disappearing political class but the proportional formula itself: it proposed a three-fourths plurality system to be applied in single-member constituencies.

It is difficult to underestimate the importance of the proportional electoral law in shaping the concrete working of the Italian political system, the composition of multi-party governmental coalitions, the dynamics of internal life in factionalized parties, the practices of state patronage and clientelism, and the very mentality of almost all the political protagonists. Suffice it to say that for most Communists and many leftists proportional representation was adamantly equated with democracy *tout court*. As a matter of fact, the first significant expansion of the suffrage was accompanied by Giovanni Giolitti (1913) with the reform of the electoral system which became proportional. One of the tangible signals that fascism was indeed an authoritarian regime was its electoral reform of 1924 that sharply curtailed the proportionality of the electoral system and distorted the outcome in a strong majoritarian direction.

The return to democracy in 1945 took place by reinstating a

proportional electoral system guaranteeing to all parties, even to the very small ones, a fair share of parliamentary seats. However, by the end of the eighties it had become clear that the variant of the proportional electoral system utilized in Italy had frozen the party system, was preventing alternation in the government, had led to improper and, indeed, corrupt exchanges between governing parties and powerful companies and pressure groups and between cliques of candidates and single or organized voters. Thus, the reform of the electoral system had become a top priority for all those who wanted the renewal of the Italian political system and was vehemently opposed by all those who wanted to retain the system as it was.

There is no better evidence that this was exactly the case than an analysis of the two alignments favouring and opposing the 1991 electoral referendum. In support of the referendum one could find several individual members of the political class and several sectors of the former Communist Party, now PDS, above all its secretary Achille Occhetto, but not the entire party as such since the proportional mentality was still largely dominant inside it. In opposition to the referendum, one could find all the parties of the *pentapartito*, the repentant reformer Bettino Craxi in the forefront and, for different reasons, the neo-fascists who feared to remain even more isolated, and Umberto Bossi, the leader of the Lega, who thought that a system different from proportional representation might block the electoral ascent of the Lega.

The opponents of the referendum invited the voters to make it void by simply not going to the polls. However, 62.5 per cent of the voters decided that the referendum was worth some of their time and more than 90 per cent of them cast a favourable vote. The positive component of the vote meant that the voters wanted a serious reform of the electoral system in a non-proportional direction. The negative component of the vote could be interpreted as a delegitimation of the governing parties and their leaders unable to understand and represent the preferences of most of their voters on such an important issue.

Encouraged by the unexpectedly resounding victory, the promoters of the referendum started yet another collection of signatures to make the national and local electoral laws almost completely winner-take-all. By April 1993 what remained of the parties of the *pentapartito* were their ashes and the indictments of their secretaries so that there was not any real opposition except that coming from a curious combination of some sectors of the very traditional left wing and of the Christian Democratic Party. The electoral referendums produced two different results. First, in order to prevent a decisive plurality law for the election of town and city councils at all levels, parliament approved a law instituting the direct popular election of the mayors with a double ballot run off system while the councils were elected using a proportional system plus a majority bonus for the list(s) supporting the winning candidate. Secondly, following the criteria deriving from the referendum approved again by about 90 per cent of the voters, a totally new electoral law was passed for the election of parliament. Leaving aside some small, though significant, differences, the new electoral law provides for three-fourths of candidates to be elected in single-member constituencies through a plurality formula and one-fourth to be elected on the basis of a proportional mechanism.

The reason why it is imperative to elaborate on the electoral referendums and their outcomes is twofold. The referendums and the subsequent laws destroyed the old style of conducting politics in Italy, almost completely burying all the dominant parties of the First Republic and opened the way to a complex process of political realignment that has not yet been completed. No understanding of Italian politics after 1993 is possible without mastering the interplay between the technical mechanisms of the electoral laws and the reactions of party leaders. In sum, the Italian political-institutional transition began when the proportional electoral system was eliminated by the voters. The transition will continue as long as party leaders are unable to design and implement modern institutions in tune with the new electoral system. In the mean time, however, momentous and unprecedented events have accompanied and marked the Italian transition.

Attempting the construction of a better democracy

Several important effects followed immediately from the drafting of the new electoral laws. The first law to be concretely utilized was the one for the election of the mayors. In the first round held in some major cities not a single representative of the traditional parties of the First Republic succeeded in reaching the run-off. In Turin a newcomer professor of engineering supported by the centre-left defeated a former Communist who had been mayor ten years before. In Milan the candidate of the League defeated a leftist professor of sociology known for being the son of General Dalla Chiesa, killed by the Sicilian Mafia eleven years before. In the next round the situation appeared already completely different, also because the cities where the voting took place were extremely different. In Naples a former Communist defeated Benito Mussolini's granddaughter; in Rome the left-wing candidate, a Green, defeated the secretary of the former neo-fascist party. The novelties introduced by these elections were many, interesting, and ripe with consequences.

In all cases the electoral competition became fully bipolar and the centre disappeared. In all cases the voters felt that their vote was more decisive than the choices made by party leaders while party leaders made an effort to take into account what they knew of the preferences of the voters when choosing the candidates. Being directly elected by the voters, the mayors took charge of the various local governments immediately without having to wait, as in the past, for the protracted negotiations among party leaders who indulged in complex allocations of local offices. Finally, contrary to its fears, the neo-fascist party that was undergoing a serious ideological and organizational reform appeared to be a viable competitor. Moreover, it was fully legitimized by a declaration by the media tycoon Silvio Berlusconi that, if he were a Roman voter, he would support Fini (the secretary of the newly created post-fascist party Alleanza nazionale, AN). Through this astonishing declaration in a context in which the neo-fascists had always been kept at the margin of the political system, Berlusconi was starting his own political campaign. He was 'taking the field', as he would later explicitly put it.

The disappearance of the old political parties and the mechanisms of the electoral law were making it possible for the left to win a sizeable majority of single-member constituencies by polling slightly more than 30 per cent of the national vote. This very likely outcome posed a serious threat to Italian moderate public opinion. Intelligently, Berlusconi understood that there was the political space and even the political need for a new movement. Utilizing the extensive network of his publicity company Publitalia and the 'fire power' of his TV company Fininvest, he founded a political movement called Forza Italia. However, not even Forza Italia alone could defeat the left in single-member constituencies. Berlusconi's masterpiece was to construct two different coalitions between partners who could not otherwise stay together. In the North, Berlusconi's Forza Italia allied itself with Bossi's Lega and presented joint candidates in a coalition called Polo della libertà. In most of the centre of Italy and in the South it was Alleanza nazionale that joined Forza Italia in a coalition called Polo del buongoverno.

When the seats were counted it was clear that Berlusconi's two-pronged coalitions had severely defeated the Left, called Progressisti, and had even prevented what remained of the Christian Democrats from retaining some bargaining power. Having a clear majority in the Chamber of Deputies and a working majority in the Senate, Berlusconi was appointed prime minister in April 1994 and received the necessary vote of confidence in May (the very day his Milan soccer team won the European Champions League). For the first time in the history of the Italian republic and for the first time in a democratic country of post-war Europe, some neo-fascists acquired ministerial portfolios. Also, for the first time in a democratic regime an entrepreneur with so many resources and economic interests acquired the highest executive office without solving his visible, massive, and encumbering conflict of interests.

Politically, the lessons were many though not all of them immediately and fully understood. Nevertheless, the first one was simple. Berlusconi won not only because he mastered the new electoral system better than the Progressisti and the Popolari who ran separately, but because he was not a professional politician but a newcomer to politics and moreover because he succeeded in inspiring more confidence in the voters than both the only slighlty renewed Left and the not much renewed Popolari. Secondly, and unquestionably,

Berlusconi won also because he appeared reassuring to the previous voters of the DC and the PSI and the other vanished parties of the *pentapartito*. Berlusconi's political message was much the same as they had listened to throughout the First Republic: keep the left away from governmental power.

Finally, Berlusconi won also because his overall political and governmental platform contained a fair amount of continuity with what the *pentapartito* had preached though not practised: trim the role of the state, give more power to individual citizens, deregulate social and economic activities of all kinds. His platform sounded more convincing because it came from a successful entrepreneur or, as Berlusconi would later put it, from a man who had been successful in everything he had done. The paradox was that the Second Republic was on the verge of being inaugurated thanks to the electoral and political victory of an entrepreneur who had constructed his economic and social fortunes in the First Republic, with the help of the now discredited parties of the First Republic, and above all with the methods, already investigated by the judges of the Clean Hands panel, of the First Republic.

The average tenure of the governments of the First Republic was ten and a half months. Berlusconi's government lasted less than average: only seven and a half months. A few days before Christmas 1994 Berlusconi resigned because the leader of the Northern League Umberto Bossi had decided to ask his ministers to abandon the government fearing that Forza Italia might undermine his electorate and spoil his political visibility. It would be wrong to deduct from this outcome the premature conclusion that Berlusconi could not last in power. The problems he experienced derived from three main sources: his personal and his collaborators' lack of political and governmental experience accompanied by 'entrepreneurial' impatience and intolerance for the tempo of politics; his inability to assuage the Lega and to work to keep together the very diversified coalitions he had constructed; and, above all, his unsolved conflict of interests that was translated into a head-on, bitter, incessant conflict with the judiciary.

Following Berlusconi's demise the Italian republic found itself again in disorder in a way not too dissimilar from when in April 1993 the Governor of the Bank of Italy Carlo Azeglio Ciampi had been appointed prime minister to run the economy while allowing parliament to draft the new electoral laws. The difference between that phase, that had a predefined goal, and the new period was fundamentally that there was no precise, predefined, and agreed goal to pursue. To some extent Ciampi (April 1993–January 1994) brought to an end the First Republic. The new government of all non-professional politicians led by Lamberto Dini (January 1995–February 1996), the former Director-General of the Bank of Italy as well as former Minister of the Treasury in Berlusconi's government, was supposed to solve the burning problem of the reform of the pension system while reconstructing the political conditions indispensable for a renewed and fair electoral competition. Dini gave a partial solution to the pension problem, while no agreement was found on the reform of the electoral mechanisms and the institutional structures.

Two fundamental political changes affected the results of the April 1996 national elections: the presence of the candidates of the Lega in all northern constituencies and the coalition of what remained of the Popolari (after a split with its internal left) and the parties of the Left under the name of the Ulivo or Olive Tree. The Lega could no longer run in alliance with Berlusconi. Hence, it decided to go alone. In spite of contrary pessimist forecasts, it did well, winning 39 single-member deputy and 18 senate constituencies and depriving Berlusconi's coalition with AN in the North of quite a number of seats. In 1994, the Progressisti had won 14 single-member constituencies (SMC) out of the entire North and the Polo della libertà had won 162 SMC. In 1996 the Olive Tree coalition won 75 of those seats and the Polo delle libertà, deprived of the support of the Lega voters, won only 62 of them. That the success of the Ulivo was largely due to its superior ability to construct a winning coalition and to put up better candidates can be seen from a very revealing comparison.

Voters for the Chamber of Deputies are given two ballots: one showing the names of the candidates in the single-member constituency; the other showing the symbols of the parties participating in the proportional allocation of seats. Altogether the Ulivo candidates in single-member constituencies collected 16 762 704 votes as compared with 16 270 935 votes collected by their parties in the proportional ballots. The results for the Polo delle libertà were the opposite: 15 097 220 for the candidates and 16 481 785 for the parties. Clearly, the Ulivo carried an added value while the Polo delle libertà showed a handicap. Finally, it may be worth noting that the centre-right still constitutes a majority of the Italian electorate. Adding the proportional votes for the Lega to those for the Polo delle libertà one gets 54.1 per cent as compared with 43.4 for the Ulivo. While this calculation may represent a meagre consolation for the losers of the 1996 elections, it indicates that there has not been a major political realignment and that a different coalitional arrangement may in fact easily return the centre-right to power.

The outcome of the political shrewdness of the leaders of the Ulivo was doubly historical. In the first place, because for the first time in Italian history since 1876 a real alternation in the government took place between a centre-right and a centre-left coalition. This peaceful alternation seemed to bode well for the functioning and even the improvement of the Italian political system. In the second place, for the first time since May 1947 when they were excluded from the government by the DC De Gasperi, the representatives of the former Communist Party could obtain ministerial portfolios and could bring into the government the interests of heretofore unrepresented sectors of Italian society. Though capable of accomplishing another historical feat, Italy's participation in European Monetary System from the beginning thanks to a sharp reduction of the inflation rate and of the state deficit, the government of the Ulivo remained dependent on the support of the unreconstructed Communists of Rifondazione and therefore somewhat constrained in its reformist activities.

On the other hand, the two oppositions, the Lega and the Polo, have so far been unable to coalesce and to offer a viable alternative to the voters. The Lega has even played with the idea of promoting the very unlikely secession from the rest of Italy of the northern regions, collectively dubbed Padania. The Polo remains prisoner of the all-out war declared by Berlusconi against the judges of Milan who have amassed enough evidence to have him sentenced for fraudulent budgets, illegal financing of political parties, and corruption of the Guardia di Finanza. Totally unwilling and, by now, even unable to distinguish between his private interests and problems as an entrepreneur and his public interests and goals as a political leader, Silvio Berlusconi prevents the emergence of a truly competitive democracy in Italy. In fact, in 1998 he has also condemned to failure the most serious attempt organically to reform the Italian constitution and institutions through a special Bicameral Committee.

There are several paradoxes of the Italian political development of the last decade, the nineties. The first one is that the majority of Italian voters consistently behaved in such a way as to get rid of the old parties, and succeeded in doing so. Then, faced with the possibility of voting the Left into government, the voters refrained and chose Berlusconi, who was able to play the newcomer to politics being at the same time the representative of much the same old interests and parties. Appalled by the leadership style of Berlusconi and his inability to reduce the tensions and the fears of the political-institutional transition a sizeable number of voters moved to give governmental power to a centre-left coalition led by yet another new-comer to active politics, Professor Romano Prodi, former chairman of the powerful state company IRI. And all Italian socio-economic actors co-operated with the government in what at the beginning seemed to be a forlorn task: satisfying the Maastricht criteria in order immediately to join the European Monetary System. By so doing, all those actors also proved wrong a very famous and frequently quoted assessment of Italian collective behaviour: that there is no need for a government; that, indeed, more progress is made in Italy in the absence of a government. On the contrary, by steering the course and providing political stability the government of the Ulivo must be considered positively responsible for an unexpectedly positive outcome.

Immediately thereafter, in October 1998, the government led by Romano Prodi was ousted, having suffered an unprecedented defeat in a vote of confidence provoked by Rifondazione comunista that declared its opposition to the budget law. Prodi was replaced by Massimo D'Alema, the secretary of the Democratic Party of the Left, and the Olive Tree coalition was *technically* enlarged, thanks to the joining of a new centrist group, the Union for the Defence of the Republic (UDR). *Politically*, the Olive Tree coalition was all but shattered. In fact, the goverment led by D'Alema represented not just the reassertion of the role of the parties and of the power of their secretaries, but also the reappearance of traditional Christian Democrats, within the UDR, and traditional Communists, a splinter group from Rifondazione—both receiving two ministries. Yet, another governmental crisis soon ensued. In December 1999 D'Alema resigned and returned, leading a weaker coalition including Prodi's Democrats, but not enjoying an absolute majority of votes in the

Chamber of Deputies. The developments that followed Prodi's ousting seem to indicate that what has been gained thanks to the political ability of a few men will not last for long if a different team takes over. Italian democracy will not work in a consistently satisfactory manner unless its constitution and its institutions are significantly modernized. Up to now the Italian transition does not simply appear unfinished. It appears never-ending. Even the two major competing coalitions are heterogeneous and litigious enough to appear fragile and unable to last for long. After all, the Polo delle libertà and the Ulivo are the product of choices and circumstances that may change following the preferences of their leaders. Both are constantly undermined by the selfish and partisan ambitions of the leaders of the different components.

Conclusions

Whither Italy? It is difficult to forget the amount of systemic corruption that characterized Italian politics in the eighties and that the judges are continuing to uncover. This corruption should not hide the many positive achievements of the Italian political system between 1945 and 1992. Not only was democracy consolidated and stabilized, but unprecedented prosperity was granted to the highest number of Italians ever. From a rather underdeveloped country with a high level of illiteracy, Italy has become the fifth industrial power of the world, ahead of Great Britain for the last ten years. And any time politics really took the post of command, significant progress and important reforms have been made. However, as regards political institutions the situation remains lamentable. To sum up bluntly: a largely imperfect proportional democracy based on excessive power held by the parties has been replaced by a still largely imperfect plurality democracy based on heterogeneous coalitions and plebiscitarian threats.

The Italian transition is not over and the risks of the reappearance of the traditional politics of party bargaining and patronage still loom large on the future of the political system. In fact, all those who would like to turn back the clock of Italian politics have reason to rejoice. On 18 April, 1999 the third referendum on the electoral law called by the promoters to strengthen the plurality component of the system failed because only 49.6 per cent of the voters went to the polls (an absolute majority is needed for the validity of a referendum). Voters' fatigue or resurrection of the 'proportionalists' and the 'partitocrats'? The setback suffered on the way to a fundamental, solid, and lasting restructuring of the political system seems to be conspicuous. While the path that has been covered by the reformists is long indeed, some of the achievements appear ephemeral. Therefore, the Italian political future is uncertain not because the existence of democracy is at stake, but because its quality and its dynamism seem to be unable to meet the forthcoming challenges.

4

Italy and the world since 1945

John L. Harper

Introduction

Italy did not cease to have a foreign policy after 1945, as is sometimes claimed. Indeed post-war foreign policy contains striking continuities with the past: the search for security and independence through a friendly connection with the dominant Mediterranean power (call it 'realism'); the impulse to go it alone in pursuit of national interests narrowly defined, and of an autonomous mission (call it 'particularism'); above all, the desire to take part in a larger political and economic project (call it 'Europeanism' or 'universalism').

It should never be forgotten that modern Italy was a latecomer to the world of nation-states, poorly endowed with natural resources, and internally divided but determined to measure up to its more advanced neighbours, and to its past achievements. Pervading the history of its foreign relations—after 1945 as well as before—are an elemental urge to retain an important place on the world stage, a fear of poverty, mediocrity, and relegation, a capacity to weather periods of adversity brought on by the vulnerability of its economy and the flaws of its political regimes, and to remain a vital part of the West.

The pre-1945 background

Italy's most important foreign minister in the 1870s, the Lombard Emilio Visconti Venosta, rejected permanent alliances in favour of a flexible non-alignment that allowed Italy to shift its weight in favour of the bigger powers. Sentiment inclined him towards France, while realism led him to cultivate good relations with Britain, the leading Mediterranean power, and like France a patron of the *Risorgimento*.

Italy's alliance with Germany and Austria-Hungary in 1882 followed the French seizure of Tunis and the passage of power to the 'Historic Left.' Anticipating Mussolini, the Left saw alliance with Germany as a way of allowing Italy to pursue its imperial dream. Francesco Crispi, a Sicilian and lieutenant of Garibaldi, despised the Francophilism of Moderates like Visconti Venosta and saw African empire as a remedy for poverty and unrest. Crispi's fall after the defeat at Adowa in 1896 led to a more prudent foreign policy, with Visconti Venosta back in office after twenty years.

Italian foreign policy between 1896 and 1940 reflected the basic tension between Visconti Venosta's prudence and Crispi's dream of power. The shifting pendulum of Fascist foreign policy reflected the conflict between the realism of Contarini and Grandi (and Mussolini himself who got US financial support in the 1920s) and the regime's Mediterranean-African ambitions. The abandonment of the former course led to the catastrophe of 1940 to 1945.

Participation in the prevailing system of European state co-operation is a third constant in Italian foreign policy. To Visconti Venosta, this meant the post-1815 Concert of Europe, a notion which competed with the more radical ideas of Giuseppe Mazzini and Francesco Cattaneo. After the First World War, the liberal economist Luigi Einaudi and Giovanni Agnelli, the founder of Fiat, combined the message of Cavour, Visconti Venosta and the Moderates—free trade and Europe's cultural unity—with Cattaneo's confederalism. The failure of Mussolini's extreme version of particularism placed the idea of European unity on the agenda once again.

Italy's defeat in 1943 also marked a brusque return to foreign policy realism, and it was fitting that Carlo Sforza (foreign minister,

1947–51), had begun his career as Visconti Venosta's secretary. Italy's connection with the new Mediterranean hegemon represented the revival of an older tradition—even if the relationship with the United States acquired an importance far outweighing that of the 'traditional friendship' with Britain.

Italy and the United States

The disgrace of the military and the discrediting of nationalism, the emergence of a party-dominated political system with a weak executive, the preoccupation with economic improvement: these factors contributed to what has been called a post-war 'process of introversion' with regard to foreign affairs (Romano 1984, 436). The 1943 Armistice, followed by the harsh Peace Treaty of 1947, reduced Italy to the status of a third-rate military power, stripped it of its empire, and produced a sense of resignation about its capacity to play an independent role. The large and well-organized Italian Communist Party (PCI) overshadowed political life and increased the sense of weakness and dependency on the United States.

But the notion of 'introversion' should not be taken too far. Sforza and the Christian Democratic leader Alcide De Gasperi were statesmen formed, after all, when Italy had considered itself a great power. Internal objectives—the need to obtain aid, to isolate the left, to secure middle class support—were obviously central to their diplomacy. But like the Moderates of the 1870s, they pursued internal consolidation hand-in-hand with membership in international society on the basis of equal dignity.

This is not to suggest that De Gasperi and Sforza were in a hurry to join the new alliances of 1948–9. Despite the worsening Cold War the Italian government considered other options, such as a kind of Westward-leaning armed neutrality, and attempted to trade Italy's participation in the nascent Atlantic Pact for the removal of peace treaty restrictions and concessions on Italy's colonies and Trieste.

The view that Italy's inclusion in the Western bloc was simply inevitable overlooks the fact that the British government and important US circles were opposed. The De Gasperi government played the card of Italy's vulnerability to communism to win State Department and ultimately White House support. Italy also received vital backing from France, which sought to extend the alliance southward to include Algeria. Italian adherence to the North Atlantic Treaty was a close-run thing, but in the end De Gasperi and Sforza accomplished their objectives in a way that Visconti Venosta, coiner of the phrase *indipendenti sempre, isolati mai* (always independent, never isolated) would have approved. Italy shed its pariah status and obtained a security guarantee through the patronage of France and the new leading power of the Mediterranean.

The American connection provided the emergency aid that helped Italy to maintain minimum levels of civilian consumption, reconstruct a shattered infrastructure, restore the export trade (beginning with textiles), modernize heavy industry (steel, cars, electricity, oil refining), and stabilize the lira—though in defiance of Marshall Plan advice. The USA revived the Italian armed forces and took practical steps to defend Italy from outside attack after 1949.

America's protective mantle also had a broader meaning. Pietro Quaroni, Italian ambassador to Paris, warned Sforza in 1948 that the alternative to a close connection with the United States was to become 'another Egypt.' Italy must accept—or pay lip service to—a controversial Marshall Plan bilateral agreement and other US-inspired '*bestialità* not for general reasons of principle but exclusively for our interests. The Americans and only the Americans can protect us.' (Harper 1986, 160). Quaroni was talking not only about the Russians, but Italy's European 'friends.' President Franklin Roosevelt had forced the British to swallow the liberalization of the Italian occupation regime during the 1944 presidential campaign. Truman had forced the French to withdraw from the Val d'Aosta in 1945. Secretary of State James Byrnes alone had risen to shake De Gasperi's hand at the Paris peace conference in 1946. State Department backing had ensured Italy's charter membership of the North Atlantic Alliance in 1949.

The Americans, in other words, helped to relieve Italy's deep preoccupation with *presenza* and diplomatic rank. Being present and treated at least formally as an equal in international forums was vital to the self-esteem and internal standing of the political class of a defeated country seeking rehabilitation just as it had been to the élite of a new and marginal 'great power' after 1861. In the early 1960s, Italian leaders looked with approval when the Americans opposed the

emergence of the kind Franco-German axis that might have threatened NATO and lowered Italy's standing in the European Economic
Community. In the 1980s and 1990s, the Italian government looked to
the United States for support to gain entry to the Group of Five
Finance Ministers and the Bosnia 'Contact Group.'

To be sure, Italy enjoyed these benefits for a price. But it was
reckoned an acceptable one from the point of view of a majority of
Italians: first, exclusion of the Communists from power, which
coincided with the interests of the moderate political forces. Secondly, Italy granted the USA access to its territory and influence over
its armed forces, entailing a kind of limited sovereignty. While
deplored by the Communists, Radicals, and neo-fascists, this did not
become a serious issue of principle for the centre-right and 'democratic left'.

There were several reasons for this: the pacifist, anti-nationalist
ideology of the Christian Democrats and lack of an equivalent to
Gaullism, the desire to live down Italy's reputation for unreliability,
and above all, perhaps, Italy's military weakness and exposed position
in the Cold War. France acquired its own nuclear weapons and could
assume that NATO would blunt an attack from the east even after US
forces and bases had been removed from its territory. Italy could not
make the same assumption.

The price of protection, finally, included US interference in Italian
politics, though this was more often than not invited by the pro-
Western political parties and trade unions. It would be wrong to
underestimate the negative effects of the freezing of the Italian political system and lack of *alternanza* (alternation in power). But
responsibility lay in part with the PCI itself, which long delayed its
transformation to social democracy. Part also lay with the proportional representation electoral system, which Italy freely adopted
in 1947–8.

In dealing with the much-discussed question of American interference it is necessary to distinguish between the basic, unalterable facts
of Italy's geographical location in the West and NATO membership—
once the De Gasperi government had decided to join—on one hand,
and purposeful American meddling on the other. The Americans,
for a start, were not always clear in their own minds about how to
react if the Communists took control. President Dwight Eisenhower
remarked that, if Italy were to elect a Communist government, 'he did

not see how we could do anything to prevent its exercise of power.' The Chairman of the Joint Chiefs of Staff complained that National Security Council papers did not answer 'the 64-dollar question of what the United States [was] prepared to do' in such a case (US Department of State 1952–4, vi. 1608, 1669). None the less, Italy's NATO membership deterred the Communists and conditioned their political strategy for over thirty years. But with the partial exception of the occupation and Marshall Plan periods, active US interference had marginal effects on the course of events and was to a degree counter-productive from the point of view of US goals.

The American campaign to influence the April 1948 elections generated support for the Christian Democrats but also protest votes for the Left. For much of the post-1945 period, the perception of US intrusion was a source of PCI strength. US leverage faded considerably after the Marshall Plan, while pressure on Italy to rearm during the Korean war, failure to deliver on a March 1948 promise to back Italy's position on Trieste in its dispute with Yugoslavia, and restrictions on Italian immigration in the 1950s cost the Americans much good will. The USA held few cards by the time of the 1953 elections. Eisenhower's ambassadress Clare Booth Luce (1953–6) misplayed an already weak hand by threatening 'grave consequences' should Italy 'fall unhappy victim to the wiles of totalitarianism' (US Department of State 1952–4, vi. 1613, 1621).

Prime Minister Mario Scelba (1953–4), a hard-line anti-communist, felt obliged to tell the hyperactive Luce that 'America ha[d] greatly exaggerated the danger' of the PCI. There is no evidence that the efforts of Luce or CIA station chief William Colby, who dispensed millions of dollars in Italy in the 1950s, had a significant effect on communist strength. Khrushchev's 1956 'secret speech' and the Hungary crisis were far more important in shaping PCI fortunes. In spite of those events, the Communists held their own at the polls in 1958. After the elections DC Secretary Amintore Fanfani pointedly thanked the US Embassy for not having 'intruded itself into the electoral contest, an intrusion which might have done a useful service to the Communists' (US Department of State 1955–7, xxvii. 1641, 1673; 1958–60, vii. 459). Christian Democratic opponents of the 'apertura a sinistra' (a DC alliance with the PSI) used US scepticism to reinforce their own arguments, but Washington played a minor part in the episode. After 1960, the Americans, while expressing concern about the PSI's position on NATO, adopted a cautious, neutral position to avoid the impression of interference in Italian affairs.

US–Italian relations in the 1960s and 1970s are still somewhat shrouded in mystery. But there is little evidence that the United States was connected with Carabinieri commander Giovanni De Lorenzo's plan to intimidate PSI and DC politicians and limit the centre-left reform programme in 1964, or involved in the Aldo Moro kidnapping in 1978. The State Department's famous 12 January 1978, statement calling for the diminution of communist influence was followed by the PCI's entry into the government majority two months later. At some level, US officials were probably aware of the activities of the Atlanticist zealots in the Italian interior ministry and military intelligence (SID) who helped to plan and cover-up the 1969–74 right-wing terrorist campaign, the 'strategy of tension.' But this does not mean that the United States was behind the strategy or that it served the purposes of those involved.

Italy chooses Europe

All things considered, the post-1945 alliance with the United States was a good bargain for Italy. Among the benefits was that friendship with the dominant Mediterranean power did not force it to sacrifice its other historic impulses. Italy, to a degree, could have its cake and eat it. Starting with the Marshall Plan (1948–51), the Americans pushed trade liberalization among the European countries while exerting the pressure on France and providing the security umbrella that allowed Franco-German reconciliation in the form of the European Coal and Steel Community (ECSC) to proceed.

The idea of European unity struck a responsive chord in Italy, where nationalism had been discredited, but the Italian government was wary of a 'Europe' that would challenge the US protectorate or prompt the Americans to leave. De Gasperi was initially cool toward the European Defence Community (EDC)—just as his pupil Giulio Andreotti was suspicious forty years later of a 'European defence identity' that created tension between Italy's Atlantic and European loyalties. But once Washington decided to support the EDC (mid-1951), De Gasperi followed suit. Revealingly, he tried to envelop it in a federal political structure (the European Political Community) that had more popular appeal than a purely military entity in which Italy would be overshadowed by Germany and France, and which was poorly suited to the public's pacifistic mood.

Italy's commitment to European economic and political integration became different things to different people. For federalist militants like Altiero Spinelli, it meant building a European state along American lines. For the Catholic, lay, and moderate socialist forces of the De Gasperi period, it was more a means to national ends—namely, modernization and stabilization—than an end in itself. 'The real core of Italy's Europeanism,' as Federico Romero writes, 'was clearly the urge to "communalize" Italy's difficulties'—in other words, a way to obtain badly needed raw materials, subsidies for its backward regions, above all, outlets for its low-cost exports and surplus population (Romero 1994). Some would argue that in stressing Italy's European vocation De Gasperi had an ulterior purpose: the need to make Atlanticism more palatable to those like the left-wing DC leader Giuseppe Dossetti, who favoured European unity but rejected the Cold War crusade. Be that as it may, 'Europe' became a kind of surrogate national identity and crutch to lean on. Italians across the political spectrum—including Socialists by the early sixties, and Communists by the mid-seventies—came to believe that Europe would bring prosperity and efficiency.

Some Italians criticized the tendency to see the requirements of membership in Europe as a source of guidance and rigour lacking at home. Invariably they pointed to the striking dichotomy between Italy's rhetorical enthusiasm for Europe, on one hand, and its inability to influence Brussels, and record of delays and infractions in implementing EC directives, on the other. But the attachment to Europe arose precisely because the Italian state was discredited and weak. There is no doubt that opening Italy to European competition had a salutary effect on Italian industry, while the need to meet European standards at times gave Italian governments much-needed leverage in their efforts to reform.

Italian support of European integration, in the end, is a case of nothing succeeding like success. Participation in the ECSC helped to underwrite the closing of most of Italy's inefficient Sardinian mines. Liberalization of the market, feared by many steel firms, occurred over a five-year period, allowing Finsider, Italy's biggest producer, to complete its ambitious modernization plans. Italian producers reliant on imported scrap benefited from ECSC policies which stabilized the price. Italian steel production increased from 3.6 million tons in 1952 to 15.8 tons in 1967, mostly to supply expanding domestic needs.

After the failure of the EDC in 1954, Italy pursued the new Benelux approach to integration: an overall common market that would sustain growing intra-European trade and lock in privileged access to the lucrative German market. Foreign Minister Gaetano Martino hosted important meetings of the 'six' at Messina (1955) and Venice (1956). The Treaty of Rome (1957) creating a customs union conformed to Italian wishes by including the harmonization of social policy and the free movement of labour. Italian diplomacy obtained a special 'Protocol concerning Italy' in which its partners recognized that the development of Italy's backward regions was in 'their common interest'. Italy also gained the commitment of the new European Economic Community (EEC) to set up a European Social Fund to pay half the cost of retraining and relocating workers from distressed areas, and the creation of the European Investment Bank to finance development and modernization projects.

The launching of the EEC in 1957 gave new impetus to Italy's remarkable export-led growth. Between 1958 and 1968, Italy's trade with its EEC partners increased by over 500 per cent and its share of world manufacturing exports nearly doubled. During the same period its Gross National Product (GNP) increased from $41.9 billion to $71.6 billion (in constant 1968 dollars).

About 1 million Italians emigrated to France, Germany, and the Benelux in the 1950s. In 1961 and 1962, EEC regulations guaranteed freedom of movement, established Community rather than national preference in hiring, and recognized the immigrant's right to bring his family and educate his children. After 1962, with more jobs available in Italy, emigration declined and greater numbers of workers returned from abroad. But twenty years later there were still 1.7 million Italians working in other Community countries and their remittances were a key item in the Italian balance of payments.

One area where European integration failed to live up to expectations was agriculture. The EEC Common Agricultural Policy (CAP), as implemented in the 1960s, provided relatively greater price support and protection for northern European products—cereals, beef, veal, and dairy products—than for Mediterranean products—oils, fruits, vegetables, and wine. The CAP financing mechanism, the European Agricultural Guidance and Guarantee Fund, or FEOGA, did not provide enough help to address the structural weaknesses of Italian agriculture, and Italy, in effect, subsidized the farmers of France and the Netherlands. Its tendency to import large amounts of food from its partners did not help. By the late 1970s, when Italy demanded that the Mediterranean products issue be addressed, it was paying in far more than it received from the FEOGA and running the largest annual food trade deficit in the Community.

Italy turns to the Mediterranean

After the Second World War the 'particularist' urge in Italian foreign policy was not a strong one for obvious reasons. It none the less found expression in progressive Catholicism in the 1950s and Craxian Socialism in the 1980s. Left-wing Christian Democrats like Giorgio La Pira saw Italy as a kind of bridge between the emerging Islamic nations and the secularized, capitalist West, and thus an ideal partner for neighbouring peoples seeking to free themselves from French and British colonialism. As President of the Republic (1955–62) the Catholic trade unionist Giovanni Gronchi sought an autonomous role for Italy in the mediation of East–West controversies like Berlin, leading to clashes with the pro-US foreign ministry and the Christian Democratic right.

Post-war particularism found its most forceful exponent in the former Christian Democratic partisan Enrico Mattei, the head of the state oil company, ENI. Mattei was sometimes compared to a Renaissance *condottiere*, but a closer antecedent was Crispi. Both were driven, imperious leaders with a mission to the South. Like Crispi, Mattei saw the old imperial powers, especially France, as Italy's natural rivals. Under his leadership, ENI conducted a semi-independent foreign policy including support for Moroccan independence and the Algerian FLN. His deals with Nasser's Egypt, Iran, and the Soviet Union won him the enmity of the established oil companies. Faced with the possibility that ENI would import and resell large amounts of cheap Soviet crude in Western Europe, Standard Oil of New Jersey complained bitterly to the State Department and asked for help in bringing Mattei under control.

Much ink has been spilled over the significance of *neo-atlanticismo*, the term coined by the conservative Christian Democrat Giuseppe Pella in 1957, but associated with Gronchi, Mattei, and ex-members of the Dossetti current like La Pira and Fanfani. It commonly denotes an Atlanticism infused with the economic and social—as opposed to purely military—purposes foreseen by Article 2 of the North Atlantic Treaty, as well as greater Italian autonomy from the United States. For some it was intended to facilitate the DC's budding alliance with the Socialist Party, and thus to restore the kind of stable governing formula lacking after the elections of 1953. After 1956, the anti-NATO Socialists under Pietro Nenni began to move towards the centre on foreign policy and away from the PCI.

Another view traces neo-Atlanticism to De Gasperi himself, and sees it, *grosso modo*, as a consensus position within the DC. De Gasperi had called for the activation of Article 2 in 1952. In this view the neo-Atlanticists would include not only Gronchi but Paolo Emilio Taviani. (For Francesco Cossiga, Taviani and Andreotti were part of Italy's post-war 'pro-American lobby.') Their aim was not to challenge US hegemony in the Mediterranean but to reinforce it *vis-à-vis* France and Britain in the wake of the Suez crisis. In so doing they hoped to consolidate Italy's role as America's privileged agent and 'brilliant second' in dealing with Nasser and the explosive problems of the Third World.

But this view glosses over the ideological differences between Christian Democrats like Gronchi who had been opponents of the Atlantic alliance and were supporters of the opening to the Socialists, and Taviani who was neither of those things. There is clear evidence that Gronchi and Mattei (though not Fanfani) were basically nationalist and neutralist in their views. Mattei told the *New York Times* journalist C. L. Sulzberger, 'I am personally against NATO and for neutralism.' Mattei's achievements came not from encouraging US hegemony but from his obsession to defy it (Sulzberger 1970, 870).

Orthodox Atlanticists and opponents of the opening to the left like Scelba and Antonio Segni abhorred Mattei, who created friction with Washington and used company revenues to advance his domestic political designs. Europeanists like Spinelli dismissed Italy's so-called Mediterranean vocation as a quixotic distraction from serious concerns. But despite the obvious limitations of Italian policy, it is hard to gainsay the attempt to play a stabilizing role in the neighbouring Arab world while securing access to oil for an energy-dependent and rapidly growing economy.

The cooler heads in the US government saw that it would be counter-productive to challenge Mattei and sought a rapprochement between ENI and American oil companies. This process was under way when Mattei's plane crashed near Milan in October 1962, though those who were unaware of it naturally suspected American involvement in his death.

Introversion and transition, 1962–1979

The early 1960s marked the end of the initial, relatively active period of post-war foreign policy. Italy's basic Atlantic and European choices had been made. Détente between the superpowers after 1962 allowed a certain disregard for international affairs and neo-Atlanticism faded in the absence of its driving force. American eyebrows were raised when Fiat built a large car factory in the Soviet Union in the mid-1960s, and when it allowed the Libyans to control 10 per cent of the company's stock during the oil crisis of the 1970s, but no one compared the self-assured and pro-American Gianni Agnelli (he sent his son to Princeton) to Mattei.

De Gaulle's early 1960s diplomacy heightened Italy's sense of dependency on the Americans to maintain its rank in the West and encouraged a kind of 'Bulgarian' conformism that contrasted with the dignified realism of De Gasperi. The DC's right-wing and centrist factions exerted pressure to follow the US line on issues like the Kennedy administration's Multilateral Nuclear Force. Without success, Italy supported British entry into the EEC to counterbalance France. The new phase in foreign policy also coincided with all-consuming internal developments—factional battles within the DC, the struggle to adopt social reforms, and economic problems starting in 1964. Italy's stronger personalities, for example Fanfani as foreign minister, were not concerned about toeing the American line on the Vietnam War. By the late sixties, however, they were too distracted by domestic matters to pay much attention to foreign affairs.

The internal crisis entered a new and critical phase with the student and workers movements of 1968–9. The economy had not recovered its balance when Italy was staggered by OPEC's quadrupling of oil prices and the world-wide recession of 1974–5. First black and then red terrorism appeared on the scene. The United States and Germany threatened Italy with a kind of quarantine within NATO and the denial of financial aid should Communists enter the cabinet after the 1976 elections. In 1979 Italy was excluded from the Guadaloupe summit where the Western powers decided (failing a negotiated settlement) to install US Pershing II and cruise missiles to counter Soviet intermediate range SS-20s. For the second time in thirty years, Italy faced a struggle to avoid relegation and to salvage its credibility within the West.

The best-known protagonist of a more assertive foreign policy was a self-styled Garibaldian, Bettino Craxi. But Aldo Moro, a former follower of the pacifistic Dossetti, set the stage. Moro was the architect of the PCI's cooptation into the majority, a strategy that helped to domesticate the Communists while calling on their great energies to combat terrorism and the economic crisis.

Before the 1976 elections the PCI secretary Enrico Berlinguer stated that Italy's withdrawal from NATO would upset the existing international equilibrium and that NATO was a shield behind which to build socialism in an atmosphere of freedom. In December 1977 the PCI signed a parliamentary resolution calling the Atlantic Alliance and European Community commitments 'a framework that represents the fundamental terms of reference of Italian foreign policy'. The new consensus did not mean Communist support of the European Monetary System and the installation of US cruise missiles, but the PCI's opposition on security issues once it had left the majority in 1979 was relatively mild.

Another protagonist of the revival was Prime Minister Giulio Andreotti. The oil crisis prompted Andreotti, like other Western leaders, to pursue a more active diplomacy towards the Arab world. Andreotti remains an enigmatic figure but it would be a mistake to identify him with the Mediterranean particularism of La Pira or Mattei. A De Gasperi protégé and leader of the DC right, Andreotti had opposed neo-Atlanticism and the opening to the left. As defense minister (1959–66), he had developed close relations with the United States. But De Gasperi had not seen friendship with the chief

Mediterranean power as an excuse for subservience. And with the apparent decline of American influence—indicated by the Iranian revolution and second oil shock in 1979—Italy found itself more exposed than at any point since the war. In those circumstances an oil-dependent country had no choice but to shoulder more direct responsibility for the protection of its interests and those of the West.

The 'new' foreign policy and its limits

A series of actions beginning in 1979 signalled the start of a new phase in Italian foreign policy. The decision in 1979 to install US cruise missiles helped to restore Italy's credit with its closest allies. The decision about the same time to join the European Monetary System and submit to the discipline of a more tightly managed currency had comparable symbolic importance. As president of the EC Council of Ministers, January–June 1980, the Italian government helped to resolve the bitter budgetary dispute between Britain and the Community and sponsored an EC démarche (the Venice declaration) on the Middle East that recognized the Palestine Liberation Organization (PLO). In 1981 foreign minister Emilio Colombo and his German colleague Hans Dietrich Genscher sponsored a 'Solemn Declaration on European Union'. Europeanists deplored the usual lack of concrete results from these initiatives. But they indicated a rekindling of the urge to concert with Europe, as did the renewed activism of the federalist Altiero Spinelli, elected to the European Parliament with PCI votes in 1979.

In June 1980, the Socialist defence minister Lelio Logorio issued a document referring to Italy's 'large and growing responsibilities' in a southerly direction. In September 1980 Italy officially guaranteed the neutrality of Malta. The sense of vulnerability to the south led to calls for a 'new defence model,' or shift in emphasis towards the Mediterranean and Middle East. In August–September 1982, 500 *Bersaglieri* helped to cover the withdrawal of the PLO from Beirut. At Italian initiative, the force returned to Lebanon after the Shaba and Chatilla massacres and remained until the abrupt US pull-out in 1984. This time a 2,000 man contingent performed the more complicated task of protecting Palestinian camps. Lagorio declared (February 1983):

'The Atlantic pact does not guarantee in a comprehensive way the defence of Italian interests.' In the early eighties Italy acquired a new generation of strike aircraft, the Tornado, and a small aircraft carrier, the *Garibaldi*.

With the formation of the Craxi government in August 1983, the 'new' foreign policy entered its most ambitious phase. Its main protagonists, Prime Minister Craxi, Defence Minister Spadolini, and (now) Foreign Minister Andreotti were all products of the post-war *partitocrazia*, a system offering little room for personal initiative, and whose stability and capacity for action rested on continuous compromise and a carefully calibrated sharing of power. But each played out—more or less consciously—a more classical historical role. As it abandoned its leftist baggage, the PSI tried to revive a decisive style of leadership semi-taboo since the war and Craxi identified himself with the great hero of Italian socialism and nationalism, Garibaldi.

Craxi's foreign policy sought greater autonomy and specificity in Italy's positions *vis-à-vis* its allies. He caused a stir in May 1984 when he suggested the possibility of suspending the installation of NATO medium-range missiles to spur negotiations with Moscow. Another theme was sympathy for Arab nationalism. In December 1984 Craxi and Andreotti met Yasser Arafat and backed a nascent accord between Jordan and the PLO. Although the EC had declined to sanction an Italian move on its behalf (the idea had been to breathe life into the Venice declaration), Craxi wanted to proceed alone.

Craxi cast himself as the patron of Tunisia, where he had a villa and close ties to the 'socialist' regime of Bourguiba, and also of Siad Barre's regime in Somalia, where the Italian taxpayer financed huge construction projects. Craxi believed that Italy must be prepared— like other 'medium powers'—to defend its interests and that military missions to Lebanon and later the Persian Gulf had a salutary effect on the national character. In all this, and in his domineering personality, Craxi resembled Crispi, an earlier Garibaldian of Sicilian origin with a mission to the South.

Andreotti, by contrast, was not concerned with Italian autonomy or specificity and even less with refurbishing military force as foreign policy tool. He wished to exploit Italy's even-handedness and his own diplomatic acumen to pursue a dialogue with radical states beyond the reach of other western countries. The Americans notoriously distrusted the 'Machiavellian' Andreotti, but Cossiga was correct in observing that, 'In his realism he [Andreotti] always believed that it was in the interest of his country to have a special relationship with the United States.' Andreotti assumed, not unreasonably, that his pro-USA record entitled him to the benefit of the doubt. His memoirs suggest that he sometimes thought he knew better what US and general western interests were than did the Americans themselves (Cossiga 1997, 9; Andreotti 1989).

Craxi and Andreotti saw eye to eye during the dramatic *Achille Lauro* incident, when a group of PLO militants hijacked a cruise ship and killed a handicapped American passenger, provoking an unprecedented confrontation between Italy and Washington in October 1985. The Italians defied an astonished US government and released Abu Abbas, PLO leader and mastermind of the ship's hijacking. One reason was the need to safeguard relations with the Egyptian government, which had taken control of the ship and its passengers. Equally important was the fact that the Americans had crudely violated Italian sovereignty by attempting to 'extradite' Abu Abbas at gunpoint from a NATO base on Italian soil. Craxi played the Crispian role to the hilt when he asserted the principle of Italian autonomy and compared Arafat with the 'noble' Mazzini. This statement was aimed at Spadolini and the strongly pro-US Republican Party— descended from Mazzini—which had just brought down the government over the release of Abbas. The Achilles' heel of Craxi's foreign policy at this point was less outright US opposition than his government's dependency on a small coalition partner, the PRI, that was more royalist—or realist—than the king.

After a Palestinian terrorist attack at Fiumicino airport (which took place in January 1986 despite Italy's pro-PLO stance) the government line shifted towards the Republican position. Craxi's original initiative evaporated when King Hussein repudiated the PLO-Jordanian accord in February 1986, while Andreotti found himself isolated in his conciliatory position on Libya. Italy undoubtedly had no choice but to pursue a more active Mediterranean policy in the 1970s and 1980s, but what Federico Chabod, writing about the late nineteenth century, had called the 'mirage of the Orient' played its tricks on Italian politicians once again (Chabod 1951, 544).

Craxi and Andreotti were more successful when they concentrated on European affairs. As president of the European Council in the first semester of 1985, the Italian government helped to conclude the entry of Spain and Portugal into the EC. At the Milan summit of the Council (June 1985) Italy put the issue of calling an Inter-Governmental Conference (IGC) to reform the EC treaties to a vote, and won. Italy was among the strongest backers of the Single European Act (February 1986) and the programme to create a single internal market by 1 January 1993. The perception of economic advantage drove Italy, as did the old urge of the political class to play an active role in a political community larger than itself.

Craxi's experiment in 'decisionist' executive leadership ended abruptly in March 1987. A fifty-six-day government crisis and early elections were a telling reminder of the political and institutional limits of the 'new' foreign policy. Indeed, if 'the ingredients, which constitute energy in the executive, are first unity, secondly duration, thirdly an adequate provision for its support, fourthly competent powers' (Hamilton 1982, 355), the Italian 'first republic' was a negative model.

Post-election infighting subsided only with the formation in July 1989 of a five-party government headed by Andreotti with the corpulent but tireless Gianni De Michelis (PSI) as foreign minister. De Michelis, a Venetian, took a special interest in the dramatic events to the north-east and launched a five-way dialogue of Italy, Austria, Hungary, Czechoslovakia and (soon to be ex-) Yugoslavia. The *Pentagonale* initiative was short on substance but Italian business took concrete advantage of new opportunities to become the second biggest foreign investor (after Germany) in post-communist Central and Eastern Europe.

In spite of the government's accomplishments during the July–December 1990 Italian presidency of the European Council (including the scheduling of an IGC on economic and monetary union and another on political union), the usual critics noted that Italy's fiscal house was becoming a shambles under the free-spending Andreotti government, while its day-to-day attitude to the implementation of single-market directives was marked by inattention or worse. In June 1991, Italy ranked last in the EC with only fifty-two out of some 300 1992 directives translated into law.

The early 1990s crisis

The growing contradiction between Italy's European aspirations and its capacity to fulfil them came to a head in 1992. The early 1990s crisis, in turn, was a consequence of the sudden end of the Cold War. The fall of the Berlin Wall, followed by the decision to reunify Germany, led to huge West German budget deficits reflecting the cost of reunification, which in turn prompted the Bundesbank to push up German interest rates. High German interest rates put downward pressure on the lira and the pound, setting the stage for the devastating speculative attack which drove those currencies out of the European Monetary System in September 1992.

Simultaneously, 1989–91 events prompted Bonn and Paris to speed up the timetable for economic and political integration in order to anchor reunified Germany in a secure European home. The Maastricht Treaty on European Union was signed in February 1992. The collapse of Italy's international credibility in 1992 was connected to the enormous gap between Italian reality and the Maastricht 'convergence criteria' requiring, *inter alia*, a public debt of no more than 60 per cent, and a budget deficit of no more than 3 per cent of GDP in order to take part in the final phase of economic and monetary union. In 1991, Italy's figures were, respectively, 102.5 and 10.7 per cent.

Coinciding with—and aggravating—the financial crisis was the political and moral crisis which also exploded in 1992. The *Tangentopoli* scandals and the disintegration of the DC and PSI between the 1992 and 1994 elections were also connected to the end of the Cold War and the collapse of communism, including the transformation of the PCI into a social democratic party, the PDS. Under the circumstances the anti-communist parties lost legitimacy and appeal. They were now vulnerable to a new protest party, the Lega Nord, and to magistrates investigating corruption that had flourished thanks in part to the lack of political alternation during the Cold War. Before 1989 public opinion would not have supported the Milan magistrates to the same degree, while Christian Democrat and Socialist politicians would have undermined their efforts—with the help of the intelligence services—in the name of anti-communism and national security.

While the public focused on the fiscal crisis, the Mafia emergency, electoral and institutional reform, and the anti-corruption drive, commentators and politicians debated the longer-term implications of the end of the Cold War. The debate followed familiar lines. Some argued, for example, that with America's role uncertain after the Cold War, 'Italian security [was] ever more an exclusively Italian problem.' According to *LiMes*, a new, self-styled 'journal of geopolitics,' Atlanticism and Europeanism had 'anaesthetized Italian geopolitical thought' and sense of nationhood and national interest. Italy had an 'important and specific role to play' in the new international context and 'must accept its new responsibility.' (*LiMes* 1993, 7–8). Indeed, the Italian armed forces regularly intervened abroad—albeit on a small scale, and as part of coalitions—in the 1990s. Operations included Iraq, Mozambique, Somalia, Bosnia (participation in IFOR and SFOR), and Macedonia. Italian troops intervened on several occasions in nearby Albania. In 1996–7, an Italian-led multinational force of 6,000 ('Operation Alba') acted to prevent anarchy and to stem the tide of immigration from the Balkans. About 13,000 Albanians arrived in Italy in March 1996 alone.

As a result of the Persian Gulf crisis, the collapse of the Warsaw Pact, and the prospect of hostile Islamic neighbours, the Mediterranean-oriented 'new defence model' was further refined and major military reforms were announced. Along with its vulnerability to mass immigration, and to the proliferation of weapons of mass destruction, Italy's vital interest in regional stability rested on the fact that it depended on North Africa and the Arabian peninsula for 69 per cent of its crude oil imports, and on Algeria for 24 per cent of its natural gas.

At a moment when Italy again faced a seemingly impossible struggle to regain international credibility and avoid relegation to the second division of a 'multi-speed' Europe (an idea floated by the German Christian Democrats in 1994), another group of politicians and commentators stressed the supreme importance of Italy's European identity and commitments. This was the view of the Socialist Giuliano Amato, whose government began to tackle Italy's budget deficit in 1992–3, a Herculean task inherited by the government of Carlo Azeglio Ciampi (the former Bank of Italy head) in 1993–4. The Ciampi government's foreign minister, the Christian Democrat Beniamino Andreatta, harshly condemned the 'deviant orientations' of unilateralism, protectionism, belief in an Italian specificity, and neo-neutralism (Andreatta 1993).

Andreatta's words were aimed at 'neo-nationalist' intellectuals, but they would have applied as well to Antonio Martino, foreign minister in Silvio Berlusconi's short-lived centre-right government (1994), who objected to the Maastricht method of achieving European Monetary Union (EMU) and held up Slovenia's associate member-ship in the EU pending the compensation of Italian wartime refugees. Another commentator argued that membership in Europe alone could guarantee 'international legitimacy' and status to Italy now that the end of the East–West confrontation had allegedly reduced the strategic value of its territory to the United States. This school of thought favoured an all-out commitment to meet the requirements of monetary union and development of the common foreign and security policy foreseen by Maastricht.

To an old realist like Andreotti the latter idea made little sense—with or without the Cold War—because Italy would count for little compared to Germany and France and because challenging NATO or raising unrealistic expectations about European capabilities might lead to isolationism in the United States. This view reflected mem-ories of the American threat to reappraise its European commitment during the agony of the EDC in 1953–4, but also the nightmare of realism since the days of Visconti Venosta: that Italy would be isolated from its main ally, or forced to choose between its friendship with Mediterranean naval power and its continental links. In 1990–91 the Andreotti government positioned itself on the 'European defence identity' issue with the Atlanticist British rather than the Germans and French. It had few problems in accepting the US-inspired 'Rome Declaration' of 1991, according to which NATO would remain the forum of discussion and locus of decision-making in the area of security—regardless of Maastricht.

In the same spirit, many argued that despite the end of the Cold War the American connection was anything but obsolete. For some, the rise of German or Franco-German power, or the shift of the EU's centre of gravity through eastward enlargement, would accentuate Italy's marginality and dependency on the USA. Nor could anyone say with certainty that the Russian threat had permanently disappeared. To these factors could be added growing American cultural influence, leading one half-facetious analyst to predict Italy's 'pure and simple annexation by the United States' (Ilari 1993). In any event, once Italy had become a 'front-line state' and staging area for NATO operations in the Balkans (beginning with Bosnia in 1995), it was clear that predictions of its declining strategic importance to the United States were highly premature.

Conclusion: a multi-partisan consensus

In May 1998, Italy's third post-war struggle back from near-relegation to renewed international credibility and respectability was crowned with success. At the Luxemburg summit of the EU, Italy was officially certified as having satisfied the Maastricht criteria and invited to be a charter member of EMU. As late as the formation of the Romano Prodi government after the 1996 elections, with Ciampi—whose name had become synonymous with dogged determination and austerity—as treasury minister, few would have bet on this result. The exceptions were those who remembered the late 1940s and late 1970s when similar 'miracles' were performed.

Strikingly, given the economic sacrifices involved, no major Italian party or interest group opposed the goal of EMU in principle or believed that Italy's exclusion would be anything other than a national humiliation and economic disaster. Indeed, despite an export boom induced by the weak lira after 1992, remaining out of EMU would have meant a defenceless currency, exposed to speculative attack and retaliation by Italy's trading partners. Italian business, with a few dissenting voices, was ready to forswear future devaluation in return for the lower inflation, falling interest rates, and free capital mobility connected with joining EMU. Thinking Italians could see that Italy's fiscal house, including its bankrupt pension system, had to be put in order to face the challenge of globalization (read cut-throat US and Asian competition), in any case, and were thankful that Europe was there to provide the indispensable lever. Practically everyone instinctively believed, as Pietro Quaroni might have put it, that it was a question of becoming 'another Egypt' or remaining in the West. It is not surprising that the Euro-scepticism of Antonio Martino and his coalition ally Gianfranco Fini, leader of the postfascist Alleanza Nazionale party (AN), was mild compared to the

British, French, German, or Danish varieties and had more to do with means than ends.

Equally evident in the 1990s was that, despite differences of emphasis, no important sector of opinion—including the new parties, AN, Berlusconi's Forza Italia, or the PDS—saw pursuit of national interests in the Mediterranean, membership in Europe, and the American connection as stark alternatives. By the late 1990s (with the exception of the Lega Nord and Rifondazione comunista) there was a multi-partisan consensus according to which Italy must balance and reconcile its Mediterranean, European, and Atlantic commitments, and that drastic choices must be avoided at all costs.

The Prodi government (1996–8) illustrated the point. No Italian government was more assiduously pro-European. It made entry into EMU its basic *raison d'etre* and it strongly supported European defence co-operation. At the same time, the government did not question the US push to enlarge NATO to the east (except to try to include Slovenia and Romania in the first round), a policy which served to reinforce American political-military hegemony over the Old World. Unlike other NATO countries, Italy made no definite move to renegotiate base agreements with the United States dating from the height of the Cold War. This was despite (or partly because of) the presence of former Communist ministers, and despite outrage over the killing of twenty people by reckless US Marine pilots flying out of the NATO base at Aviano in 1998.

By and large, the centre-left coalition followed the US lead in dealing with the Balkans, and it sided with the Americans in a US–French dispute over who should head NATO's Southern Command (AFSOUTH), based in Naples. The explanation given by Luigi Vittorio Ferraris, a former diplomat, would not have surprised Quaroni: 'if he [the commanding officer] were French we would come down a step in rank.' A late 1990s opinion poll asked Italians, 'Who would come to our defence if we were ever in any danger?' For 37.5 per cent of respondents the answer was the United States; for 17.9 per cent, nobody; for 11 per cent, Europe (Ferraris *et al.* 1996). Because of an ingrained realism and sense of military weakness, though not necessarily their deep preferences, Italians would continue to look to the United States as their main protector as long as the United States was available to play the role.

The Prodi government, finally, realized the importance of stabilizing the mainly Islamic countries on the southern and eastern shores of the Mediterranean. This did not mean Italian unilateralism or 'particularism;' rather, co-operation with the United States and joint European action through the 'Euro-Mediterranean Partnership,' a programme combining aid, gradual economic liberalization, and political dialogue inaugurated by the EU in 1995. This multilateral approach reflected the lesson of the 1980s that Italy could not accomplish a great deal in the Mediterranean on its own. Still, Prodi—whose background linked him to the Dossetti–La Pira wing of Christian Democracy—emphasized that Italy had 'a unique role in constructing a progressive dialogue between the Islamic world and the Christian world. This must be our commitment in the coming years. For peace. For the economy of our *Mezzogiorno*. In order to regulate flows of immigration' (Prodi 1998). Old notions die hard, especially when they contain a solid grain of truth.

5

Italian environmental policies in the post-war period

Simonetta Tunesi

Nature repairs her ravages—repairs them with her sunshine, and with human labour.

(G. Eliot, *The Mill on the Floss*)

We are not living in a landscape but in a collective project.

(Sebastian Matta)

To trace the main elements in the history of the Italian environment two hypotheses are proposed. First, that the economic and political choices that shape the natural landscape and the urban environments after Second World War predate this era and testify to a deep divide, first of all intellectual and emotional, between the characteristics of environmental and historical resources and the way they were used. Secondly, that the implementation of environmental policies similar to those adopted by other western governments revealed extremely damaging effects in Italy, the land known as the *Bel paese*, home to more than 60 per cent of the world's architectural and cultural heritage.

Since the eighteenth century, Italy had been the destination of artists and wealthy young people on study tours. They came to enjoy the natural beauty and climate, to learn the formal rules of aesthetics, and to admire a country in which 'limited and domestic scenarios acquire a universal meaning' (Benevolo 1998). But by the latter half of the nineteenth century, owing to the advancing industrialization and the social overturns produced by the Napoleonic and Austro-Hungarian administrations, the organic relationship between the local, rural, urban, and craft communities and the landscape, the very relationship that made Italy so sought after and well loved, was already shattered.

The fifty years that followed the Second World War were characterized by a general indifference of public administrators, either at local or at national level, to safeguarding natural resources and the threads of human activities intertwined with them. While throughout this period, citizens have shown an increasing awareness of the delicate environmental equilibria and the need to protect public health, from the forming of sound grass-roots organizations to the founding of Green political parties in the 1960s, environmentalists' proposals have not had much influence on the policies for economic and urban development in Italy.

The divide between civil society and the natural environment is deep-rooted. Following the unification of Italy (1861), national efforts concentrated on creating administrative structures and on providing support to the manufacturing industry of the North. They marked the detachment of Italian intellectuals from their natural environment. This trend was accentuated as a result of the idealist approach characteristic of Italian culture in the twentieth century and the eclipse of scientific culture. It had irreversible effects on land organization and native natural resources.

In describing the history of the Italian environment it is important to trace the changes wrought on the delicate natural environment which had been embroidered by human labour over centuries; to look at the relationship between the people and the artistic heritage surrounding them; to record the effects that the destruction of beauty has on the quality of life of Italians. The challenge facing the common weal administrators is even harder than that given by other national realities. The economic, cultural, and political choices necessary to sustain the industrialization and the development of the Italian economy should rise to the level of the cultural and artistic heritage of a civilization so finely expressed by the harmony of Renaissance cities.

In post-war Italy the needs for reconstruction were pressing. The demand for industrial manual labour moved millions of Italians from the south to the north, from the mountains and the countryside to the cities. Urban development around historic centres was frenetic and unplanned. After the Second World War, urban planning regulations required the drawing up of detailed city plans. But in practice privileges were granted to private land owners and the way was left open to irrational building speculation, which failed to take into account the integration of the different urban functions. No control was put on the occupation of agricultural land on the outskirts of urban areas, not even historic areas. A glaring example is the degradation, since the 1950s, of the ancient Appian Way, where petrol stations, private villas and blocks of flats have been superimposed on ancient monuments. An urban park, planned for the last forty years, may never see the light of day.

Dormitory urban outskirts laid siege to artistic cities, invaded during the course of the time by bank counters and emptied of their old craft functions; monuments were degraded by air pollution; urban green areas were dismembered. By the seventies no Italian city could boast more than three square metres of green areas per inhabitant. European planning experiences, such as the British, Dutch, Danish, and Swedish, integrating the development of building areas with open spaces and green zones, were studied and applied, both in the construction of new peripheral neighbourhoods and in the preservation of historic cent. These efforts, undertaken during the seventies by left-wing public administrators in a few central north Italian towns, were a result of the transfer of several territorial control functions to the regions. They were just isolated examples that were not followed elsewhere.

Private and road freight transportation was encouraged in the name of the national car industries and supported by the construction of highways, viaducts, connecting roads, bridges, underpasses. During the fifties and the sixties more than 100 000 trees were cut down to allow for the enlargement of roads. This spread of concrete was more a result of favouring specific industrial, political, or local groups' interest than of meeting real needs. It has contributed to transforming Italy into the nation with the highest number of tons of concrete per inhabitant. Because of these activities vunerable Apennine mountains were pierced; springs were intercepted and polluted; natural areas and parks were not respected. It could even happen that, through design and execution mistakes, two highways branches would never link up. These stumps were left undisturbed and are a perennial warning of the damage caused by the unconditional support of private transportation. The railway system, constructed during the fascist period all over the territory, had great potential, but was never placed at the disposal of freight transportation. In the eighties, the flow of trucks coming from Italy was so intense as to generate conflicts with bordering alpine countries, which started protesting at the pollution. As for private car use, in the seventies Italy was refining three times the amount of oil necessary to internal consumption; refineries robbed hectares of coastal land of their primary vocation, for tourism or the enjoyment of nature, causing air, sea, and inland water pollution.

Industrial centres, created in the nineteenth century, were enlarged without effective controls of polluting emissions. From the end of the sixties, as awareness of the damage caused to workers' and citizens' health grew, a conflict developed between the need to alleviate the damage caused by industrial discharges and the requirements of maintaining high employment. In the post-war period, the national governments created other industrial centres in the South. Because of inadequate services and the absence of links with a wider production sector, these plants became 'cathedrals in the desert', a reminder of the failure of industrial policy in creating steady employment.

From the calm beaches at the mouth of the Po river, frequented by mass tourism from all over Europe, to the most exclusive shorelines and southern islands, coastal land has been covered in concrete. Rivers have been filled with concrete, with the aim of imposing order in the distribution of water resources, thus producing regular flooding in the cities and the countryside during autumnal rains. Mountains zones are invaded by ski-lifts, and the mountain agricultural and social framework is deconstructed by the requirements of winter tourism.

Control over land, natural resources and cultural heritage

Some events can take on symbolic meaning if the causes that determine them are representative of a whole system. In describing the evolution of the natural environment in post-war Italy it is useful to refer to the events of 5 May 1998 in Quindici and Sarno, two townships in the Campania region clinging to the slopes of the Apennine mountains. After very heavy rainfall, these two townships were covered by a mud-flow almost four metres deep, originating from a landslide and advancing at the impressive speed of about 300 metres per minute. The mass of mud caused the destruction of an entire community and over 200 casualties. The inhabitants who had not left their homes, partly because they were not warned, were overwhelmed by the solid mass.

The explanation of this occurrence reveals the limitations of the environmental policies implemented across the national territory for decades. The soil of the mountain was bare following arson which caused complete deforestation the previous summer. This allowed infiltration of rainwater in a natural fault and caused the swelling and consequent detachment of surface layers. This area, like the rest of the Apennine chain, is particularly vulnerable hydro-geologically, and subject to floods and landslides. The first national hydro-geological ordinance on all land 'whose stability may be jeopardized by intervention on the forest coverage or by transformation involving perturbation of the water regime' dates back to 1923 (royal decree).

Italy's natural conformation is extremely delicate. It is transected by two mountain chains, Alps and Apennines, which present an enormous variety of ecosystems. It has 8,000 kilometres of shores going from sand dunes to volcanic headlands. Rivers have a torrential character, and are exposed to autumn floods and summer droughts. Cultivated plains have been extracted from marshy environments through intense human labour. From the end of the war up until 1990, there were 3,488 casualties due to landslides; 4,600 municipalities are at hydro-geological risk, accounting for 65 per cent of the national land area.

During the sixties, Italian legislators' attention to water regimes intensified. They eventually produced a 1989 soil protection law that affirmed the need to confront the serious problems of land disruption through a sound knowledge of the territory. It also aimed at ensuring coordination among water policy makers and established that land planning should be based on the watershed, a physical and natural element transcending administrative boundaries. This approach emphasized the protection of natural features, and integrated soil quality control with the rational distribution and use of all water resources. The responsibility for the planning of the hydrogeological rearrangement of local watersheds was handed over to the regions. But the implementation of this law has not been ubiquitous, in Campania the 'watershed plan', which would have defined landslide risk zones, has never been formulated.

In spite of their physical structure, the zones where the townships of Quindici and Sarno are found had for years been selected as the locations for large building contracts: restructuring of ancient canals, straightening of canals and rivers with concrete walls, construction of a mega power station, highway construction. In the absence of planning decisions, an avalanche of concrete was deposited on an area whose natural vocation was agriculture and sheep-rearing.

Another peculiar element of recent Italian life which has had effects on its physiography is the presence of covert and illegal organizations which have for decades exerted almost total control over the southern territory, and which for the last two decades have shown the ability to expand to the north. In Quindici (population 3,000) two powerful Camorra clans were at war for control of the wild urbanization and indiscriminate cementification of the area. In the early eighties, a mayor allied with the 'new Camorra' was elected. During this period, illegal houses and building yards kept popping up on the fringes of the town. This mayor was eventually removed by the intervention of the President of the Republic, Sandro Pertini. But in 1990 the town council was again dissolved owing to serious Camorra infiltration. Sarno (population 15,000) was home for years to illegal traffic of waste, to illegal excavation of quarries, and to use as dumps. Waste from other regions, most likely the more industrialized northern ones, was buried in these areas. The Naples prosecutor's office declared that what happened in those areas was an 'example of the extreme interest of organized crime to achieve control of large building contracts at the expense of land upkeep'.

The Sarno town council was also dissolved because of Camorra infiltration. While the town had never drawn up a design for an urban development plan, it listed 3,000 building legalization requests. In this atmosphere, a new business that could enrich the Camorra materialized: mud removal, landfill deposits, and building reconstruction. In Quindici, on 23 May 1998, only eighteen days after the disaster, a few gunshots were aimed at the trucks of a company engaged in mud transport.

For a few days it was difficult to estimate the number of casualties and missing people, because the landslide took place in an area subject to illegal urban development. Here local administrations had allowed for building of houses, often by future residents, that would never have taken place had there been any land planning. Since officially those houses did not exist, and neither the birth nor the electoral registry was up to date, it was not immediately possible to find out how many citizens had inhabited the area.

Illegal building was also the result of urban development and of the reconstruction efforts undertaken to repair war bomb damage. The building of houses and facilities was entrusted to private enterprises that freely established what and how much to build. Suburbs developed outside of any planning framework both in the authorized and in the unauthorized areas. These constructions often occupy zones of natural, historic, or architectural value, and permanently disrupt a landscape shaped by centuries of cultural and social superimposition.

Illegal building was not a phenomenon of the past. In the period 1994–7 alone, 207, 000 illegal houses were erected, corresponding to 29 million square metres of illegal cement, 76.3 per cent of which was concentrated in the Southern regions. This is on top of those built during another illegal building boom in 1983 to 1984, when 230,000 illegal houses were built. These peaks were the result of announcing in advance administrative amnesties on illegal building (in 1993 and 1985 respectively). This resulted in many fines being paid into the treasury but at the same time it cancelled out illegal situations accumulated over the previous fifty years. These announcements of amnesties generated even more illegal building as private builders, relying on the state's lack of control on dating constructions, begun furiously building illegally in time to be granted a waiver. To these numbers should be added those relating to illegal construction dating from the post-war period located on state property or in areas subject to landscape or historical limitations, that have never been pardoned and are still waiting to be demolished.

Another aspect of Italian social and economic development that strongly affected environmental conditions has been the abandonment of mountain areas. This reached its height in the beginning of the twentieth century and during the 1950s and 1960s, and was matched by the depopulation of the countryside when marginal agriculture practices were not enough to sustain farming families. This process led to the disintegration of the hydraulic structures built by human patience and labour over the centuries, that guaranteed a well diffused water control and channelled rain in river beds, mitigating its impact. In turn this facilitated arson and lack of reforestation.

The occupation of land by buildings, roads, bridges, and tunnels in Italy is indicative of the more general world ruling classes' unawareness of the relationships existing between the human occupation of land and the degradation of natural resources, between the restriction of enjoyment of the countryside and the lowering in quality of life suffered by populations detached from natural beauty. Given the concentration of valuable historic buildings and artworks in urban centres and the countryside, damage to the natural environment extends to the historical heritage.

Floods in Italy have been innumerable and constant, but in November 1966 Florence was submerged and Agrigento suffered a landslide. In Florence the loss of artworks was irreplaceable and the significance of this event was demonstrated by the huge assistance provided by young volunteers coming from all over the world. In Agrigento, the Italian public discovered that the landslide in the Valley of Temples, where splendid evidence of Greek civilization remains, was caused by the weight of illegal building which occupied vulnerable areas provoking their collapse. It emerged that 8,500 rooms had been built in defiance of all existing norms. In 1997 in Agrigento, the demolition of several buildings was proposed by environmental organizations and government offices, but at the end of a long legal battle they were not touched.

One positive trend in policy is the national government's increasing attention (and thus the mass media's) to safeguarding the artistic and natural heritage of the country and implementing the demolition of illegal constructions. In 1998 the Council of State agreed to the demolition of the 'Monster of Vietri', a hotel built by pulverizing an ilex wood and the shoreline on the Amalfi coast. This area represents 'eighty prodigious kilometres that put these shores among the most splendid and famous in the world, where impressive nature and human toil have created through the centuries an admirable landscape equilibrium, from the historical centres to citrus grove terraces' (Cederna 1995). The demolition finally took place at the end of 1999. Meanwhile, to the satisfaction of locals, several illegal second homes of people with ties to the local Camorra have been demolished in Eboli, where Christ had stopped.

Ecomafia

The cement sector is one in which big illegal interests are aligned with legal activities. According to a report by Legambiente (1998), the number of Mafia clans that have a direct interest in the 'concrete cycle' and in waste management is growing and the connection between these activities and usury, extortion, and recycling of illegal capital is becoming apparent. In 1994 the neologism Ecomafia was coined. This term refers to a convergence of three criminal sectors: organized, economic, and environmental.

It is estimated that in 1998 the income flow from illegal building, illegal dumping of hazardous waste, and animals racket was 11,850 billion lire (6.12 million Euro). These illegal activities translated into a tax evasion equal to 2,342 billion lire (1.2 million Euro). Investments subject to Ecomafia involvement, that is, huge public projects which Mafia companies may infiltrate, amounted to 18,868 billion lire. The link between the environmental and social aspects of these phenomena is evident: as a huge amount of public wealth was taken from the open market and the treasury, permanent and widespread destruction of natural collective riches was perpetrated.

Legislators and environmental grass-roots organizations which have constantly denounced and fought against illegal waste traffic have been calling attention to this problem. A 1997 law has reorganized waste management and, in accordance with European Union directives, calls for the reduction of waste production, recycling, and energy recovery. Further support is found in the citizens of the different cities where recycling experiments are undertaken.

The great industrial centres

Just as the landslide in Sarno can be considered the symbol of the degeneration of national and local land control policies, so the history of a few industrial installations is sufficient to describe the economic development of post-war Italy and its impact on natural environment and on the quality of life of workers and citizens.

Post-war industrial development policies endorsed those adopted since the beginning of the industrialization process. Existing northern industrial centres were strengthened and enlarged. The development by big industrial centres, the localization of which ran counter to any planning consistency and economical use of the territory, was encouraged in the South. Aggravating the environmental impacts of these processes is the fact that all over Italy, as economic activities spread, artisan installations and small and medium-size industries proliferate in highly visible positions all along main communication routes. This growth has failed to take into consideration the integration of urban functions with the safeguarding of environmental quality and has produced ribbon-like barriers which obscure the surrounding landscape for kilometres at a time.

For those who associate Venice with the ability of man to produce objects which at the same time give the pleasure of real beauty and evoke a dream dimension, the installations of Porto Marghera are an example of how industrial policies in Italy produce more intense and far-ranging effects than in other countries. By their behaviour, policy makers exhibited their schizophrenia with respect to the physical and cultural environment on which they acted, modifying it irreversibly.

In March 1997 a suit for offences ranging from fraudulent omission of precautions against accidents to first degree murder, including the hypothesis of massacre, was brought against two companies operating in the chemical sector. These investigations were based on statistical data regarding the high death and disease rate for workers assigned to the production and treatment of vinyl chloride. As prosecutors confirmed a series of environmental legislation violations, the inquiry widened.

The shift of productive activities by Venetian entrepreneurs from the mainland to the lagoon shore had occurred at the beginning of the twentieth century. By 1910 the shore housed almost seventy firms with about 5,000 workers; the location of Porto Marghera dates to 1917. At present, the industrial centre occupies 6 kilometres of the shore, with an average width of four kilometres, thus covering almost 2,000 hectares, compared to the 200 of historic Venice. The list of industrial activities concentrated in Porto Marghera is impressive: chemical, aluminium production, shipyard, oil refinery, metalworks, electrical energy production, and oil products sale. There are 2,000 chimney stacks in the industrial zone, which emitted 240,000 tons of various chemical substances per year, some of which are well-known carcinogens. Since 1917, 80 million tons of waste have been dumped in the Adriatic Sea; liquid discharges in the surface waters at present amount to 20 000 tons per year. In the sixties, the construction of the 'oils channel' in the middle of the lagoon helped to increase the competitiveness of local industries. At that time the petrochemical installations employed about 60,000 workers and the average income of Venetians was among the highest of the region. Meanwhile, the density of high-risk industries in this area was among the highest of Italy, not counting the number of plants which handled industrial and toxic waste.

The Venice Urban Development Plan of 1962, which was in force until 1990, contained this paragraph: 'Those plants diffusing in the atmosphere smoke, dust, or exhalation hazardous to human health, discharging poisonous substances in the water, producing vibration and noise will be located primarily in the industrial zone.' Toxic vapours and dust emitted in the atmosphere formed a yellowish pall which robbed locals of their health; the management of industrial plants was carried out without due attention to working conditions. By the end of the sixties, it could be proved that children dwelling in the zones surrounding the plants had a high incidence of respiratory diseases; from 1971 to 1973, fifty-one accidents took place and more than 1,200 workers were poisoned, scalded, or subjected to toxic exhalations. Workers assigned to a peculiar step of vinyl chloride production died of liver cancer with a frequency 600 times higher than the national average. This information was provided as a result of a private investigation conducted for years by a single worker. Meanwhile, official studies, performed without isolating the statistically most exposed workers, were showing only a slight increase in cancer occurrence.

The depth of the 'oil channel' entails that it must be regularly dredged. In the single year of 1996, 20 billion lire (10.3 million Euro) were earmarked to dredge the channel. Beginning in the sixties, an island was created from the sediment and it was illegally enlarged during the seventies. For decades the development of this area was supported, without concern for environmental degradation, or damage to monuments, because of the employment it guaranteed. But due to the constant streamlining of chemical production in Italy, in 1997 the workers in Porto Marghera were reduced to about 12,000.

In the spring of 1998 the magistrates ordered the closure of plants because the law on industrial discharges had not been observed. Tons of soil and sediments had been polluted. In all, including wastes, there were 5 million tons of material to clean up. These events highlight the tension between the well-developed Italian legislation on water and air pollution, and the actual capacity to ensure institutional controls on its implementation. Industrial waste-water containing hazardous substances in concentrations higher than that allowed by the 1976 law have been discharged in the lagoon waters for years, but employment concerns had led citizens and trade unions to neglect the failure of industrialists to apply environmental laws.

In the seventies, adopting the same development scheme, the construction of industrial centres began in the South of Italy. The pattern adopted in the North was reproduced as a result of national policy makers' inability to comply with the propensity of Italian territory to agriculture, and to natural and cultural tourism. Moreover the capital flow supporting these enterprises remained external to these areas. A self-supporting development, respecting environmental resources, could have been based on the development of small and medium-size industries which would have benefited from local knowledge, natural resources, and historical heritage, thus allowing for the diffuse growth of sustained income and permanent employment for local residents.

As an answer to the social uproar (which would eventually become urban warfare) in the face of high unemployment rates, it was decided to build an iron metallurgy centre on Gioia Tauro. The plant was to be located in what had been a splendid olive and citrus area in

Calabria that produced high incomes for the landowners and season-
al work for olive pickers. To help industry a harbour was built by
destroying a pine wood that protected citrus from sea-salt spray. In
the end, the industrial plant was never built, but the land had been
expropriated and trees uprooted. The shore, once green and scented,
had become a wasteland. Ten years later it was proposed to transform
the undeveloped centre into a coal power plant. Even in this case the
industrial zone never saw the dawn, and not a single industrial job
was created, while many jobs in the agricultural sector and food
production were lost. Unexpectedly, the harbour started functioning
in 1995 thanks to a private initiative. A thousand jobs were created
and it has since become the most important port in the Mediterranean Sea for the transportation of containers, thus redressing a
strategic error which had lasted for two decades.

For the Sicilian industrial centre of Priolo, Syracuse, the list of
disasters will suffice. From 1949, an area which at the beginning of
the twentieth century had seen the building of a harbour, added to
that three refineries, plants for the production of cement, chemical
plants, and a power station which were lined up along a coastal line
of almost 20 kilometres. This area was archaeologically invaluable
because of a long and complex human history. The following remains
were engulfed among installations: coastal caves serving as homes to
Palaeolithic populations; a Neolithic village; a vast dwelling and a
necropolis from the Bronze Age (fifteenth to twelfth centuries BC);
the Greek colony of Megara Hyblea founded in the eighth century
BC; a palaeochristian basilica; and Roman and Norman dwellings.
There were repeated accidents that caused toxic emissions in the
atmosphere and polluted rainfall; oil product fires and sea water pollution. Industrial accidents caused casualties and intoxication. One
thousand people from a fishing village were forced to move to give
room to a refinery plant which was never built. Among the archaeo-
logical remains even an industrial wastes landfill found its place.
Water consumption was so heavy as to cause the infiltration of sea
water into the groundwater.

An Italian case

A peculiar example of the intertwining of Italian cultural and social characteristics and the perception of environmental damage is offered by the Seveso accident. On 10 July 1976 a ICMESA chemical reactor exploded producing dioxin and the emission into the atmosphere of a toxic chemical mix. The multinational owner kept silent about the presence of dioxin in the vapour, and even today it is not possible to know either the exact amount emitted from the stack or the fate of the forty-one barrels filled with contaminated materials. Spurred by animal deaths, on 20 July the mayor issued a first ordinance forbidding the use of garden produce. Beginning on the 15th, children were being admitted to the hospital for skin lesions. On the basis of contamination estimates, on the 25th the forced evacuation from houses began. News on chronic effects and foetal damage begun to spread. At the end of August, the first episodes of chloracne were recorded. The accident was so serious that it generated the European law 'Major accident hazard of certain industrial activities', the so-called Seveso directive (82/501/EEC).

In the weeks following the accident, a debate raged in the local community and at the national level on the question of whether to allow women exposed to the toxic cloud to undergo therapeutic abortion. The disagreement of clerical voices with the declaration of the local, Catholic, councillor, who gave freedom of choice and free public medical examinations to pregnant women, was strong and aimed at throwing a social stigma on the abortion choice. In Seveso, private and painful decisions were made more confusing by the uncertainty concerning the toxic effects of chemicals, by the lack of knowledge on the contaminant dispersion phenomena, and by the suffering caused to inhabitants by the relocation prudently imposed by local administrators, on the basis of scanty scientific information, to reduce the accident damage.

The strength of the values expressed by the local Catholic community was woven into the difficulties pertaining to the communication of environmental and health risk. This was a community of craftsmen who were industrious and strongly bound to their land and work. Had there been an examination confirming women's exposure to dioxin, they would have been inclined to accept the results, in order to take a step towards finding a solution. On top of all this was added the intervention of Catholic local authorities and fundamentalist national organizations, with the intention of minimizing and denying danger. Minimization of the problem found fertile ground, owing to the great inconvenience of a relocation/evacuation that had interrupted work and fragmented the community. To local people the denial of the hazard meant obtaining permission to return to their homes and the life they knew. On the other hand, a push in favour of clean-up and recognition of health damage was charged with a symbolic value that would have implied criticism of the economic and social model that had shaped that community. The locals preferred not to push for industrial liability in the accident and to silence those who expressed their awareness of the damage and who were in favour of the disrupting interventions.

The most polluted area was cleaned up and currently there is an innocent oak wood, one form of economic compensation that citizens accepted for the environmental and health damage caused. The local community preferred to remove the memory of the accident 'because we must progress and not let ourselves get depressed by misfortunes' (Conti 1979).

6

The Church in post-war Italy

Patrick McCarthy

The Catholic Church describes itself as universal and eternal but it also lives and hence changes in space and time. The Italian Church is different from the Irish and French Churches. The post-war Italian Church is no longer the Church that Cavour or Mussolini faced. There is also much geographical and cultural diversity within the national Church: in central Italy Catholics are fewer and more likely to have centre-left political views; Romano Prodi is only one of many examples. In the Veneto the Church acted as an intermediary between the peasants and the Habsburg rulers, and it was rewarded with a mass following. In Calabria, however, the middle classes were agnostic and the peasantry superstitious.

Popular Catholicism is rich in weeping but heartening Madonnas, of whom one of the most recent appeared at Civitavecchia in February 1995, and in dubious but useful miracles such as the liquefying of San Gennaro's blood at Naples, which takes place at important moments of civic life. In contrast with this belief that heaven intervenes in the affairs of earth, the Christian Democrat leader, Giulio Andreotti, displays a cold, indifferent view of human nature: he bears witness to the Fall but not to the Resurrection.

The distinctive trait of the Italian Church is that it includes the Vatican which governs the world-wide Church. Pope Paul VI felt that Italy should be a model for Catholics in other countries. John-Paul II ceded some power to the Italian Council of Bishops (Conferenza

I wish to thank Kathleen Turner and Stefano Frascani who worked as my research assistants on this chapter.

episcopale italiana, CEI) but he still chooses the president and defines the goals the CEI should adopt, as he did in his 1985 Loreto declaration. Moreover, when he feels that great moral or social issues are involved, he intervenes in a language that leaves little space for ambiguity. His journeys and his actions as head of the world-wide Church are widely discussed in Italy although his words are not necessarily heeded.

Whereas the Irish state was constructed with the backing of the Church, the Italian state was created against the Church. But, unlike the French Republic, Unified Italy did not defeat the Church in the battle for legitimacy. Both suffered: the unofficial culture of the state was Benedetto Croce's historicism which had little use for Catholicism. Meanwhile the Church weakened the state by not allowing Catholics to participate in politics.

To organize this chapter around Church–State relations leaves one open to the criticism of blindly reproducing the traditional vertical structure of the Church itself and of underestimating the many movements at the grass roots, such as the volunteer workers who are active in areas like drug addiction. After all, the Second Vatican Council defined the Church as 'God's people', shifting weight from the Vatican towards the bishops and from them towards the laity.

If we were writing only about the contemporary Church, it might be more appropriate to start with the volunteers. But, in the years after Mussolini fell in 1943, the major decisions about the Church's role in Italy were made at the Vatican, which also helped make the major decisions about Italy. In the first three sections of this chapter we shall concentrate on the tale of three Popes and their dealings with the Italian republic, although for reasons of space we shall have to treat the second and third with great brevity. In the last section we shall start in the same way before switching to a view from below and to popular Catholicism.

An angelic but hard-headed pastor

Under Fascism the Church had deigned to recognize the Italian state and to sign an agreement with it. The Vatican cordially despised the Fascists but it co-operated with them. It also reinforced Azione cattolica (AC) a lay organization which has its roots in the Society of Catholic Youth, founded to protect the Church against the Liberal state and to ensure a Catholic presence in society. AC could be hurled into battle when the right moment came.

It came in 1943. The Vatican had considered Mussolini foolish to enter the war in 1940 and it was not surprised by his defeats. Pius XII, elected pope in 1939, had a clear vision of a new post-war order. He was guided primarily by his role as leader of the world-wide Church but he saw no contradiction between this and his second role as Bishop of Rome and head of the Italian Church. His goal was to increase the Church's power over the Italian state by using a Catholic party. He had two concerns which were noted by that connoisseur of political power, Charles de Gaulle: Pius 'foresees a long period of confusion in Italy but this does not greatly trouble him. He may think that after the collapse of Fascism and the end of the monarchy the Church, which exerts great moral influence in Italy, remains the only force for order and unity. The prospect rather pleases him' (de Gaulle 1956, 286–7)

In fact Mussolini's overthrow and the King's flight from Rome did leave a vacuum. Pius, who remained in Rome, who tried to negotiate with the Nazis and the Allies, and who ordered the Church to devote its resources to the victims of the war, saw his prestige rise.

In 1943, a month before Mussolini fell, Pius published the encyclical *Mystici corporis* which defines the Church as the mystical body of Christ. The encyclical gives meaning to the suffering of millions—which is 'not useless but fertile'—because it is linked with Christ's Passion (Pius XII 1995, 237). Pius goes on to offer the Church, which is at one with Christ and hence is endowed with a legitimacy to which no earthly organization like a state can aspire, as the principle of order.

Pius also possessed a charisma of his own. In the film *Pastor angelicus* he is tall, his face is ascetic, and his body is tense, as if he were crucified. He wears a flowing white robe and extends his arms towards the faithful but also towards the heavens. He is the antithesis of Mussolini: the short, burly Duce with his crude, belligerent rhetoric had suited the victory in Ethiopia. Pius offered to a powerless, defeated nation human compassion and divine help.

From his ordination in 1899 on, Pius had been a diplomat, accustomed to complex negotiations behind well-guarded doors. But his very remoteness from the people strengthened their admiration for him. Only a man of God could confront the destruction caused by the war. Pius 'was convinced that he—and only he—could interpret the feelings and aspirations of the masses' (Tardini 1960, 126). De Valera thought he could do the same for the Irish masses. By monopolizing the role of charismatic leader he, however, left no space to Church leaders.

Pius united charisma with organizational ability. In 1940 AC had been restructured and the control of the hierarchy had been increased. In 1943 Luigi Gedda proposed to the Badoglio government that AC simply take over the buildings and the activities of the Fascist organizations. This was, however, too crude a solution. Meanwhile Alcide De Gasperi left the Vatican library to become the leader of a new Catholic party, the Democrazia cristiana (DC). All the organizational might of a great Church, its parishes, and their priests, a grassroots network of disciplined militants that made Togliatti's new Communist Party seem weak, was placed behind the DC. The party overlapped with AC, which Pius XII held in reserve in case the DC should disappoint him. AC grew: in 1946 it had nearly 2 million members, while by 1954 it had grown to 3 million. What sort of Italy did the Vatican want? It wanted to retain its own freedom, as the Concordat, signed with Mussolini had established it. For this reason the Communists were tolerated in government until March 1947 when they voted to include the Concordat in the new constitution. Then they could be dismissed without thanks. Next the Vatican wanted greater power in the post-war Italian state than it had had previously. To obtain it Pius was willing to concede democracy, although only the Church could decide where the common good lay. In the Rome local elections of 1952 the Vatican wanted the DC to ally with the Monarchists and the Fascist Movimento sociale italiano (MSI). But it allowed itself to be convinced by De Gasperi that this was a political error.

In return the Vatican wanted to control what it considered the vital issues of birth, sex, and death; hence the dissolution of marriage and the use of contraception were to be restricted. The Vatican sought to discipline the human body by setting norms for clothing, by censoring love scenes in the cinema, and by discouraging dancing. On economic issues the Church accepted the need for capitalism, unenthusiastically. Its relationship with Italy's small group of industrial and financial magnates, like the Agnelli, was distant. The Church liked family farms and the DC took cautious measures to increase their number by breaking up the big estates. To keep the farmers going, the DC strengthened the network of rural savings banks and co-operatives. Pius recognized the need to win over recruits from the industrial workers who would otherwise be monopolized by the Partito comunista italiano (PCI). In 1946 the Church formed the Associazione cattolica dei lavoratori italiani (ACLI), which quickly became anti-Communist and helped to split the trade union movement and to form the Confederazione italiana dei sindacati dei lavoratori (CISL). Pius distrusted the French worker-priest movement and the Marxist concept of class. The ACLI called for worker participation in industry and used the idealist language of personalism—'dignity' and 'harmony.'

Italian Catholicism did not produce a great upsurge of culture. In France the clash between the individual Catholic's freedom and God's plan for her/him produced the tension in Paul Claudel's masterpiece *Le soulier de satin*, while Mauriac's *Thérèse Desqueyroux* satirizes tepid, middle-class Catholicism from the viewpoint of a soul that is, unknown to itself, in search of God. Separation of Church and State turned French Catholics like Georges Bernanos into dissidents. His Italian counterparts were rare. The political thought of the Italian Church taught it to distrust liberal individualism which considered man sufficient unto himself, but in fact limited him to the physical world. The Catholic concept of personalism placed man in the context of God and sought to liberate his full potential. A bold version of such thinking, Jacques Maritain's *Humanisme intégral*, held the view that all society could be 'humanized' (Rossi 1956). Giuseppe Dossetti, the leader of the DC left, adopted Maritain as a guide in the task of transforming post-war Italy into Christ's kingdom.

The more concrete Pius wanted an Italy where the PCI had as little influence as possible. This was the second trait that de Gaulle had noted: 'It is the actions of the Soviet Union . . . that are the cause of the Holy Father's torment.' The origins of the Vatican's tenacious anti-communism go back to Pius XII's predecessor, who condemned the persecution of Catholics by the Soviet and Chinese Communists in 1927 but who signed a Concordat with the new Nazi government in 1933. Pius XI's anti-Nazi encyclical *Mit brennender Sorge* is vaguer than the anti-Soviet *Divini Redemptoris promissio*, both published in 1937.

The distinction was accentuated under Pius XII, who viewed Germany as a diplomat, who had negotiated Concordats with Bavaria (1925) and with Prussia (1929), and who was willing, in order to protect German Catholics against persecution by the Nazis, to remain silent on the Holocaust. Pius clearly liked some aspects of German life, whereas in the Soviet Union he could see nothing but materialism and a determination to destroy all religion. He and his chief foreign policy advisers, Monsignori Tardini and Montini, the future Pope Paul Vl, never wavered in their view that Roosevelt was naïve in thinking that the USSR, if consulted and rewarded, would become a responsible world power. They feared that the Communists would exploit the chaos which would ensue after the war ended: Pius had been in Germany during the Spartacus uprising. The advance of the Red Army through Eastern Europe seemed to the Vatican a proof that its view was correct and, as head of the world-wide Church, Pius XII had as his prime aim was to block the spread of Communism in Western Europe. For this reason Pius wanted the Americans to remain in Europe: he even considered making the Archbishop of New York, Francis J. Spellman, Secretary of State but wisely backed off. Pius supported the Truman doctrine in Greece and US diplomats reciprocated by calling the Catholic Church a great bulwark of democracy. The Pope was unenthusiastic about NATO, which may hark back to the Church's traditional neutrality and/or foreshadow the concern for peace shown by his successors.

Italy was to play a vital role in the struggle against Communism by strengthening its ties with the USA and by shunning its own Communist Party. In turn this meant that Catholics should unite in the DC which would base its policies on the principles laid down by the Pope. The Church organizations, AC and Gedda's civic committees, worked tirelessly in the crucial 1948 election campaign. No resource was wasted: even the skills of the cyclist Gino Bartali were exploited, Pius telling an AC rally to go out and win like Bartali.

The consequences of the Vatican's effort were varied and lasting. It can take much credit for the establishment of a democratic republic but must accept some blame for the shortcomings of Italian democracy. The mass parties, the DC and the PCI, were supposed to root democracy in strata of society that Liberal Italy had not reached and that Mussolini had won over to Fascism. Neither party was ideally suited to the task and it is hard to see how the DC could become a beacon of democracy while it remained subordinate to a Church that was authoritarian in its 'top-down' organization and that defined itself as the supreme arbiter of right and wrong. The Italian state was strengthened in the short run by the Vatican's ability to gain both popular support and foreign backing for 'its' government. In the long run, however, the state's dependence on another organization, which had greater legitimacy, served to weaken it.

As one learns more about the views of Tardini and other Church officials, so the PCI's strategy of working with the Church and the DC, on the grounds that they represented the Catholic masses, seems implausible. A figure like Franco Rodano, a leader of the Catholic Communists, is intriguing but his influence should not be overestimated. Cardinal Ottaviani slapped down the Catholic Communists when they tried to form their own party and to run in the 1946 elections as an ally of the PCI. Togliatti's decision to co-operate with the DC rather than press for economic and social reform and even the Berlinguerian historic compromise appear strategies born of weakness, tacit admissions of Pius XII's victory.

Is there any truth in the notion that Catholics and Communists have similar world views and that they can work together? One Catholic Communist argues that both oppose the 'unrestrained, frenetic form of individualism' that inspires capitalism.[1] The statement could be turned around: both Catholics and Communists have obstructed the transformation of Italy into an advanced capitalist society. Small industries have flourished but not grown bigger in red Emilia-Romagna and in the white Veneto. Yet there are differences in the way the PCI and the DC regional and local governments treated their industries. Anyway the parallels do not outweigh the dislike that the members feel for each other. Pius excommunicated the Communists; a poll of thirty PCI officeholders in Bologna in the early 1970s shows that twenty-eight never attended church and that the remaining two went to mass only at Easter and Christmas (Kertzer 1980, 71).

In the 1950s the Vatican paid a price for its success. Both DC rule and the alliance with the US, which were weapons in the war on communism, helped launch a process of modernization which threatened the Church. By the time Pope John-Paul II was elected, it was evident that consumer capitalism was a more insidious enemy of

---

[1] Tatò 1988, 83. Tatò became a close collaborator of Enrico Berlinguer and had some influence on the historic compromise.

Catholic values than Marxism. Pius XII lived to dislike the boom in the mid-1950s. The Pope had also left his mark on the sensibility of his followers. He was an authoritarian who promoted other conservatives like Cardinal Siri of Genova and Cardinal Ottaviani, leader of the Curia conservatives in the Second Vatican Council.

Aquinas's thought continued to represent Catholic orthodoxy and the Vatican discouraged theological innovation. Yet Pius understood the need to provide an emotional outlet for a population that was emerging from a lost war and that he was hurling into a crusade. So he emphasized the figure of Mary. In itself this was no great innovation. Popular Catholicism, whether in Italy or elsewhere, has always attached great importance to Mary and to the saints. This is orthodox Church teaching as long as both Mary and the saints are intermediaries between humans and God. The Council of Trent placed them clearly below Christ. But since they are human, popular Catholicism has felt less awe and more familiarity for them. Their humanity even means that they may be lazy in offering help and greedy in their demands for shrines and churches. They belong to the world of magic rather than of religion and Mary may be traced back to the the great mother-figures of Mediterranean mythology.

Pius XII was certainly not the man to permit heresy but neither did he neglect a valuable weapon. Italy had more apparitions of Mary than any other country and they were also the best organized. During the 1948 elections thirty-six Madonnas wept in Naples alone at the prospect of a Communist victory. Pius had created his own Mary: in *Mystici corporis* she is a model for European mothers because she transcends her suffering at the foot of the cross.

Pius fused new apparitions with the old. He repeated the Fatima warning and took the Assumption as an integral part of Church teaching which the faithful must accept. He thus followed in the path of Pius IX who had declared the Immaculate Conception to be an article of faith in 1854, six years after he had to flee from the 1848 revolution. Devotion to Mary is suited to periods when the Church is struggling because her purity offers an example of discipline, while the love and the grief she shows at Christ's suffering legitimize strong feelings.

In 1950 Maria Goretti was canonized. A 12-year-old peasant girl murdered by a man whose sexual advances she had resisted, Maria Goretti was a model of purity, courage, and the disciplined body.

That both she and her murderer were stranded in a poverty-stricken, undrained marshland infested with malaria served only as an example of how free will could triumph over the environment. The murderer, who was still alive and who campaigned for his victim's canonization, was a model of penitence. Both symbolized values that were the antithesis of Soviet Marxism and Americanized consumerism. The PCI also displayed admiration for Maria Goretti, which must surely be an example of subordination to Catholic hegemony.

Pius thus shaped Italian Catholicism into a strong political force with a Manichaean world-view. A dissenter like Don Lorenzo Milani could dislike the parish cinemas and the cult of Gino Bartali, behind which he discerned the 'religious indifference' of the people and the 'inner emptiness' of the priest (Milani 1957, 138, 153).

Two popes, much ambiguity, and a barely Italian Vatican Council

Pius gave no ground on the most important issue the DC faced: the opening to the Socialist Party. The lack of a majority–minority system pushed segments of the DC in this direction. The Church, however, would have no truck with a party that claimed to be Marxist and was allied with the PCI. In January 1958 Cardinal Ottaviani threatened the DC with the withdrawal of Church support, while two years before Cardinal Angelo Roncalli of Venice had used strong language to denounce the DC for ruling his city with Socialist support. One could be with or against the Church, he affirmed, but tolerance was not a virtue. Roncalli did not, like neighbouring bishops, call on the faithful to stop reading the DC's Venice newspaper and a year later, when the DC congress took place in his city, he made a statement that seemed less hostile to the notion of a centre-left coalition (Baget Bozzo 1977, 78–9).

When the cardinals elected Roncalli, they were not voting for a reforming pope. John XXIII was 77 years old and he had spent many years executing Pius XII's foreign policy. He had been rewarded with a cardinal's hat and the splendour of Venice. Retrospectively John's liberalism has been exaggerated. He felt that Pius's austere authority could not be maintained and he had sufficient trust in God—and in himself—to launch a process of change without foreseeing the outcome.

Angelo Roncalli was born in a village, Sotto il Monte, in Bergamo. In an Italy transformed by the boom, he incarnated an earlier, peasant society supposedly associated with simplicity, with a shared poverty, and with an absence of greed. In reality Roncalli could both take pride in his background and welcome prosperity. He reconciled the Church with the new refrigerators and Fiat 600s. Since he was not a Roman, he sought to shift power away from the Curia and towards local bishops. He named the conservative but independent Tardini as his Secretary of State, much to Tardini's surprise.

The Second Vatican Council constituted, along with the opening to the centre-left, the great events of John's papacy. They were very different: John put all his energy into the first and allowed the second to happen. The Council was designed for the universal Church, whereas the centre-left was an Italian affair. The alliance with the PSI was a milestone in the DC's long, never completed march towards autonomy from the Church. The project of clientelism was designed to provide the party with an alternative source of funding and votes. Moro, who followed Fanfani as party secretary, endowed his party with a different identity. No longer was it to be the political arm of the Church; instead it would mediate among the various social groups.

Cardinals Ottaviani and Siri maintained their opposition to the centre-left but they were reluctant to take on the DC. Local elections revealed a widespread desire for change. Anyway the PSI was not a credible red menace. The Italian bishops' response to the Pope's appeal for suggestions on the work of the Council was unenthusiastic. But they had to respect the call for liberty that arose from the universal Church. The result was that, while the Council infused new life into the German or American Church, the Italian Church remained locked into its alliance with an increasingly corrupt and powerful DC.

The Council got going, although the Curia, *Osservatore romano*, the Jesuit magazine *Civiltà cattolica*, and even Cardinal Montini were unenthusiastic. The Pope's political views were set out in two encyclicals. *Mater e magistra* (1961) repeated the traditional Catholic view that work must be an expression of the human personality but also called specifically for state intervention in the economy on behalf of the working class. John defended worker participation in industry and the extension of welfare. The shift towards what might be called a social democratic world-view was clear, as was the conventional belief in economic growth and technological innovation. John made a special plea on behalf of the Third World, which moved the Church away from the Manichaean vision of the Free World and the Communist threat. In *Pacem in terris* John substituted peace for anti-communism as the goal of Church foreign policy and he challenged NATO's view that nuclear weapons simply deterred.

Vatican II began in October 1962 and ended in December 1965. Perhaps the major Italian contribution was made by Cardinal Lercaro, who developed the theme that the Bologna working classes spurned the Church because it was remote. One solution lay in bringing the liturgy to the people. The use of the vernacular rather than Latin in the mass, the priest who faced the people rather than turn his back on them, and the increased use of the Bible rather than commentaries on it are just a few innovations.

The Council produced a more humble church: the 'people of God' sought out truth in history; they did not assume that the Church already possessed all truth. The Italian Church would take up some of the Council's themes: greater power for bishops and a partial recognition that Italy was missionary territory. A lay observer argued that the relationship between the Vatican and the Italian state could now proceed in a more distant and correct manner (Cavallari 1966). But Italy did not become just another Catholic country.

By the time Vatican II ended there was a new pope. Paul VI came from a middle-class Catholic family in Brescia, where the Church was traditionally liberal. His father, Giorgio Montini, was the editor of a newspaper and the family supported the Partito popolare italiano (PPI). Ordained in 1920, Montini became chaplain to the Federazione degli Universitari italiani (FUCI) and hence knew the future DC leaders.

Montini was in the foreign affairs department of the Vatican during and after the war. He received the cardinal's hat from John XXIII, who was in many ways his opposite. Montini was ill-at-ease with crowds and with himself. Appointed to the Central Preparatory Commission of the Council, he brokered compromises between the Italian conservatives and foreign liberals. When John died in 1963 Montini was the centrist candidate between Cardinal Siri and the

Belgian Cardinal Suenens. A vote for him meant accepting, without wild enthusiasm, both the Council and the centre-left.

Pope Paul VI found himself in an impossible position. The Council had gone too far and not far enough. As leader of the world-wide Church, Paul VI sought to expand his predecessor's foreign policy by speaking at the United Nations and by opening to Eastern European countries. He succeeded in bringing the Council to a conclusion, although disappointments lingered behind documents like *Gaudium et spes*. But when the Council enthusiasts went out into Italy they discovered a country that was changing faster than they were.

The integralism of the late 1960s found expression in Mgr. Luigi Giussani's *Comunione e Liberazione*. Based on the drama of the encounter with Christ, it was, however, quickly swallowed up by the mainstream DC. Retrospectively, the late 1960s period important less for its messianic Marxism than for its emphasis on greater individual freedom. One of the key areas was the emotional-sexual domain, where Paul published the encyclical *Humanae vitae* which reasserted the ban on contraception. This was a case where Paul could have done otherwise. Indeed he went against the majority view on a commission he had set up. He paid a high price for his stand. He was never able to shake off the reputation of being a conservative. Moreover, since a large number of Italian Catholics paid no attention to his ruling, the gulf between the hierarchy and the faithful widened.

In 1970 Italy finally legalized divorce and Paul had to protest. He took a strong stand on the referendum of 1974 which called for repeal of the 1970 law. Many of the actors misjudged the speed with which Italy was changing: the DC secretary, Amintore Fanfani, thought that his party could gain votes on the right, while Enrico Berlinguer did not want a referendum where the PCI would be accused of destroying the Italian family. The 59 per cent of the voters who wanted to retain divorce was another indication of the secularization of Italy.

The logical next step was the abortion law passed by the PCI-backed Andreotti governments of 1976–9. Once more Paul was left in painful and powerless opposition. By now his image was fixed: not only was he branded as a conservative but he was considered indecisive and incapable of leading the Church. Both judgements are too harsh and the real issue was that the Italian Church could not be true to itself and yet make the concessions to individual judgement which large sectors of the population were demanding.

Paul lived one moment of grandeur when in 1978 he made an impassioned appeal to the Red Brigades to release Aldo Moro. His intense emotion bestowed on him the dignity of a supplicant who wants nothing for himself. His grandeur was enhanced by the fact that he was obviously dying.

Italy's crisis and the foreign pope

The Church was seen as drifting and what better way to relaunch it than to choose a non-Italian, a cardinal who was fighting on the hardest front and whose national religious culture was combative? Polish Catholicism is more Irish than Italian. In the election the Italian cardinals did not come over to Wojtila until the eighth ballot (Szulc 1995, 295–303). The election of a non-Italian—the first since 1523—raised the issues of whether the new Pope would grant the Italian Church greater autonomy and how the CEI would use it. Yet the way John-Paul II would govern the world-wide Church would still be an important example.

The special trait of John-Paul's theological views is that God—in the person of Christ—is not only within this world but is immediately present within each of us. For example, whereas prayer may be seen as a monologue in search of an interlocutor, Pope John-Paul maintains that, because God is within us, the 'I' is already merged with the 'Thou.' Prayer is not a quest but a union that liberates man and glorifies the divine.

In the 1998 encyclical *Ratio et fides* John-Paul defends philosophy. But, as well as feeling that the Pope's real concern is to weaken the hegemony of science and technology, the reader is taken aback at the restrictions placed on reason. Far from being a free force of criticism and the inventor of its own conclusions, reason is subordinate to faith and, if it struggles against its master, then it is denounced for alienating man from the only true happiness which is found in God's love.

John-Paul II does not shrink from stating that the Church is not a democracy.[2] Nor has he hesitated to take strong stands against

[2] *La Repubblica* 23 Nov. 1998.

contraception and especially abortion. He dislikes biotechnology. Yet since Western culture is dominated by consumer capitalism, which dissuades man from seeking salvation, the Pope seems left-wing when he excoriates European individualism and the exploitation of the Third World. Moreover in his refusal of fertility treatment which requires third-party donors of sperm or eggs John-Paul II can legitimately claim to be defending not merely the family but the very coherence of human existence against those who would create a motherless and fatherless race.

Jean-Paul II is a forceful critic of his age and an inspiring if difficult leader. Susceptible to charisma but also sceptical of it, most of the 85 per cent of Italians who declare themselves Catholics and even some of the 35 per cent who claim to be practising Catholics (the corresponding statistics for France are 70 per cent and 10 per cent, which indicates the strength of the Italian Church) disregard the Pope's teaching on sexual issues. Only 32 per cent of voters followed him in the 1981 abortion referendum. His style of leadership provokes and its content heartens, but he does not always persuade.

Meanwhile some power has passed to the CEI, as the revised Concordat of 1984 envisaged. The CEI is divided but although one may distinguish between a left and a right, of which Monsignor Luigi Bettazzi of Ivrea and Cardinal Giacomo Biffi of Bologna would furnish examples, this is not very meaningful. Another, more useful distinction might be between bishops who believe that the CEI should take specific stands at election time, which usually means calling on all Catholics to vote for one party, and those who prefer to see the CEI take general positions based on the Church's moral teaching.

A bishop does not run his diocese with absolute authority, although the parish priest can hardly do more than mediate between bishop and base. There are around 26,000 parishes serving an average of 2,200 people. Some 70 per cent of them have no resident priest. There are about 37,300 priests, excluding the 20,000 who are in religious orders. The most striking statistic is that 43 per cent of priests are over the age of 60 and 61 per cent are over the age of 50. The decline in vocations, which began under Pius XII, has not been reversed and there is now one seminarist for every twelve priests. The Church has tried to cope by naming lay deacons, exclusively male, who take minor orders and help the priest (Garelli 1991, 16–26).

Despite this decline it is hard to think of a social group in Italy that is as strong as the parish.

Until 1992 the CEI continued to support the DC. Cardinal Ruini informed the faithful that the end of the Cold War did not leave them free to vote as they pleased. As the DC-led coalitions stumbled into the 1990s, relying on ever larger doses of systemic clientelism, neither the Pope nor the CEI issued strong moral or political warnings against corruption. The last prime minister of the old regime (1989–92) was Giulio Andreotti, who has been described as 'indifferent towards politics' (Baget Bozzo 1996, 143). It is tempting to see him as the incarnation of the pessimistic, Augustinian strand that is present in Italian Catholicism. For much of his career he was on the DC right but in 1976 he became prime minister of the national solidarity governments. Opportunism was involved but it was rooted in a limitless scepticism that embraces all ideologies and projects. For Andreotti there remained power for power's sake, stripped of ostentation and ceremony.

This world-view is only one strand in Italian Catholic culture. It is very different from what one might call the Manzonian strand which holds that, while good may not win out in a historical period, God's grace is sufficient to allow any individual who perseveres to lead a good life.

The Italian Church was unprepared for the 1992 crisis and yet it might have been more prescient. In 1991 a referendum on institutional reform—reducing the number of preference votes—was organized by Mario Segni, a Christian Democrat who was outside the party's ruling group. Although the Church took no official position and the hierarchy showed little interest in reforming a voting system that had brought it such power, a surprisingly high number of Italians voted—62.5 per cent—and 95.6 per cent of them said yes. Among them was a strong Catholic contingent, won over by the ACLI and the grass-roots movements.

In the same year Sicilian Catholics, who were outraged by the DC's ties with the Mafia, lined up behind the ex-DC mayor of Palermo, Leoluca Orlando. Advised by a group of Palermo Jesuits, they formed a political movement, La Rete, which shifted to the left but retained a strong moral strand. The Catholic militants were ahead of their leaders.

Rather than inventing a new identity for itself and a new project for Italy, the CEI showed caution in analysing the origins and consequences of the 1992 crisis. Some bishops admitted that corruption had gone beyond the moral shortcomings of specific individuals and constituted a 'structure of sin'. Obviously this left the Church open to accusations that its own responsibility was great.

During the period up to the elections of March 1994 the CEI's only idea was to relaunch the DC. It threw its weight behind Mino Martinazzoli's Partito Popolare Italiano, a rebaptized and partially reformed DC. Segni, who had abandoned the party, suddenly discovered that he wanted to form an electoral alliance with it. Cardinal Ruini declared that the Italians' soul lay in their faith and the Pope used the coded expression 'Catholic unity.' The hierarchy made it clear to all who were willing to understand that it favoured the PPI, that it continued to distrust the ex-Communists of the Partito democratico della sinistra (PDS, now called DS—Democratici di sinistra) and that it did not approve of the Cristiani sociali, the small band of Catholics that was allied with the PDS. Yet the CEI did not launch a crusade for Martinazzoli as it had done for De Gaspari.

One reason lay in the gulf that separates the Italian Catholics of 1948 from the present generation. A 1992 survey showed the reality behind that figure of 85 per cent. Only 49 per cent of Italians believed in heaven and only 37 per cent in hell. The percentage that saw nothing wrong in contraception stood at 67. Only 50 per cent of Catholics went to confession regularly. If so many of the faithful did not follow the hierarchy in the spheres of faith and morality, why should they be more disciplined politically? And indeed 50 per cent thought that Catholics could support any party they chose, while 83 per cent thought the Church should not try to influence their vote. Only 13 per cent thought there should be a Catholic party, while 37 per cent thought there should not (Garelli 1992, 111–22). One may conclude that the hierarchy could influence about 15 per cent of the electorate, which is far from negligible but not enough for a crusade.

For the next two years the CEI continued to hesitate. Forza Italia supported public funding for Catholic schools, which was tempting. But Berlusconi's wealth, his legal problems, and his habit of comparing himself with Christ made him an implausible ally for the Church. Despite uncertainty about its role, the CEI was guided by two time-worn principles. The first was a distrust of the PDS because its Communist past made it too statist in education and healthcare and too libertarian on abortion. The second was a nostalgia for the old DC.

When Romano Prodi cycled onto the political stage in 1995 the CEI's dilemma was sharpened. The group of PPI leaders associated with Prodi were mostly convinced that the culture of Italy—and especially Catholic Italy—needed an injection of liberalism. But they believed this could best be done in a language of dialogue and serenity that also spoke of solidarity. Solidarity formed the link between this segment of the PPI and the PDS, although the term has very different hinterlands for the two allies. The hierarchy could hardly find fault with Prodi's cultural baggage, except on the key point that it led to the centre-left coalition. This included the shrunken PPI, the supposedly gigantic but in reality crumbling PDS, and a motley crew of minor parties, with Rifondazione comunista both included and excluded.

An exemplary Catholic (and an admirer of Gino Bartali), Prodi could not be opposed openly. So, by winning the 1996 elections, the Olive Tree coalition brought to power the 'Democratic Catholics'. This does not mean that the Church enjoys the power it possessed in the post-war period. In daily politics Prodi was far freer of the Vatican than De Gasperi had been. The PDS's presence in the government does not mean this is a new historic compromise: it rather indicates that Catholics and Communists both had to change before they could collaborate.

Avvenire, however, has spoken, in mild language that masks a Cold War vision, of 'parties whose physical make-up leads them to behave differently from the way Christians behave'.[3] Perhaps, but, although the PDS is not sure what it is, it is sure it is not a communist party. The CEI remains equally unsure of what it is but it still looks right rather than left. The more subtle bishops may, however, remember how weak the PCI was in dealing with the Church in the post-war years.

When Prodi fell in October 1998 and D'Alema became prime minister, *Osservatore romano* expressed outrage. It reminded its readers that D'Alema was no ordinary ex-Communist but had been a party bureaucrat and head of the Young Communists. *Avvenire* added that he was now the head of the PDS bureaucracy.[4] On 20 October

---

[3] *Avvenire* 23 April 1996.
[4] *Osservatore Romano* 18 Oct. 1998, and *Avvenire* 16 Oct. 1998.

Avvenire even suggested that D'Alema was an ally of the big, private companies: the Communists and the capitalists were ganging up on the Church. The CEI realized, however, that they were strengthening D'Alema's position and they became more tolerant. It remains unclear to what degree the Church was taking a tough line in order to win better treatment from the D'Alema government on funding for Catholic schools and social issues like abortion. At the time of writing (April 1999) the Church has kept up its campaign for state funding for Catholic schools and tax breaks for families. Cardinal Ruini has been kinder to D'Alema, who has stated in the pages of *Famiglia cristiana* that he stands by the abortion law but will work with the bishops on the schools and family issues.[5]

John-Paul has called on the bishops to be present everywhere in society. In its response the CEI agreed that Italy was no longer a Christian country and therefore the Church must become a 'missionary' force. This meant that its most important duty was pastoral and that it would serve society, especially the weaker or excluded groups. The notion of such a role gained ground after the new Concordat was signed in 1984. The key tenet was not the freedom of the Church from the Italian nation-state but State and Church working together for the common good of the Italian people.

This leads back to the question of how the Church might deliver its message. In his 1995 Palermo speech, John-Paul repeated his Polish message: Italian Catholics lacked faith; there were too many Mafiosi and too few babies; the Church must stress its social policy and insist on workers' rights, as restated in the encyclical *Centesimus annus*, issued for the hundredth anniversary of *Rerum novarum*.

This last exhortation seemed remote from the Italy of the tripartite agreement. Other themes were better-suited: the anti-Mafia stand, symbolized by the choice of Palermo, the sympathy for the Third World, and the aversion to wars. In 1990 the Pope condemned the Gulf War and found support especially among Catholics and among supporters of the PCI-PDS. When Clinton and Blair bombed Iraq again in December 1998, the Pope's condemnation was stronger and close to the views of the D'Alema government. The NATO bombing of Serbia has brought fresh condemnation from John-Paul who has helped create an energetic protest movement and won the backing of

[5] *Famiglia cristiana* 8 Nov. 1998, 32–5.

Rifondazione comunista. Another good issue for the Church is national unity. After Bossi's relative success in the 1996 elections, the Pope set the tone by speaking of the common good of the entire nation, while Ruini was more explicit in condemning all secessionist movements. One of the Church's many arguments is the moral evil of a separatism that abandons the weaker part of the nation, the South. Although there is a certain irony in the Church as the champion of Italian unity, the CEI's stand hints at the Chuch's reconciliation with the state born of Unification.

Two perspectives

A group of Catholic thinkers sees a particular role for the Church in the post-1992 crisis. P.-P. Donati argues that the state has had too much influence, as has the Gramscian anti-state. The liberalism of a Locke could not penetrate Italy where, even after the Second World War, the parties succeeded in gaining control of and for the state. Now, however, a space has opened up which the Church may occupy in the name of civil society.

Such a church would identify with the third or non-profit sector. The growth of the third sector, which is also historically weak in Italy, would demonstrate that capitalist and public-sector economies are not the only kind and that the non-profit sector might offer new approaches to such problems as health care.

Similarly the Church is rich in volunteer workers who give up to ten hours a week to various services: old people's homes, centres for the handicapped, AIDS victims, as well as shelters for drug and alcohol abuse. The volunteers make a directly religious contribution in their goal, which is the reinsertion of their patient in mainstream society, and in their method, a direct confrontation with those being treated.

Both the volunteers and the followers of the Madonna of Civitavecchia reveal the Italian Church's capacity to inspire people. For reasons of space we shall limit ourselves to three examples of popular Catholicism: Padre Pio, the blood of San Gennaro, and the Madonna.

Of the participants Padre Pio is the dominating figure. Beatified on 2 May 1999, he has ample miracles and no lack of popular devotion.

An unusual group of believers is the Allied pilots who tried to bomb his home and his people but were sent away in confusion by a priest sitting next to them. Of the army of pilgrims who come to San Giovanni Rotondo each year, many bring Southern Italy with them: old-fashioned clothes, worn faces, and the accents of the *Mezzogiorno*. Padre Pio's religion was the same. He said mass and heard confessions, he could be hard like the countryside. Yet seventy-four prayer-groups arrived from Ireland alone for his beatification. There is no shortage of money: his church at San Giovanni will cost £10 million.

Padre Pio is invoked in exceptional moments, whereas the liquefying of San Gennaro's blood confirms and reinforces the civic order of Naples. This is too simple since the origins of Naples are a tale of bloodshed and of the constant threat from Vesuvius. If Naples was to survive, its civic feast days needed all the social and spiritual support they could find. Despite the Bassolino Renaissance little has changed, so Naples awaits with confidence but anguish the two Saturdays when San Gennaro's blood is to liquefy. Rarely does it fail 'its' citizens.

The continuity of this tradition is assumed by the Madonna of Civitavecchia, born or at any rate fabricated in Medjugorje (Herzegovina 1981), itself the site of a supposed apparition of the Madonna. By first appearing and weeping in 1995 the Madonna has assumed an array of troubles both domestic—the post-1992 political crisis—and international: from Civitavecchia the boat leaves for Sardinia, a participant in the EU's as yet unrewarding Barcelona project. The Virgin chose a crowded, concrete area—gone are the shepherdesses of Lourdes and Fatima—where the shrine to be built for her will constitute a rare relief not from poverty but from the restrictions of modernity. Mary's message is no longer harsh as it was at La Salette (France, 1846). It is an appeal for spiritual values to survive into the third millennium.

In its basic traditional form as in its novelties, the Madonna of Civitavecchia marks the Church's ability to project itself beyond the regime it helped found in the 1940s. It is still fighting for its brand of truth against the 'inevitable' victory of secularization.

7

The Mafia

Salvatore Lupo

In the fifties, the South of Italy, like the North, underwent a great transformation of its own. People emigrated to Germany and Northern Italy while within the *Mezzogiorno* there was a generalized shift from mountains to plains and from rural areas to the cities where new buildings were springing up everywhere as wages started to grow. Above all, this was the start of state funding to foster economic development: it was the time of agricultural reform and its implementation, the redistribution of property and (in the more fortunate areas) land reclamation and irrigation. The Southern Italy Development Fund and its projects were to set up infrastructure in Sicily, one of the regions enjoying greater autonomy, in often Gargantuan projects to free the island from alleged exploitation by the capital in the north. It was the era of the Christian Democrat (DC) party-state, which was to make the South a part of the modern world, thanks to a singular notion of political participation and the myriad government institutions for the economy and welfare.

Surveying these events some years later, many observers and experts were to pronounce the end of the clientelism that had characterized the *Mezzogiorno* up to then. In their view, the networks outside politics itself, those of personal clientele created in the past by the notables, no longer represented a decisive means of accessing the funds distributed by the welfare state and the patronage offered by the party machine led by Amintore Fanfani's DC party. For political historians of the seventies, the manner in which Silvio

Translated from Italian by Anne Collins.

Gava (father of Antonio who was to become Minister of Home Affairs), in Naples, and Nino Drago, in Catania, dismantled the clientele of the old agrarian right inside and outside the DC party was emblematic.[1]

The argument went that with the new society there was no room for organized crime nor the power of the Mafia and the Camorra which were now universally considered remnants of traditional rural society. There views were grossly wrong, however. According to the records of the case recently studied by Francesco Barbagallo, Antonio Gava in person once justified his own relations with members of the Camorra, saying to Professor Lavitola: 'Peppino, you too have been in politics and you made use of these people just as I did and as my father did before me' (Barbagallo 1997, 17). It is particularly interesting that these dangerous liaisons linked Gava's father not to some old forgotten thug, but to men of consequence close to those who were to be become the opposing factions of the Camorra at the end of the seventies, for and against Cutolo. Among Cutolo's supporters, the businessman Alfonso Rosanova, considered the leading influence behind the head of the new Camorra, Raffaele Cutolo, played a key role in extending the Camorra's links with politics. Among Cutolo's enemies, Ciro Maresca, scion of a well-established Camorra family, was said to have been an 'intimate friend' of Gava junior since childhood, whereas the father of Pasquale Gallaso, who was to become a leading figure in the eighties, through the grand chief of vote procurement Ciccio Liguori, was a supporter of both Gavas. This close-knit network led to Pascalone 'e Nola, Maresca's brother-in-law, the most famous member of the Camorra in post-war years who appears to have had control over 2,000 votes which were bestowed upon the Christian Democrat Giovanni Leone, future President of the Italian Republic, a leading criminal lawyer and defence counsel for numerous representatives of organized crime brought to trial during the fifties (Barbagallo 1997, 18–20).

Leone himself went to Catania in the early sixties to defend a gangster, Franco Ferrera, accused of murder. The episode caused a stir even then, but it would have caused a scandal had it been known that Ferrera belonged to a Mafia group linked to the Palermo Mafia, entrenched in the city of Etna since the twenties, which had been

---

[1] 'Technically', Gava is referring to the 'Dorotei', a centrist current within the DC. Allum 1975; Caciagli 1977; but cf. also Chubb 1982.

gaining ground while the Fanfani political machine was consolidating its power, even in areas hitherto refractory to Mafia influence. Far greater prominence was given to the Reggio Calabria Mafia and the clamp-down by security forces during the 'Marzano operation' in 1955, similar to the more famous Mori operation carried out in Sicily in the twenties, aimed at crippling a traditional political system by attacking its peripheral ramifications. Here too Fanfani's supporters led the operation and profited from it at the expense of the right inside and outside the DC party, but also at the expense of the socialist-communist Left which many Mafia 'firms' had backed since the early fifties.[2] In any event, the operation in no way halted the growth of the *'ndrangheta*, which has gone from strength to strength since the war.

The war ends, the Mafia continues

Again from the standpoint of political analysis of the seventies, 'Milazzismo'—the split in the Sicilian DC party over the figure of Silvio Milazzo[3]— has been construed as a revolt of the notables against the centralized party; the defeat meant the fall of the last bastion against the accession of Fanfani's 'young Turks': Drago, Nino Gullotti from Messina, Giuseppe La Loggia from Agrigento, Giovanni Gioia, and Salvo Lima from Palermo. In actual fact, the new men in the party system sometimes had strong links outside the party and with the past. Giovanni Gioia, for example, was the scion of the nineteenth to twentieth-century Palermo establishment, grandson of the famous founder of the milling industry Filippo Pecoraino, related to the Tagliavia, a family of shipowners, landowners, and famous politicians. Giuseppe La Loggia, perhaps the most important representative of the Fanfani group, was the son of Enrico La Loggia, mason, rabid anticleric, and old stalwart of social reform in Agrigento who had played a central role in drafting Sicily's regional statute, but

---

[2] Albeit with much in-fighting: cf. 'Il caso di una cosca reggina' in Cervigni 1956, 64.
[3] Scion of a notable family, godson of Sturzo, once tied to the separatists, he set up the USCS (Sicilian Christian-Social Union) and became head of the region in 1959 leading a mixed coalition backed by the right and, outside, by the Socialist-Communists on a Sicilianist platform.

later converted suddenly to the DC party. Moreover, in the clash over Milazzo, both sides accused each other of enjoying Mafia backing. In fact, there is no doubt that subsequently the Fanfani supporters Gioia and Lima did not lack that support. It appears that the Milazzo experiment was initially supported by Paolino Bontate, the influential Palermo Mafia chief, and by businessmen destined to join the Mafia network like the Salvos from the Palermo establishment and the Costanzos of the new Catania élite. These figures subsequently worked to overthrow Milazzo, thereby earning the undying gratitude of the Christian Democrats.

If confirmed, this would mark the last emblematic episode in the great transformation which from the end of the war and throughout the fifties brought into the fold of the majority party right-wing groups and organized patronage systems, and along with them, the Mafia. In western Sicily, the Mafia's inheritance was strong and well-stratified. During the feverish crisis of 1944–5, the Mafia had tried to support old politicians with whom they had been in league before the fascist era, men like Vittorio Emanuele Orlando and Andrea Finocchiaro Aprile and prominent landowners like Lucio Tasca Bordonaro. It had supported the latter two and their Movement for Sicilian Independence (MIS), a move that may have appeared rational when the war was still under way, but which subsequently proved ingenuously extremist in the face of the success of national parties and the defeat of the separatists in the first elections. Subsequently, Mafia representatives once active in the MIS ended up joining the DC party, often after an intermediate move to the right. Calogero Vizzini and Giuseppe Genco Russo, influential Mafia chiefs in the province of Caltanissetta, and Michele Navarra from Corleone belonged for a time to the Italian Liberal party; Paolino Bontate, father of Stefano who was to be among top level bosses of Cosa nostra in the sixties and seventies, took DC membership after a period as a monarchist. The same path was taken by the twenty-four palermo mafia chiefs cited in the report drafted in 1963 by Carabinieri Captain Malausa. In one of his files (the one on Benedetto Targia), the official wrote: 'He was a keen supporter of separatism, but when that movement lost its influence, he followed in the wake of other Mafia members going from party to party (liberal–monarchic–Christian democrat)'.[4]

---

[4] Rapporto Malausa 1972, 40. All these findings are discussed in detail in Lupo 1996a.

The political system was thus in a state of flux. The groups trad-itionally linked to the Mafia were in decline, but the Mafia found a more solid prop in the DC party. However, whereas the large landed estates ceased to exist after the peasant struggles and agrarian reform, the Mafia continued to be in excellent health despite all the predic-tions of those who saw it as merely a by-product of the landed estate system. Not many realized that the classical Mafia figures of the land-ed estates, Vizzini and Genco Russo, had already set up co-operatives to benefit from the sharing out of land at the end of the First World War. After 1950, we find Mafia figures in key positions in land reclam-ation consortiums and land reform agencies under the leadership of the DC party. This was the case, amongst others, of Genco Russo and Vanni Sacco.

The left was the only voice to protest against the Mafia: to pay homage to the peasants killed in Portella della Ginestra, shot down by the bandit Salvatore Giuliano, victims of a sordid episode of political terrorism constantly shrouded by the establishment; to mourn the many others, including numerous trade unionists murdered by the Mafia during the peasant struggles and occupation of the land; to denounce conspiracies and shady business dealings involving the government of the region and the Palermo municipality. Intellectuals like Simone Gatto, Danilo Dolci, and the young Leonardo Sciascia wrote important analyses; Palermo's pro-Communist evening paper *L'Ora* published courageous inquiries and was also victim of intimi-datory attacks. Yet Cardinal Ruffini, who was not even Sicilian, took up the crassest line of Sicilianist defence, claiming that the Mafia did not exist except in the slanderous inventions of the Communists. He was joined by the silent consensus of the whole of national and regional conservative opinion. Alternatively, he would launch into misleading speeches on the customs of Sicilians and their hot-bloodedness which led them to react violently when offended. The close ties between the Mafia and the majority political party triggered what is probably a unique phenomenon in the centuries-old relations between organized crime and a national state: the total suspension of any attention or alarm on the part of the authorities. The minimalism of the reports by prefects from 1957 to 1959, studied by Guido Crainz, contrasts sharply with the worries recorded continuously in equiva-lent documents of the pre-Fascist era. 'Murders committed or attempted killings constitute as always isolated episodes of a personal nature, originating from anomalous vents of private vendetta', stated the prefect of Agrigento. The relations between the Mafia and a DC member of parliament 'were part of normal dealings' claimed his counterpart in Enna. Even in Palermo, this was the line adopted. Each of the eleven [sic!] killings in June 1959 'should be considered a separate criminal episode lacking [...] the typical features of Mafia crimes'; the cluster was a 'mere coincidence'. The triple murder in broad daylight in Corleone in September 1958 was no cause for worry because it was 'linked to internal struggles among representatives of certain factions of the underworld' (Crainz 1997, 17–18).

Let criminals kill each other, because basically this does not affect respectable law-abiding people, thought the Sicilian bourgeoisie in those years, just as their forefathers had done. In this climate of total unconcern and impunity, the cancer was destined to spread.

Is the Mafia irrelevant?

As we have seen, in the early seventies organized crime may have seemed to play an irrelevant role in the construction of Fanfani's political machine, hidden—yet again!—by the 'modernity' of the new political style (Barbagallo 1997, 17). Political science failed to glimpse the looming shadows which, in the late nineties, were apparent. Indeed, it was the Mafia-watchers themselves who pronounced their subject of study extinct along with traditional society, because it was historically out of date. 'Yesterday there was the Mafia, today there is politics',[5] wrote the Dutch anthropologist Anton Blok, leaving his topic on the threshold of the 'great transformation', evidently convinced that the 'modern' political machine would provide answers better suited to the times and needs of representation and social protection fulfilled by the Mafia in the past. As Pino Arlacchi wrote in 1983:

'Sociologists, anthropologists and historians who were doing research between the late fifties and sixties all pointed to the same elements of decline in Mafia power and behaviour in both Sicily and Calabria. They saw the central state appropriating the mandate previously granted the Mafia to take

[5] Blok 1986, 207; along the same lines Sabetti 1993.

care of public order and emigration to Northern Italy and Europe. This and the involvement of Mafia strongholds in the post-war 'cultural revolution' had led to a generalized delegitimation of the Mafia's authority. Mafia members were being thrust from the centre to the outer edge of the social system. The role of the man of honour is growing dangerously close to that of a common criminal' (Arlacchi 1983, 12).

Arlacchi's solution is well known: the 'old' Mafia, characterized by its honour and its notables, was dead; a 'new' Mafia, enterprising, bloodthirsty and drug-dealing was about to be born (Arlacchi 1992, 127). In fact, Arlacchi's sources pushed him in that direction. On the other hand, the British historian Hobsbawm (1966), the German sociologist Hess (1970), and the Italian De Masi (1963, 17–40), together with Blok, continued to announce the demise of the honourable society. Faced with the evidence that Mafia members were thriving, they pointed to the birth of a form of gangsterism which had little to do with the past. In many descriptions of Southern crime, the term 'new' was used emphatically to denote the increased danger of groups and key figures. In reality, in many cases those with the oldest pedigree were the most efficient. Plainly, the critics and virtually all those in the front line had in mind a simplistic, often subtly apologetic, concept of the society of the past. Vice versa, they espoused an all too linear concept of modernization in which there was little room for hybrids and that exceptional capacity for mutual contamination of old and new which imbues the Mafia.

In western Sicily, especially in the city of Palermo and surrounding towns, the elements of continuity were extremely strong. According to one interpretation, sanctioned by the reports of the anti-Mafia commission, the old rural Mafia in the central part of the island had conquered the city in the fifties, changing its outward appearance and abandoning the landed estates for the more lucrative business of building development. This is yet another variation on the theme of setting the old Mafia against the new. The fact that the Badalamenti family in Cinisi, the Panzeca family in Caccamo, and above all the Corleonesi had enormous influence in Palermo should not be construed as a conquest of the city by the countryside, but as yet further proof of the integrated provincial-wide nature of the Mafia organization. During the nineteenth century the rents of the entire area of the surrounding landed estates were decided in Palermo and Mafia tenant farmers and herdsmen often moved from Palermo: 'What a network! What a tangle!' exclaimed the angry Bernardino Verro in 1911 from Palermo where he had temporarily escaped the Corleone Mafia who were plotting his death.[6] Looking at things from Palermo, he realized how compact their provincial support network was. Likewise, fifty years later, an unknown police sergeant linked the murder in 1958 of Michele Navarra, a doctor and local Mafia chief in the last years of the Fascist regime, not to the specific context of his town, but to issues and interests on a subprovincial scale and the struggle for control of the dams bringing water to Palermo, in 'that chain which, along the main road, leads to the island's capital'. On the topic of continuity, a study of the network of Navarra's relations led back in time to the murderers of Verro in 1915 and forwards to Luciano Leggio, initially his right-hand hired killer, later his implacable enemy, and further on to Toto Riina himself.[7]

Cesare Terranova, the magistrate and Communist member of parliament destined to die under Mafia fire, emphasized that the Mafia was characterized by the same ancient system of relations: in his court decisions he used to refer to 'one single Mafia, neither old nor young, neither good nor bad', 'efficient and dangerous, grouped into clans or groups or "families", or better still, "cosche", organized bands'.[8] Of the two opposing groups in Palermo during the 'first Mafia war' (1962), the La Barbera family (the losers) 'came from nowhere and their strength lay mainly in their enterprise and later in being a resolute band of hired killers', whereas the Greco family (the winners) 'represented the traditional Mafia, the Mafia playing the part of respectability [. . .], linked by a close-knit network of friends, interests and protection with the leading Mafia figures of the Palermo region'.[9] From the turn of the century to the present day, the Greco family has held a place of honour in the Mafia hierarchy. 'The Greco family', claimed the informant, Calderone 'has always had more influence than any other family. The Greco family has long held the real power in the Sicilian Mafia', irrespective of who was in charge of

[6] Verro to N. Colajanni, 27 May 1912, in Barone 1993, 255.

[7] On the Corleone affair, see Lupo 1996a, 199–200. The citation is from a report by the police sergeant Vignali in Commissione antimafia, 1972, 4. 16. 164.

[8] Palermo Court. Committal for trial against L. Leggio + 115, 14 Aug 1965, in Commissione antimafia, 1972, 4. 26. 208–9.

[9] Palermo. Committal for trial against La Barbera + 42, 23 June 1964, ibid. 27. 543. The Commission also devotes a monograph to the Greco family, *Relazione sull'indagine riguardante casi di singoli mafiosi*, Rome 1972.

the organization at the time. The other informant, Contorno, when asked what should be done to defeat the Mafia, answered from the standpoint of a peon who longs to attack the castle: 'It's simple, but nobody takes any notice. How many roads lead to Ciaculli? Two in all. All you have to do is close them off and start the approach because that's where they all are'.

Mafia garden parties

Since the end of the nineteenth century the Greco family have been the tenants of huge citrus plantations belonging to the famous Tagliavia family in the Palermo village of Ciaculli. Their century-old history takes us back to the Palermo Mafia's main area of influence during the past century: the villages outside the city, the traditional stronghold of citrus growing, where the Mafia had the same role as they had in the landed estates as herdsmen, tenant farmers, intermediaries, sometimes even major exporters and landowners, as in the case of the Bontate and Greco families. The villages remained the focuses of an infection destined to reappear with the urban sprawl of the fifties and sixties. Hence it was not the rural Mafia which moved to the city in conquest, rather the city that offered the Mafia new opportunities for profit in the suburban areas which had always been the strongholds of the 'garden' or 'citrus orchard' bands. Even the Mafia 'businessmen' came from this same environment. This is the case, for example, of a 'new man' of the post-war period like Francesco Vassallo, born in the same Palermo village as Tommaso Natale and closely related with an ancient Mafia family there. He gradually rose to become a well-known figure in the construction industry thanks to his dealings with the leaders of the large organized bands and the Palermo political and business establishment for whom he acted as right-hand man and sometimes front man (Deaglio 1995, 62).

These new developers were not very different from their predecessors. It was the society around them that had changed and is still changing. Their greatest skill was using the network of political, business, and criminal relations to clinch deals. The revelations of subsequent informants likened them in some sense to diplomats acting as intermediaries among territorial potentates, involving the groups in the most lucrative deals organized with Byzantine intricacy, always party to secret matters, like unpublished town planning schemes and possible exceptions to their dictates. They were always expected to deliver, however, supplying bribes and business opportunities in sub-contracting for materials and in hiring workers to the band which controlled the territory in question. This was not always possible, which explains the bloody wars which affected the fruit and vegetable wholesale markets in 1955. In many cases, though, outside firms (from Northern Italy) acquiesced to the territorial Mafia landlords. The fifties then did not mark a genetic mutation in the Mafia, but an important turning-point, with the consolidation of political–business groups under the safe umbrella of the Palermo municipality or the Sicilian region. One example is the great fortunes accumulated by the firms of the famous regional tax collectors, the cousins Nino and Ignazio Salvo, originally linked to a Mafia group in Salemi (a town outside Trapani) and later playing a pivotal role in complex networks of relations with the most dangerous groups of the Palermo Mafia.

Relatively more innovative was the business linked to cigarette smuggling and drugs dealing. Here too, we must beware of the cliché of the 'traditional' Mafia member shut within the narrow confines of some small village in central Sicily. Ties with the United States of America, in the wake of illegal immigration and a series of licit and illicit activities, had always been an essential part of the Sicilian Mafia's dealings, as for its American counterpart. The return of a series of influential Mafia figures, expelled from the USA after the war as 'undesirables', served to revive that relationship. Lucky Luciano, the famous New York Mafia boss, was sent back to Italy and settled in Naples, starting up the trafficking of narcotics which was already under way in the twenties and thirties and forging links with the Marseilles underworld. Gaetano Badalamenti, a Mafia boss from Cinisi, exported heroin in partnership with his relatives across the Atlantic. A member of the Greco family, Salvatore Greco, known as 'the engineer', became the drugs and contraband baron of the fifties, confidential information reports of the finance police describing him as the 'backer in charge of contacts with foreign organisations',[10] in

---

[10] Report by the finance police for the year 1963, in Commissione antimafia 1972, 4. 14. 287–8.

particular with the Marseilles clan. The refineries were in Marseilles; the Sicilians exploited only their ancient tradition of a united criminal front and their relations of trust with their American counterpart. Again, it was American businessmen based in Tangiers who involved the Sicilians in contraband. But it was in this sector that the Mafia was to start widening its net of relations towards other forms of regional Southern crime, in particular forging links with the new Camorra.

A thoroughly modern Mafia

The Mafia thus adapted well to modernity. It fitted into modern America, where it had prospered since the twenties. It blended into modern international trafficking, actively participating with North American Mafia groups and entwined with other mafias from South America and the Far East. The Mafia adapted to modern Italy of the fifties and sixties, but also to that of the seventies and eighties when corruption in business and politics became wholesale and the very idea of public interest was lost in a spiral of bargaining among secret organizations and representatives of illicit activities of all kinds. The affair of the Italo-American banker Michele Sindona and that of the Milanese banker Roberto Calvi are good examples of how the Mafia already had a foothold in international finance, being able to count on pressure and political groups actively working to safeguard this deadly organization.

An analysis of these episodes reveals a complex, variegated picture where sensational features blend in with blurred, barely visible elements. Yet alongside the more modern and most profitable activities there remained others which some may (erroneously) judge less important because more traditional, like contraband and even cattle-stealing, or prostitution and protection rackets. In particular, extortion remains a sign of territorial control and the key to Mafia members' entry into many other sectors and control of enterprises and legal business activities of different kinds. Building and public works contracts have been all-important for the drug-trafficking Mafia, indeed probably more important in terms of asserting power which, it should not be forgotten, is not only economic but also political and 'military'. While capital flows through offshore banks and investment funds in the seas of international finance, Mafia members continue their 'simple' trade in the field of protection and extortion, monopoly mediation in illicit but also licit activities, with even greater commitment (and even more disastrous results) than their counterparts forty years earlier. Of course the various mafias have their financial advisers and rely on sophisticated money-laundering channels, but members of the Mafia essentially belong to an organization deeply entrenched in its local setting, with its internal channels of solidarity and criminal fraternity, enshrined in ancient membership rites.

These rituals, described by famous ex-Mafia informants like Tommaso Buscetta, are just like those revealed by past American plea-bargained informers like Joe Valachi and are surprisingly similar to the ceremonials meticulously recorded in police reports of nineteenth-century Sicily. Here, the Mafia is described as an organization practising initiation rites, possibly derived from the Freemasons. This is in sharp contrast with all the socio-anthropological interpretations of the Mafia at least until the seventies, which insisted on its fluid, non-corporate character, a mere reflection of Sicilian regional culture. There may also have been a feedback effect from America just after the Second World War. For example, the New World seems to have given rise to the term 'Family' used to denote the organization's elementary unity which in nineteenth-century Sicily was referred to as band, net, party, society, and brotherhood, even though the Mafia has no exclusive familial connotations either in America or in Sicily. Buscetta and many other subsequent informants have also related how Sicilian Mafia members refer to their organization by a name which had never appeared in Sicily, but was used in the thirties in the USA: Cosa nostra ('Our thing'). It would appear that the Sicilian (Italian)-American Mafia meant to emphasize, or better, invent a pseudo-noble and pseudo-patriotic tradition, something distinctly 'ours' which immigrants could set against the incomprehensible demands of 'theirs'. Joe Bonanno simply called it the Tradition to indicate practices that probably grew up in America out of traditions from the old country. Indeed, the conventional view according to which traditional Sicily exported the Mafia could even be inverted by asking how much of that tradition was generated in the New World and re-exported.

In Palermo, as in New York, a Commission representing the different families or bands supervised the dealings of Cosa nostra. Various police sources already referred to the activities of such a Commission at the turn of the century. This gives the lie to statements by Bonanno and Buscetta that nothing of the kind existed in the Sicilian tradition before the Second World War. Yet it is significant that after the period of Fascist repression—deemed a watershed within the Mafia itself— the American model was considered crucial for the post-war recovery of the Sicilian Mafia after Fascist repression by the island's prefect Mori.

One wonders to what extent the criminal organizations were unified following the political and institutional centralization of island life when Sicily became one of the Italian Special Statute Regions enjoying greater autonomy. There is definitely a link between these two events. It may even be that the involvement of members of Cosa nostra in widescale criminal trafficking required stable coordination among Mafia groups and between the latter and other sectors of organized crime, for example, between Mafia members in Palermo and Catania, between members of the Sicilian Mafia and the Camorra around Naples who are sometimes found among the affiliates of Cosa nostra.

Whatever the motive, the centralization of the Palermo Mafia was without doubt the primary concern of the judicial inquiries of the seventies and eighties and was the main focus of the passion and intelligence of Italy's leading anti-Mafia magistrate, Giovanni Falcone. The renewal of inquiries, the 'maxitrials' of the Sicilian Mafia and the final emergence (in the late seventies) of an opposition to the Mafia, came from an awareness that the organization must be countered. This could not be achieved simply by prosecuting individual criminal offences committed by members of the Mafia, whose internal workings, rules, and equilibrium would remain inscrutable to the outside world. The idea that the Mafia was a vague cultural code not an organization was a scientific error which was to be politically and legally detrimental. Today, journalists' reports tend to exaggerate, depicting the Sicilian Mafia as a single unit governed by top-level Palermo bosses; the organization has important and even autonomous centres in Trapani, Caltanisetta, Agrigento, and Catania. The history of the years spanning the seventies and eighties is one of territorial expansion and reproduction by imitation, a generalization of the Mafia model by other components of Sicilian crime and its encroachment on other regional settings. An example is the 'rebirth' of the Camorra, the boom in the '*ndrangheta* and the proliferation of Mafia-like groups all over Italy, well beyond the traditional geographical confines of Mafia influence. This has not made organized crime uniform, nor does it authorize us to liken it to a giant octopus with one head and a thousand tentacles.

Dealings with other criminals

In long-distance trafficking, Mafia businessmen broadened their dealings with Mafia members to encompass larger crime networks. Buscetta explained how in his era, unlike what occurred for extortion, the bands simply gave their members 'permission' to operate. Every member had the 'right' to share in the business dealings of co-members, but in practice 'those with the most economic means were those who worked most'.[11] This accounts for the differences in earnings in the Mafia universe: the big dealers, even when affiliates, did not always have a 'rank' within the bands corresponding to their financial and managerial strength. In running the contraband rings and drug rackets the Sicilian Mafia, like its American counterpart on an even more daily basis, had to contend with criminal groups far-removed from its own (Sicilian or Italo-American) environment, strategies and 'values'. This has led to a potential contradiction between the two spheres, the Mafia on the one hand and business dealings on the other: the clan's solidarity could clash with solidarity among business partners from different clans and relations with non-Mafia members belonging to the network could prevail over solidarity within the Mafia. Buscetta related that in 1958 he was temporarily expelled from his family for having too many contacts in cigarette-smuggling with 'people who did not have the Mafia mentality'.[12]

The 'second Mafia war' which wrought havoc among the Palermo Mafia in 1981–2, with possibly a thousand casualties, reflects just this situation. On the one side was the Sicilian-American drugs-dealing

---

[11] Text of Buscetta at the 'maxitrial' (1986), citing from the text stored in the files of the anti-Mafia commission, p. 218.

[12] Text of Buscetta at the 'maxitrial', 1. 41.

ring well represented by the 'boss of two worlds' Tommaso Buscetta and by Badalamenti, with the Gambino family and Sindona on the other side of the Atlantic and the Inzerillo family in Palermo (related to the Gambino family) and Stefano Bontate. On the other, there was the Commission dominated by the Corleone family led by Riina and strongly allied with the Greco family. In the middle were the individual families which shared out the city among themselves and represented the basic cell of the organization but which in fact appears an empty shell devoid of power and group strength. As virtually all the dead belonged to the Bontate–Inzerillo side, rather than a war (like the 'first Mafia war' in the early sixties), it would be more correct to speak of a coup by the Commission which concentrated military strength in its own hands, expropriating the family clans and taking over control of drugs-dealing.[13]

In the same period, from 1979, the Mafia abandoned the deferential attitude to the establishment which had characterized all its past dealings, and commenced a period of top-level assassinations, killing leading policemen, businessmen, honest politicians, corrupt politicians, and magistrates, culminating in the slaying of the two masterminds of anti-Mafia strategy, magistrates Falcone and Borsellino. Was this due to the effect of political terrorism sweeping through Italy at the time? Had the years of unbridled success and the process of centralization led the Mafia pseudo-state to think it could replace the real state? What is certain is that the whole of Italy risked falling hostage to this mighty criminal organization and its many allies in the world of business and corrupt politics.

It is likely that Cosa nostra's centralizing thrust, the 'totalitarian' drive of its leadership, was excessive and counter-productive both inside and outside the Mafia environment. In short, the Mafia over-exposed itself when it abandoned its reserve, admitting, as it were, its existence *urbi et orbi* with the bloody second Mafia war and above all in its offensive against the country's institutions.

As a result, the losing factions within the Mafia, exposed to the now unlimited power of the Commission, began to break their conspiracy of silence, claiming the alleged Mafia values 'of the past' and eschewing the degenerate ones 'of the present'. This ideological slant led the media to label them *Pentiti* (the 'repentant'), a term already in use

---

[13] For a more detailed analysis see Lupo 1996a, 237 ff.

for former terrorists turned informants. Leaving aside its seldom convincing ideological and moral justifications, the repentant/ informant phenomenon rapidly snowballed and has now reached epidemic proportions, shedding doubt on the capability of an organization grounded on century-old continuity to reproduce further. Accounts of informants on daily life within the Mafia reveal how even the slightest suspicion of betrayal (and now, repentance) can trigger the ultimate penalty, death, and how the Mafia (like all primitive and inefficient legal systems) implements this penalty on the basis of vague and arbitrary elements of 'proof'. This has had the opposite effect from that envisaged, of the self-limitation of violence, indeed it implies a de-personalization by which Mafia members are called to implement judgements whose motivation is unknown and, they suspect, bizarre, generating the reasonable fear that they will be the future victims. Attempts to regulate community life by murdering homosexuals, punishing rapists, adulterers, or those who killed for personal reasons without the mandate of Mafia tribunals,[14] are all propaganda ploys, carried out unsystematically and therefore unsuited to control deviant behaviour. The Mafia has proved unable to implement the protection inherent in its ideology, an indictment implicit in the informants' accusations (be they sincere or scheming) of the alleged degeneration of their organization.

Equally important changes have occurred in the relations between Cosa nostra and the surrounding world. The Mafia offensive has narrowed the space for silence and indulgence by members of the establishment. Outrage at episodes of terrorism has led many in national institutions to abandon the line of indifference. On the anti-Mafia front, the struggle has been carried on by a minority of front-line magistrates and policemen, who have paid an intolerably high price in terms of bloodshed, especially in Palermo. Their fight has been backed by public opinion movements to create an indispensable 'party of judges' and stimulate moral reawakening in infected areas and elsewhere, thereby refuting the idea of a generalized conspiracy of silence on the part of Sicilians as a whole. In addition, the front has been supported by the Left and by the anti-Mafia Parliamentary Commission, mainly during Violante's chairmanship, even if, as a

[14] Scarpinato 1996, 175–95. During the 'maxitrial' hearing Michele Greco issued an outrageous death sentence against the kidnappers of a child (Lodato 1992, 202–5).

rule, political circles have only called for prompt and effective action after the most tragic outbreaks of Mafia violence.[15] The anti-Mafia front is not vast and only since *Tangentopoli* has it found a less unfavourable general political climate (and for how much longer?). Yet Cosa nostra has been radically undermined; it has lost its compact front in the face of increasingly numerous defections, its leaders have been arrested and convicted and to date many of them are still in prison.

In the past too much emphasis was placed on Mafia superpower, perhaps a self-justification by public opinion, the institutions, the government, and even the opposition forces, unable to fight against Mafia activity. We read astonishing figures on the turnover of Mafia Inc., but on closer scrutiny it becomes evident that these are guestimates of all illicit markets, which are hardly run by a single Mafia corporation. A lot has been said about the totalitarian control of the southern vote by Mafia organizations, but, as far as I know, there is no serious study on electoral turn-outs and the influence of the Mafia on the political machine, but only the mechanical multiplication of the alleged number of clan members by x number of votes which may be influenced. From the little we have gleaned from some first-hand accounts, members of the Mafia and the Camorra exercise a somewhat elementary function of electoral canvassing (see Lupo 1996*b*, 74–5, and 1997, 5–23).

I do not wish to deny the danger of the ties between organized crime and politics and it is true that, with this system, the two have mutually reinforced each other, giving rise to a monstrous politics–business–Mafia system. However, it is also true that the Mafia groups compactly aligned in the MIS have failed to achieve any electoral success since the last war and recent attempts by the Mafia leadership to shift their votes from the Christian Democrats to the Socialist Party and the radicals do not seem to have resulted in any great changeover in electoral geography. At the time, the Christian Democrat Party gained its electoral success not because of Mafia support, but because of its ability to embody collective myths, projects, and ideals. The Sicilian electorate can be involved in projects for political and moral renewal, as demonstrated a few years ago with the election

[15] Two reports on Mafia and politics and Camorra and politics date back to this period, 1993 and 1994 respectively. On the topic of the anti-Mafia see the monographic issue of *Meridiana*, 25 (1996).

as mayor in two major Sicilian cities of candidates whose battle-cry was the fight against the Mafia. The current cuts in public spending have squeezed the Southern economy, but they have also created a pressure for renewal and set in motion economic circuits more resistant to Mafia aggression.

In the last twenty years, the Mafia has taken on a virulence without precedent in more than a century of Italian history. Yet nowadays the conditions for its defeat do exist, thanks to the fact that for the first time the Mafia has revealed to the Italian people just how dangerous it really is.

8

Sport

Stefano Pivato

When describing the Italian political system, historians, journalists, and foreign commentators resort to the word 'anomaly'. Italy is commonly construed by Europeans as the country which produced a political system like Fascism but, at the same time, the nation which nurtured the largest Communist Party in the West. It is also the country whose frequent government upheavals are more reminiscent of South America than of Europe.

Italy seems to confirm its vocation as an anomaly even in the sporting arena. Unlike other European countries, Italy's management of sport is not delegated to a ministry but to an independent body, the Italian National Olympic Committee (CONI). The anomalies of Italian sport do not stop with its management. Italy is the only country in the world to have three daily newspapers devoted to sport. Even more exemplary is the fact that in autumn 1993, after years of intellectual ostracism towards sport, one of the most authoritative national dailies, *La Repubblica*, opted to publish an edition on Mondays and to devote much of it to sport. Italy is the country where sports programmes have the highest TV audience ratings. Last but not least, it is the country which hosts what has been called the 'best football championship in the world' thanks to a policy, later imitated by other European nations such as Great Britain and Spain, which has allowed clubs to import the most skilled (and most highly paid) world football stars such as Maradona, Platini, Falcao, Rumenigge, Ronaldo and Batistuta.

One of the most peculiar characteristics of Italian football is its ties with the world of politics—ties which first took shape in Italy in the twenties and thirties as part of a whole communication strategy. With Fascism, Italy was the first nation to implement a model—later imitated elsewhere—for the management of leisure and sport in particular. Sporting images played an important role in constructing the myth of Mussolini as a popular hero, displaying speed, youth, sport, and contempt for danger: for Fascist propaganda, Mussolini embodied the qualities of Nietszche's superman as no other political figure had done before. The Duce's iconography, which the Fascist propaganda machine circulated around the world, seems to embody the ideal that Filippo Tommaso Marinetti, prophet of Italian Futurism, had laid down in a programme to regenerate the Italian nation through the 'domination of gymnastics over the book'.

Values such as youth, fearlessness, character, and dynamism emerge as personal traits in the works that most successfully spread the myth and image of Mussolini abroad. More than a classical political figure, Mussolini seems to symbolize the consummate qualities of the athlete. The American historian John Hoberman has defined Mussolini as the ultimate expression of twentieth century 'political athleticism'.

Politics and sport seem, thus, to represent two long-standing facets of Italian life. So much so that it came as no surprise to hear the unprecedented remarks made by the then prime minister, Silvio Berlusconi, in a speech to the Senate during a debate before a vote of confidence in spring 1994: 'In a few weeks, and this . . . is an issue of national interest, the World Cup will take place in the USA. I do not know if this is standard practice, but first of all I would like to convey my warmest good wishes to our players.' The unprecedented good wishes inserted in a highly official speech were, however, in line with a political style which stressed the close ties between enthusiasm for sport and national sentiment in much of Berlusconi's electoral propaganda.

The symbol, the battle-cry of Berlusconi's new political movement (Forza Italia), the language used by its members ('take the field', 'score a goal'), the name to be given to Forza Italia members of parliament (the *azzurri*), show how widely Berlusconi has applied sports metaphors to the language of political mobilization.

The popularity of sport in Italy explains Silvio Berlusconi's strategy. It also explains another characteristic: the appropriation by those wielding political power of a consensus-creating phenomenon. In fact, through the presidency of sports federations and related organisations, some of the more dubious Italian politicians have made use of the world of sport as a means of wielding favouritism and patronage.

In the eighties, the Socialist minister of foreign affairs, Gianni de Michelis, was president of the Basketball League; Enzo Scotti, a Christian Democrat and frequent government minister, acted as president of the League of Cycling. Franco Carraro, already president of AC Milan and of CONI, owes to the world of sport the beginning of a brilliant political career which was to take him to the office of mayor of Rome from 1989 to 1993. Giulio Andreotti himself, the longest-lasting post-war politician, for years presided over the football team of his electoral constituency, the city of Rome, bestowing favours and patronage.

Interestingly, the divide between the supporters of opposing football teams also extends into the political arena. Sharp divisions are not always possible, however: Juventus, the team which could be dubbed the status symbol of Italian capitalism, was supported, at different times, by the secretary of the Communist Party, Palmiro Togliatti, and one of the foremost trade union leaders since the war, Luciano Lama.

None the less, for other football teams the distinction is more clear-cut. Historically the two teams of the capital, Roma and Lazio, have always been supported by left- and right-wing fans respectively. Lazio's tradition of right-wing support dates back to Fascist Italy: it is no coincidence that despite his Emilian origin the leader of the Italian Right, Gianfranco Fini, makes a show of his support for the team of the 'sons of Mussolini'.

Starting with the eighties, a period which saw the birth of football violence, hooliganism in the stands took its cue to some extent from certain forms of political extremism in both rituals and language. The 'ultras' or hooligans (the 'Red-Black Brigades' of AC Milan , 'Black-White September' of Ascoli, the 'Violet Collective' of Fiorentina) chanted slogans reminiscent of the extremist Italian left in the seventies and eighties. The very rituals adopted by the fans themselves often mimic the symbolism of political extremism: banners with the five-pointed star (the emblem of the Red Brigades), the swastika, and other Nazi symbols. This infiltration of sport into Italian politics seems a common feature right across the political spectrum.

It has been claimed that in a country whose traditional points of reference for national sentiment have waned, the *azzurro* of the national team signifies much more than competitive spirit and constitutes one of the strongest symbols of national identity. This does not only apply to football. In 1996, in the heat of the call for secession launched by the leader of the Lombard League, Umberto Bossi, the most popular Italian cycling race, the Giro d'Italia, set off from Venice, one of the cities symbolizing Italian unity, under a banner with the slogan 'Green divides, rose unites'.

On the occasion of the European Football Championship in 1996 the two leaders of the coalition which had just defeated Silvio Berlusconi, Romano Prodi and Walter Veltroni, were to use the national team as a call to the Italian tricolour flag and the values of Italian unity against the separatist aims of Bossi and the League. It therefore came as no surprise when Romano Prodi, who succeeded Silvio Berlusconi as prime minister leading a centre-left coalition in 1996 based part of his media campaign on a sporting metaphor.

One of the most popular images in the Italy of the Olive Tree coalition is that of Prime Minister Romano Prodi portrayed as a keen cyclist. Television and magazines showing him pedalling round hairpin mountain bends on his bike have come to embody a country that must 'pedal hard' and put aside the Berlusconi-inspired dreams and illusions of easy money and any facile optimism about a smooth passage into Europe. Romano Prodi's Italy is synonymous with exertion and fatigue and links up with one of the most vivid images of the collective Italian memory: the Giro d'Italia and its heroes. The heroes of the Giro seem taken from the pages of a popular novel or from the script of a soap opera. Indeed, some of the most acclaimed early heroes of the race, Giovanni Brunero, the two Azzini brothers, and Libero Ferrario died of tuberculosis. As in a popular novel or soap opera, the man in the street immediately identifies with the cycling hero since not only is the Giro part of the collective memory, but, like soap opera, it strikes a very modern chord in the popular imagination of today.

The end of the forties saw one of the masterpieces of neo-realist cinema, *Ladri di biciclette* (Bicycle Thieves), being slated by the government press because the main character in the film, who steals a bicycle to keep his job and support his family, portrayed a negative and pessimistic image of Italy to the world. At the same time, however, the sporting victories of two cycling champions, Bartali and Coppi, were redeeming the image of makeshift Italy as a loser in rags.

In the Italy of Peppone and Don Camillo[1] and of the Manichaean opposition between Communists and Christian Democrats, these two cycling champions attained cult status in the popular imagination also in political terms: the Communist Coppi versus the Christian Democrat Bartali. Nevertheless, to grasp this peculiar opposition we need to go back to the second half of the thirties when the Catholic propaganda machine created the myth of the 'perfect Christian athlete'.

Following Gino Bartali's first great sporting victory in the Giro d'Italia in 1936, the Catholic press swiftly created the image of the 'perfect Christian athlete' around the Tuscan cyclist, a figure who became the alternative to the archetypal Fascist athlete. Bartali became a model figure expounding the ideal virtues of the Catholic militant: a sense of sacrifice and subjugation, chastity and prayer.

In 1946, when sporting events were resumed after the Second World War, Gino Bartali won the Giro d'Italia. Coming second by only 47 seconds was one of his former team mates, Fausto Coppi. Gino Bartali was then 32, a relatively advanced age for an athlete. Fausto Coppi was five years younger than his rival. The 1946 Giro d'Italia was depicted as a victory of the 'old' Bartali over the 'young' Coppi. After the 1946 Giro d'Italia, at the age of 33, Bartali won the Milan–San Remo race and came second behind Coppi in the Giro d'Italia; in 1948 he seized his second victory in the Tour de France, ten years after his first win in 1938. This victory was greeted by the Italian sports press as the 'greatest sporting victory of all time'. In 1949, Coppi's triumphal year, Bartali came second behind the 'champion of champions' in both the Giro d'Italia and the Tour de France. The following year he won the Milan–San Remo race for the fourth time and was again second in the Giro d'Italia behind Koblet. Lastly, in 1952, at the age of thirty-eight, he wore the tricolour jersey of champion of Italy yet again.

It was on this athletic longevity that Catholic propaganda built the myth of Gino Bartali's 'eternal Christian youth'. The Catholic press, at the time, presented Bartali not only as a 'sportsman to imitate' but,

---

[1] The two well-known characters of Guareschi's novels: Don Camillo the genial parish priest and Peppone the Communist mayor of a small northern Italian town.

most of all, as 'an exemplary Catholic'. It explained that his athletic vigour was the result of a 'pious religious life that enabled his moral and physical fibre to work like a clock' because 'a Christian life lived in a Christian way is the ideal way to gain earthly successes'. In post-war Italy the public image of Bartali was not just that of a sportsman but one of a 'moral athlete' thanks to the blanket recognition he had received from the highest political and religious authorities. In September 1947, in front of a huge crowd gathered in St Peter's Square in Rome, Pius XII praised Bartali as the epitome of Catholic, Christian Democratic, anti-Communist Italy in these terms:

Now is the time for action . . . it is the hour of trial. The strenuous race St Paul refers to is now under way; it is the hour of utmost effort. A few moments can mean victory. Look at your Gino Bartali, member of 'Azione Cattolica': many times he has won the longed-for 'jersey'. You too must run in this championship of ideals to win a far nobler palm: *Sic currite ut comprendehatis* (1 Cor. 9: 24).

Following that speech, Bartali started to launch appeals and calls for votes for the Christian Democrats against the 'red peril'. Joining the electoral propaganda machine in favour of the Catholic Party was a natural political dénouement to Bartali's ideal journey. However, the presence of Fausto Coppi at his side on the electoral billboards would have raised eyebrows. This is because in the post-war years the popular imagination had cast Coppi as the 'Communist' or at least as a sympathizer of left-wing parties.

To explain the reasons behind the Communist support for Coppi it should be noted that this transposition largely occurred after the period when the two champions were rivals. This is especially the case of the famous 'lady in white' affair of the early fifties,[2] which alienated Catholic public opinion. In a still prevalently Catholic country, Coppi's private life clashed with entrenched and widely shared moral standards. Even if the figure of a libertine Coppi drew him closer in the popular imagination to secular anti-clerical feeling, the events all happened after the period of rivalry between the two champions and their heroic duels. Besides, until the 'lady in white' affair, the Catholic mass media had depicted Coppi as a devout athlete, far removed from any Communist or anti-clerical taint. How then, did the image

---

[2] Coppi's alleged mistress always seen in public wearing white.

of a 'Communist' Coppi, without a doubt present in the popular imagination, arise?

From a sports standpoint, the press exalted Gino Bartali's victory in the Tour de France as a 'wholly Catholic' triumph. His win was the first great achievement of Italian sport at international level since the end of the Second World War. Italian nationalist pride had not celebrated a similar victory since the Italian football team's second World Cup victory in 1938. By winning the most prestigious international cycling race, Bartali not only gave Italy a sporting victory, but at the same time avenged national pride humiliated by the war. In addition, Bartali's sporting victory took place in France, in that same city where some months earlier national pride had been humiliated at the table of peace negotiations. On that occasion, the Italian press greeted Bartali as a 'peace-maker' between the French and the Italian peoples. It is reasonable to suggest therefore that Bartali's victory helped to heal the wounds of injured national pride.

Bartali's heroic image was fuelled by the fact that the victory coincided with an attempt on the life of Communist leader Palmiro Togliatti. The attempted assassination took place as Gino Bartali secured his triumph in the Tour de France with a memorable series of stage victories to win the yellow jersey. It is difficult to look behind the popular myth and gauge the extent to which revolution was averted by Bartali's victory in the heated climate of that period. The Catholic press did not hesitate to claim that this victory had kept Italy from revolution and social turmoil 'quashed by Bartoli's effort'.

The emphasis by the Catholic press on Bartali's victory helped to widen the political divisions between supporters of Coppi on the one hand and Bartali on the other. In a period in which the Catholic Party had cast the left-wing parties out of political life, the popular imagination may have interpreted the defeats that Coppi inflicted on Bartali as a symbolic victory over one of the most popular symbols of Catholic Italy. The victories were again celebrated as a triumph of the 'new' over the 'traditional', 'young' over 'old', 'modernity' and 'progress' over the traditionalism of clerical Christian Democrat Italy. The public imagination may well have created the myth of Communist Coppi not only to counteract the cycling champion but also to demolish, at least idealistically, the symbol of Catholic Italy: Gino Bartali, 'God's cyclist'.

The Coppi and Bartali duel, which from the late forties and early fifties divided popular support into two opposing factions, came at a time when sport still had a romantic aura and yet was about to be projected into the world of post-war modernity.

Starting from the end of the fifties, the Giro reflected the economic boom under way in Italy. The car had become the new means of transport and television had entered most living-rooms. And seen on television the Giro lost the essential emotional charge transmitted by the live event on the road. By an uninterrupted repetition of images, photo finishes, slow-motion shots that scrutinized every move, revealed every secret, probed into every detail, television, first in black and white then in colour, numbed the fancy and imagination that had made the Giro so popular for decades.

A metaphor of Italy's modernization, the race took the products of the first Italian economic boom all over Italy: brilliantine, coffee machines, liqueurs, salami, toothpaste, refrigerators, and cookers. This was the start of the Giro show: no longer a soap opera, but a consumerist saga. No longer poetry, but tawdry prose. Lenticular wheels, ever more sophisticated bicycle models, flatter and flatter routes have today removed the Giro from that genetic code of physical fatigue which had made it a myth. Those values have only recently been rekindled by a champion like Marco Pantani who in 1998 won the Giro and the Tour de France in the same year like Coppi in 1949 and in 1952. The diminutive Italian cyclist became the toast of press and media celebrating almost the re-discovery of a sport which in the popular mind evokes exertion, sweat, and provincial life: the Giro d'Italia was once again proposed as a quest for time lost.

With the disappearance from the scene of Coppi and Bartali in the early fifties, a profound change took place in Italian sport. Cycling gave way to football as the most popular sport.

On 4 May 1949 the entire Torino football team perished in an air crash over the Superga hills. Winners of the previous five championships, Torino had the highest number of players in the national team. In the transition from cycling to football as the most popular sport, the Superga disaster had a huge emotional impact on the collective imagination.

In the space of a decade, from 1953 to 1963, the number of spectators at First Division Football Championship matches increased by 30 per cent. In addition, one of the major features of post-war Italian life, 'Totocalcio' (football pools) played no small role in shifting Italy's sporting preference. When it was launched in 1946, Totocalcio achieved an annual profit of little over 7 million lire. A decade later, this figure had risen fivefold and in 1975, when the football pools announced an annual turnover of 150 billion lire, surveys estimated that 35 per cent of Italians did the pools.

The final sign of change in Italian sport came with the staging of the 1960 Olympic Games in Italy. Italy took part in the first post-war Olympics (London, 1948) after overcoming initial protest by the British, who did not want to admit a former ally of Japan and Germany. Holding the Olympic Games in Italy fifteen years after the end of the conflict not only signified the readmission of Italy into the international community (the Olympic Games had been assigned to Italy in 1955) but also confirmed the organizational skills of a country which had just emerged from post-war reconstruction.

The Rome Olympics were not only a success at the political and diplomatic level but also a triumph of sport and spectacle. They exceeded all previous records for number of nations and competing athletes and also marked the transformation of the Games into a global event with the mobilization of the media: 1,500 journalists followed the Games which, most importantly, were to be broadcast almost all over the world by some hundred TV channels.

The Olympic medals won by the *azzurri* (36 in all: 13 gold, 10 silver, and 13 bronze medals) placed Italy in third place behind the Soviet Union and the USA. This was Italy's best Olympic Games result ever. The 1960 Rome Olympics opened up a new era for Italian sport. The impact of mass media broadcasting and the impressive performance of the *azzurri* athletes further popularized sport in a nation which was now well on its way towards unprecedented economic prosperity. Sport and its rituals became the new status symbol for the average Italian.

In the fifties, the number of Italians practising sports fluctuated between 2 and 3 per cent. By the mid-seventies, this percentage had doubled, and in 1985 exceeded 22 per cent of the population. From the seventies onwards, with the advent of sponsors, sport became a vehicle for advertising, making sport a consumer commodity. In fact, by the end of the eighties, annual per capita expenditure on sport in Italy was the highest in Europe: US$293, against US$230 in Holland and US$210 in Germany.

Often, speculative business interests went hand in hand with those of politics. The overlap between the worlds of sport, politics, and business deals became macroscopic during the organization of the Football World Cup by Italy in 1990. According to the findings of various judicial inquiries, the actual expenditure for the facilities, financed by ad hoc legislation, was 83 per cent greater than the amount originally budgeted—increasing from an initial allocation of 570 billion to 1,248 billion lire. The unjustified rise in these costs was frequently pushed through by political figures eager to reap the attendant political consensus sport creates.

The link between sport and politics since the eighties is exemplified by Silvio Berlusconi. A little-known entrepreneur until the early eighties, Silvio Berlusconi suddenly became popular when he became president of one of the best-established football clubs, AC Milan. Berlusconi transformed the Milanese club into a business enterprise, making huge investments to ensure its supremacy in national and international football for years to come. As owner of Italy's largest private TV network Berlusconi turned sport into an event generating primarily advertising revenue. Subsequently, coverage of major sporting events was gradually shifted away from state channels, starting from 1993 when one of the most popular events, the Giro d'Italia, was awarded to one of Berlusconi's networks. This was followed in winter 1996 by an attempt to snatch the Football Championship from the RAI by the networks owned by Vittorio Cecchi Gori, another individual to combine sport, politics, and the mass media from the eighties on. Cecchi Gori was at the same time president of one of the most prestigious football clubs, Fiorentina, a member of parliament, and the owner of a TV network.

The Berlusconi–Cecchi Gori model, the mixture of sport, politics, and business, was to constitute an example for many European football clubs. Between the eighties and nineties Bernard Tapie transformed his football club, the Olimpique Marseille, into a springboard for his political career; in Spain a prominent businessman, Jesus Gill, became the owner of Atletico Madrid and mayor of Marbella at the same time. Sport, not only football, seems now on its way towards a sort of globalization of its management following universally applied business criteria.

Against a backdrop provided by the mass media, the faces of sports heroes have also changed. Up to the sixties, one of the most popular characterizations of Italian sport was the cyclist, a provincial lad whose interviews were crammed with dubious syntax and dialect expressions. Today's sporting hero is, by contrast, a TV personality who speaks to the press in the language of the global market, English—a far cry from the cyclist of a popular TV sketch in the fifties who always ended his interviews with a homely 'ciao mama'.

Sport has become another consumer product largely on account of TV coverage. In Britain the average number of tickets sold during a season was around 40 million in the fifties; by the mid-Eighties this number had dwindled to little over 15 million. A similar fall has occurred in Italy, where the average number of spectators per First Division Championship match has fallen from 38,872 during the 1984–5 season to 29,454 in 1988. The substantial drop in spectators of such a popular sport does not, however, reflect a decline in public interest. Television has undoubtedly helped keep the crowds away from the football grounds. But the fall-off in ground attendance is also the result of deep-rooted changes in culture and customs which have influenced sport as a commodity. Proof of this is the fact that, during the eighties lower attendance at football matches coincided with a marked increase in the number of people regularly engaged in sports, the overall percentage increasing during the period 1982 to 1986 from 15.4 per cent to 22.3 per cent.

The increase in people playing sports is linked with a vast range of 'new sports' which have been transformed into mass sporting activities thanks to the inducements of the sportswear industry and sports accessories market. Between the late seventies and early eighties, sports like skiing and tennis, once the prerogative of the few, became mass sports spurred on, respectively, by the victories by Gustavo Thoeni first and Alberto Tomba later and the Davies Cup victories of Adriano Panatta and Attilio Bertolucci. During the eighties, sports like basketball and volleyball enjoyed a popularity previously unknown.

Other sports have contributed to the redistribution of the sporting interests of Italians between the late eighties and early nineties. The health mania of the eighties, physical fitness, and a new cult of the body beautiful have not only triggered widespread changes in attitude towards physical activities and sports, but focused attention on sports and values hitherto unheard of in Italy. The so-called Californian sports (free-climbing, wind-surfing, and beach-volley ball), burst onto the Italian sports scene in the eighties, symbolizing eternal American youth, and a taste for risk and extreme challenge. Health, beauty, well-being, and physical efficiency have been—and in part still are—among the emerging values of Italian society in the eighties and nineties.

This trend has been consolidated in recent years. According to 1998 figures released by the leading economic daily, *Il Sole 24 ore*, as part of a quality of life survey, the highest average percapita expenditure among leisure-time activities went on sport. In 1998, Italians spent an average of 12,726 lire as spectators at sporting events, against 12,147 lire on theatre or concert tickets. In addition, the same survey reported 10.72 gyms for every 100,000 people against 8.25 bookshops and 2.96 cinemas. Italy was once known for its 'heroes, saints, and sailors'. It would appear that this old adage should perhaps be updated to include 'sports enthusiasts'.

9

Memory and identity: popular culture in post-war Italy

Stephen Gundle

For Gramsci, Italian popular culture was a construction of the country's social divisions; it existed as the culture of the lower classes and consisted of all that was not artistic or high culture. This separation was maintained and reproduced by capitalist control of cultural production and distribution. It was the task of the Communist Party, as Gramsci saw it, to work towards a correction of this situation by promoting a 'national popular' culture. This would take shape as the working class assumed the functions and responsibilities of a hegemonic class and gave rise to its own organic intellectuals, who would challenge those of the dominant class. As part of the process whereby rule passed from the bourgeoisie to the working class, old cultural stratifications would be overcome and a new culture capable of integrating different interests and practices would emerge. Although Gramsci did not specify what form the national popular culture of the future would take, he indicated the need for a struggle against the isolation of conventional intellectuals and for action to combat the localisms and folk customs that stood in the way of the development of a national consciousness among the common people.

In the post-war years, the PCI implemented a cultural policy which broadly took on board this project. Although there were problems and setbacks in the party's political strategy, and rather more weight than Gramsci intended was placed on traditional intellectuals, the party set about promoting a culture in which writers and artists were encouraged to communicate with the mass of the people and take note of their concerns. Workers were simultaneously invited to improve themselves by attending classes and engaging with the books and films the party recommended. Generally, the party was too prescriptive in its interpretation of the national popular—realism was always preferred to modernism—but it did not ignore Gramsci's injunction that the new culture should 'sink its roots in the subsoil of popular culture as it is, with its tastes, its tendencies etc.' (Gramsci 1975, 1822). Taking as its model the Catholic Church, the PCI established itself as a pole of community life. It gave rise to sports and musical activities, it promoted festivals and celebrations, and it provided opportunities for women and children to pursue their interests together. In line with Gramsci's concerns, it paid particular attention to the South, although the encounter with folklore was not always sympathetic.

The problem for the Communists was that their vision of national development, which they continued to believe could only be led by the working class even after the Left was heavily defeated in the 1948 election, was rapidly displaced in the 1950s by a process of capitalist development. Far from leading Italy to ruin, as the Left had warned, the United States provided aid and know-how to promote recovery and growth. Imported culture made an important contribution to this. David Ellwood has suggested that, while the Marshall Plan and the politics of productivity 'stood as the key to the supply side', conveying the promise of future prosperity, Hollywood 'worked on the demand side of the economic and social transformation, speeding and channelling the changes in mentality and behaviour' (Ellwood 1992, 227). More than anything else, it offered appealing images of possible lifestyles. Already in the 1920s and 1930s American films, comics, and popular music, as well as broader cultural techniques, had been embraced by younger members of the urban middle class. Following the American role in the Liberation and the reconstruction, which included a propaganda campaign to persuade Italians that they should resist the seductions of communism and aspire to an American way of life, American influences became a structural feature of Italian life, although not always in the forms and ways that the American authorities would have wished. Films, magazine articles, popular music, and consumer goods all furnished raw material from which Italians selected and appropriated at will. Only the populations of the large cities could engage with this in the 1940s, but in the 1950s many more cinemas were built in the South and in rural areas, with the result that the dream of individual and familial prosperity was carried to poorer sections of the population.

Although the term *cultura popolare* is still predominantly used in Italian to refer to folklore and popular traditions, from at least the 1950s, the extension of consumption ensured that the leisure and culture of the common people took a different form. Nevertheless, in seeking to analyse consumption, there are certain difficulties in applying the sort of approach which has characterized British cultural studies. Starting in the 1970s, this focused on the study of the ways in which 'the objects and contexts of commercial popular culture . . . could be transformed and molded by the particular realities of *this* time and *this* place'. In other words, it tried to show how people (young, working-class men above all) 'rendered consumption into a precise and imaginative conquest of their circumstances' (Chambers 1986, 7–8; see also Hall and Jefferson 1976 and Hebdidge 1979). While this method yielded notable results in understanding the complexities of cultural consumption in determinate contexts, it overemphasized overtly creative appropriations on the part of highly visible and semiotically articulate sub-groups such as Mods and Punks as against the less active, non-appropriated consumption that prevailed in most people's lives.

In Italy individual consumer styles were important but general modernizing trends were skilfully manipulated by the Catholics to dovetail with conventional norms and values. The Catholic Church and the Christian Democrats had their own view of national development which involved intense competition with the Communists. Not only did they possess an extensive network of institutions and associations, as well as symbols and rituals which had a consolidated presence in Italian life, they also had at their disposition the state cultural apparatuses. The schools and universities, the state leisure organization inherited from Fascism, national radio and later television all provided tools for forging consent on the basis of old values and new experiences. Given that business provided the DC with support, private cultural industries including the press also contributed to the creation of a new, media-dominated cultural model. This was much easier to form than the Communists' idea of the *nazionale popolare* (national popular culture) because it did not require any change in economic and social relations or belief systems. Indeed the emphasis on individual or mediated solutions to problems, rather than the collective ones of the Communist tradition, was well suited to the real dynamic of modernization. In so far as it was 'national', this arose out of the processes of integration that were a consequence of urbanization and development. To this extent, Italian mass culture was given a conservative inflection.

It is impossible in a brief chapter to explore in depth the complexity of popular culture in post-war Italy. However, there are three issues which require attention. First, there is the way in which the media formed important moments of shared experience through which common cultural reference points were forged. Secondly, it is necessary to explore how identities were constructed through individual moments of consumption. Thirdly, account must be taken of forms of collective association which are structured through the state or voluntary organizations. In order to explore more fully these aspects of popular culture, a typical manifestation of the cultural configuration of Christian Democratic Italy, the San Remo Festival of Italian popular song, will be considered. In addition, two important moments will be examined: the Rome wedding of Hollywood stars Tyrone Power and Linda Christian in 1949 and the funeral of the Communist leader Enrico Berlinguer in 1984.

The San Remo Festival of Italian popular song

Over time, visual broadcasting became by far the most important tool of the Christian Democrats in forging consent. For the first twenty or so years of its existence, television conveyed information and entertainment to audiences which had often previously been excluded from cultural circuits, either because of their age, health, or poverty, or because they lived in remote areas. Because it was basically free in public places, and relatively low-cost in private homes, television had an immediate impact. It extended familiarity with the Italian language, it gave people a common texture of experiences and appointments, it provided models of dress and behaviour. In part television looked out on to the world; it transmitted events like the 1960 Rome Olympics and the 1969 moon landing and turned them into significant collective experiences. It also offered popular education and supplied entertainment which drew on theatre, the revues, music, and cinema.

The rise of commercial television from the late 1970s witnessed the emergence of a new style of broadcasting, which Umberto Eco (1990) memorably described as neo-television. Whereas early television talked about the external world, neo-television was largely self-referential. With its entertainment-oriented ethos, it offered viewers an alternative reality consisting largely of itself. Simultaneously with these changes, television also took a central position in social and political communication. As Alberto Abruzzese has written, 'there is no episode of daily life or of the social system which is not mediated by television. There is no aesthetic or ethic, ideology or policy, passion or conflict, that does not act in terms of television' (Abruzzese 1995).

There have been few attempts to study the impact of these and other changes in Italian television on audiences and therefore on popular culture. In her study of the history of the television audience, Francesca Anania talks of the 'disappearing audience'. One reason for this is the end of the clear separation of the two sides of the screen. 'Ordinary people' (*la gente*) are continually drawn into television through games, quizzes, talk-shows, phone-ins, polls, people shows, and interviews. In these contexts people act out roles and conform to expectations that they know television has of them. Lorenzo Fantini, a selector of participants for such shows, has even wondered if it is Italian society which appears on television or, rather, if it is television which invented Italian society.

An example of the changing nature of the mediation of television is offered by the San Remo festival. First held in 1951 to promote the casino of the Ligurian resort town of San Remo, the festival quickly established itself as an annual radio appointment of great moment. It offered an important forum for the reassertion of the national melodic tradition (which draws from both the operatic tradition and Neapolitan popular song) after the intrusion of jazz and swing in the war and post-war years. The festival produced many new singers, including Claudio Villa, Nilla Pizzi, and Luciano Tajoli, nearly all of whom were of humble origins and whose fine voices became widely known. In keeping with the atmosphere of restoration which marked nearly all state-sponsored and commercial culture in the 1950s, the songs were banal and consolatory; they spoke of motherly love, bell-towers, village life, and doves. This coincided with the shift of the axis of popular music broadcasting from Turin, where EIAR had been based, to Rome. As the presenter in the early years, Nunzio Filogamo, said many years later, the festival had, in the minds of RAI managers, to be an event for *all* Italians, including priests and nuns; it had to avoid hurting the sensibilities of anyone (Fortichiare and Mayer 1997, 99). As a result, Gianfranco Baldazzi has written, San Remo became 'the triumph of nothing, framed by violins and rose petals' (Baldazzi 1989, 77). Its mediocrity and the emphasis on rural traditions matched the conservative ideology of De Gasperi's Italy.

But the festivals were none the less examples of popular culture. The competition between the songs fired public interest and gave rise to heated divisions of opinion. Moreover, owing to magazines and television, people paid great attention to the costumes of female singers and the general elegance of the occasion. Record companies, which were industrializing with the advent of the 45 and 33 r.p.m. records, benefited from a boom in sales. Although the broad appeal of commercial popular music was not at all what Gramsci had in mind as a possible common culture when he advanced the idea of the national-popular, the success of the festival in the 1950s and 1960s pro-vided Italians with moments of collective identification that retained a prominent place in national memory. The innovation heralded by the success in 1958 of Domenico Modugno's unconventional song 'Nel blu dipinto nel blu' (better known as 'Volare') signalled the opening of Sanremo's most creative season. Through the 1960s, up-tempo rhythms, pop music, and singer-songwriters were all repre-sented. However, the suicide in 1967 of Luigi Tenco following the exclusion of his song from the final at the expense of one entitled 'You, Me, and the Roses' marked a watershed. It showed that there were strict limits to the extent of acceptable diversity.

After a period of decline in the 1970s, the festival was revived in the 1980s and 1990s as a weapon RAI-TV could use in its ratings battle with Berlusconi's Fininvest channels. As a national festival with a tradition behind it, it was relatively easy to create sufficient interest to turn it once more into a success. The festival featured old glories who embodied memory, foreign guests of honour including Liza Minelli and Ray Charles, but also Madonna and Sting. However, the Italian music it offered was of a very conventional type. Major singer-songwriters and rock singers kept their distance, while the dominant current was a mixture of the melodic tradition, carried forward by Mino Reitano, Massimo Ranieri, Amedeo Minghi and others, and the international soft-rock/easy listening of I Pooh and Ricchi e Poveri. This tradition was nearly moribund, as was especially evident in the spectacular kitsch of regulars such as the Apulian songster Al Bano and his (now separated) wife Romina Power and the poor quality of the few young hopefuls who subscribed to it. The competition ensured a modicum of entertainment value, but it was not helped by the fact that the rules and their application were rarely clear or transparent.

San Remo became almost entirely a television event, the success or otherwise of which was measured in terms of viewing figures. The stars of the show were not the singers but the avuncular male presenter (whose identity varied from year to year) and his beautiful female assistants. This was appropriate because they were much more famous than the contenders, whose records generally failed to sell. With no memorable tunes to offer, the festival traded on nostalgia, spiced with the antics of a few licensed jokers and the picturesque framework of the city of flowers.

As an example of how élites tried to control the process of modernization by making it conform culturally to tradition, eliminating controversy and promoting the bland, the festival had few equals. But its reduction to no more than this rendered it a ritual without content, a 'non-place' of popular culture which everyone passed through passively: there was no creative appropriation or absorption of songs into a patrimony of memory. Instead the ethos of neo-television dominated. Interest was aroused by tricks and stunts, unexpected appearances, the mixing of genres, phone polls, and the inclusion of figures from the external world. Like the 'hold-all' programmes (such as the Sunday afternoon marathon *Domenica In*) referred to by Eco, San Remo seemed to be interminable (it stretched over five days) and to include everything. On one occasion the presenter Pippo Baudo brought striking workers onto the stage, on another he helped prevent a suicide during transmission. Fashion was incorporated in 1995, with parades taking place between songs. In 1999 presenter Fabio Fazio was flanked by the French top model Laetitia Casta and the 85-year-old Nobel prize-winning scientist Dulbecco. Songs were introduced by television journalists, a lawyer, and a postmistress, as well as the former Soviet president Mikhail Gorbachev.

The wedding of Tyrone Power and Linda Christian, January 1949

The culture of consumption which played such an important part in reshaping the lives of Italians was driven by Hollywood films, television, advertising, and fashion. It may seem forced to try and link the impact of these aspects to a single event, but, in so far as that is possible, the event which best symbolized the way in which it was not only politics which aroused the enthusiasm of Italians in the years after the war was the Rome marriage on 27 January 1949 of the American film stars Tyrone Power and Linda Christian.[1]

This commercialism reflected the nature of the event as one which was publicity-driven. Tyrone Power was the leading hearthrob of the moment, whose film *Blood and Sand* had been hugely successful in Italy, and magazines and newsreels had talked for months of the forthcoming 'wedding of the century'. The Settimana Incom newsreel company had milked his popularity to increase its audiences. Cameras filmed several of his six stag nights and the hen night of his bride. They also pictured him preparing for the wedding as his butler dressed him. Magazines devoted great space to the dress that the Fontana sisters made for Linda Christian.

Newspaper accounts of the wedding spoke of the huge crowd which filled the pavements along Via dei Fori Imperiali, from Piazza Venezia to the Colosseum. 'For once the crowd did not gather to protest and the police did not have to protect ministries or politicians,' wrote Nantas Salvalaggio in *Il Tempo* of 28 January. He also could not remember seeing a gathering of similar size in Rome since before the war—'it had what might be termed an "oceanic" character.

---

[1] Romina Power, mentioned above, is the Italian-raised daughter of this couple.

At bottom, one could say that Tyrone Power has beaten Palmiro Togliatti.'

This crowd was composed of people rarely seen at demonstrations: 'gossiping girls and mop-headed adolescents' (*Il Tempo*), 'hundreds of youths who wear their hair like [Power] and who gesticulate and walk in a manner copied from his films . . . hundreds of girls who had bunked school or slipped out of offices . . . elderly ladies, women of the people, and old folk' (*Il Corriere della sera*), 'modern girls, hysterical widows, and young dandies covered with brillantine right down to their toe-nails' (*L'Unità*), 'groups of young girls carrying books under their arms', 'smart young guys wearing sky blue ties, striped nylon socks, scruffy hair, and suede moccasins', and 'distinguished ladies in furs' (*Avanti*). It was a lively gathering which 'hundreds of Carabinieri, policemen, and police on horseback struggled to keep in check' (*Corriere della sera*). Comments and appreciations were shouted, especially by the 'youths with greased-back hair' at the arrival of Linda Christian, although cries of 'Come on Tyrò' were heard from the girls. But it was also a gathering which had a commercial side. While many of the young people present had clearly abandoned the classroom in order to attend, others had merely taken time out from shopping ('the halls of the big stores were rather empty yesterday morning, like during the' flu epidemic', *Il Tempo* wrote). Newsvendors waved copies of a one-off paper bearing the enormous headline 'Ty e Linda sposi' (Ty and Linda Marry) while tradesmen sold coloured balloons, almond bars, and other confectionery.

The wedding itself was an event conceived and executed as one to be consumed by a mass, world-wide audience. Although people were held back by police and the stars were whisked away for an audience with the Pope following the ceremony, Italian and foreign broadcasting companies fought hard to win unprecedented permission for radio equipment to be installed in the Church of Santa Francesca Romana and photographers took shots during the ceremony; the films were then rushed by motorcycle to the central telegraph office from where they were wired to newpapers around the globe. Indiscreet photographers emerged from the bushes and hedges around the church as soon as the couple appeared outside and made towards a waiting limousine.

For many Italian commentators all this was new and undesirable. They spoke of it as an American B-film, vulgar and commercial, and they disapproved of the unusual enthusiasm of the crowd. The fact that Power's divorce from the French actress Annabella only became legally effective hours *after* the wedding added to these feelings. The event was described by *Avanti* as 'a saga for readers of *Grand Hotel*' and by *Il Messagero* as 'more picturesque than a technicolor film'. In consequence the 'wedding of the century' was widely seen, perhaps particularly by the older women and the young girls who were there, as a modern fairy-tale. The romance and marriage of the handsome actor and his beautiful starlet bride captured the imagination of the readers of romantic fiction. In the absence following the referendum of 1946 of the royal family or any aristocratic figures of wide renown, it offered an escape, a distraction from the troubles of the moment. That the dream was an eminently material one was evident, however, in the extraordinary publicity machine that surrounded it. In addition, it offered Italy's Christian Democratic leaders an example of how spectacle could be manipulated to conceal or obscure less appealing or conflicting topics from the press and the media. Although De Gasperi did not attend the wedding, he appeared on the front cover of *Oggi* in the company of Linda Christian.

Moreover, the wedding remained for many years in the collective memory of the Roman people. It offered a high-profile event, a rare chance to see with one's own eyes and recount to friends and relatives one's experience of Hollywood royalty. Although the crowd soon broke up, leaving the roadway and pavements clear once more, it was a significant if momentary public coming-together of film fans, magazine readers, shoppers, and cultivators of celebrity. It showed how events could add a realistic dimension to the experience of cinema and connect at various levels with popular culture. People did not at the time see the Power–Christian wedding as part of the drive towards lifestyles based on American kitchens, electrical appliances, and motorized transport—what Raymond Williams called mobile privatization—but with hindsight it can certainly be read in this way.

The funeral of Enrico Berlinguer, June 1984

After the defeat of the Left in the watershed elections of 1948, the Communist world took on the features of a subculture. Yet the PCI prospered as a result of sharpening class inequalities and the remarkable wave of protest that swept through the country between 1968 and 1973. At that time, not only did the PCI expand electorally, its membership grew, subscriptions to its press increased, and all its festivals and related activities flourished. For the first time, Communist culture entered the mainstream. Following the conquest of local government in 1975, some even theorized the possibility in the short term of the Left's culture of collective participation and solidarity becoming hegemonic.

The triumphs of this period were identified with Berlinguer, a man whose sadly cast good looks and evident sincerity endeared him to many Italians who were not Communists. As the architect of the Historic Compromise, the scheme whereby the Communists would ally with the Christian Democrats and gradually usher in a peaceful and democratic transition to socialism, he was personally responsible for leading the PCI out of the ghetto. Although his proposal eventually came to naught, and the PCI saw its vote decline in the elections of 1979 and 1983, Berlinguer retained a special place in the affections and the estimation of Communists and non-Communists alike. When he was suddenly taken ill and died in June 1984, he was given an extraordinary public valediction in Rome.

Berlinguer's funeral was a mixture of spontaneity and orchestration, in keeping with the party's regimented view of civil society. Because of the more central place the Communists had acquired in national life, it was attended by all leading public figures and state authorities, including President Pertini, who publicly laid hands on the coffin and spoke of Berlinguer as a political son. International figures including Yasser Arafat, Gorbachev, and the president of the European Parliament, who delivered one of the orations, were also in attendance. Even political adversaries like the MSI leader Almirante paid tribute. Public participation was enormous, in part due to the efficiency of the PCI machine, which arranged transport to Rome for party members and supporters from all over Italy. So full were the streets of Rome between Piazza Venezia and Piazza San Giovanni that the funeral cortège passed with difficulty through a crowd that was estimated variously at between one and two million people.

The press picked out the banners of delegations from Sardinia, Piedmont, and other regions; many activists carried party flags or copies of the PCI daily *L'Unità*; nearly all those interviewed had some recollection of having seen Berlinguer in person, usually when he was visiting their region or city for a rally. In the descriptions which appeared in the Communist press, attention was drawn to the popular nature of participation. References were not made to an undifferentiated mass presence, but rather to the heterogeneity of the crowd, with photographs of single individuals or descriptive vignettes bringing out the different experiences which led people to attend. The same technique was used in the film of the funeral, made by a team of directors including Ettore Scola and the Taviani brothers, which was subsequently distributed with *L'Unità*.

Overall, the event presented an impressive picture of the PCI as a genuinely national force, whose members and sympathizers were drawn from all regions and a wide range of backgrounds. The following day, 14 June 1984, *L'Unità* ran a red headline which read, in giant letters, 'TUTTI' (ALL); on an inside page another title read 'That large sea of righteous men'. Although the occasion was marked by deep sadness, there was also vitality in the bonds of comradeship and shared affection for a much-loved leader which united the massive crowd present under the Roman sun. From one point of view the event was an extraordinary testimony to the power and nobility of Communist popular culture. Symbolically, the crowd was composed of the tens of thousands of people who ran the hundreds of festivals which the PCI ran every year in towns and villages, who attended section meetings on cold nights, who sold the party press door-to-door on Sundays, who whipped up support for given campaigns or for Communist candidates in elections. According to a conventional image, they were people motivated by public values, who placed collective goals over private desires and who were prepared to sacrifice time for ends larger than themselves.

However, it is also possible to view at least aspects of the participation in a different way. While there were a significant number of older people at Berlinguer's funeral, most Communist activists were no longer, by 1984, hardened militants schooled in the confrontational politics of the early Cold War years. Many were quite young, men and women who had taken part in the protests of the late 1960s or 1970s and had joined or voted for the PCI in recent years. While these people viewed Berlinguer with respect, there was also a quasi-egalitarian affection or friendship ('We have come from the Mirafiori factory to greet a friend of ours once more', read one headline) that led them to chant his first name, something that would have been inconceivable with Togliatti. Some observers also detected feelings of regret among activists that they had not been as selfless as Berlinguer had assumed they were (or wanted them to be).

Also present in the streets of Rome were many people, including teenagers and students, who had perhaps never voted for the PCI but who were either vaguely left-wing or who were in some way drawn to the figure of Berlinguer. Their presence was not part of a broader pattern of life which consisted even partially of party meetings and *L'Unità* festivals; rather it was a one-off, an exceptional moment in a life that was organized entirely around different experiences and values. These people had not been present at Togliatti's funeral in 1964, but they turned Berlinguer's into a mass gathering without precedent in the history of the republic. Ottavio Cecchi wrote in the party daily that 'the young people standing around me are, I suppose, the same ones who fill the stadiums for rock concerts, those who celebrate in the streets after a football match'. 'I have the impression (perhaps illusory)', he continued, 'that a metamorphosis is happening: these young people, these "masses", are about to transform themselves into "societas".'

In fact this was not occurring. Even for many Communists the event had an artificial quality about it and its very scale ensured that, for non-Communists, it was simply a phenomenon to be consumed. For the week prior to Berlinguer's death, television and the press had built up expectations and emotions. Moreover, the whole event was broadcast live on the main public television channel, RAI-1. If the PCI momentarily became Italy's largest party in the European elections held a few days later, it was because a collective feeling had been built up which transcended the event itself.

By the mid-1980s Communist culture was no longer marked by the noble, alternative features that were once attributed to it. Thanks to secularization, prosperity and greater individualism, society was not organized in a way that could readily sustain hierarchical subcultures.

Moreover, the decline of left-wing ideology eroded the motivations of many who might once have given up time and money to support the party. In Rome itself, the Communist-led local administration in the early 1980s did not attempt to extend the typical features of left-wing culture to a broader audience; instead the culture assessor Renato Nicolini organized 'Roman Summers' in which popular films, discos, comics, and old television shows were the staple fare.

'The sudden death of Enrico Berlinguer in 1984 deprived the Communists of the one man of sufficient political ability and international stature to guide them through the doldrums of the eighties,' Paul Ginsborg has written. 'The extraordinary demonstration at his funeral, with well over a million people in the streets of Rome, was the last moment when the PCI held the centre of the national stage' (Ginsborg 1990, 420).

10

Impegno and the encounter with modernity: 'high' culture in post-war Italy

Robert S. C. Gordon

Culture and politics

The history of 'high' culture in Italy since 1945 is a history of radical change. This is not least because the boundaries and parameters of the field that constituted culture itself changed almost beyond recognition in this period, in large part owing to the rapid growth in mass media (cinema, radio, popular magazines, and television after 1954). For 'high' culture in particular, this meant a massive degree of cross-fertilization with 'lower' or broader cultural forms and a constant transformation of styles, practices, and audiences. Boundaries between high and low, élite and mass, traditional and modern, national and international, aesthetic and commercial, and so on became highly porous. One manifestation of this was the filtering through of American cultural models into local culture, high and low. Even in a film like *Riso amaro*, made in 1948 by a communist, neo-realist director (Giuseppe De Santis), the influence of Hollywood cinema and American mass culture is apparent in the music, eroticism, and gangster-movie plot. This is not to say, however, that 'high' culture disappeared in this period: on the contrary, it retained many aspects of its traditional autonomy and prestige and indeed flourished, even if increasingly as a 'niche' within a wider culture market.

This is well illustrated by the wave of successful 'auteuriste' films in the 1960s (by names such as Fellini, Antonioni, Visconti, Pasolini, Bertolucci, Rosi). Producers invested in the prestige of these film-makers. They marketed their work as 'art', and audiences, perhaps for the first time in large numbers, took pleasure in the difficulty and complexity of the films, frequented film clubs and the like, so that 'art house' cinema became a viable proposition (at worst as a sort of 'loss leader') and directors maintained a high degree of creative autonomy.

The most influential factors in bringing about these and other profound changes in the cultural arena originated in the wider society beyond it. The rapid expansion of education at secondary and tertiary level in the 1960s resulted in a rapid decline in illiteracy; traditional and new forms of culture became accessible to large sectors of the population for the first time, as both producers and consumers (aided by the widespread prosperity following the 'economic miracle' of the late 1950s to early 1960s) and, with the added influence of television, standard Italian for the first time became a genuinely national language. Certain categories of writers and artists ploughed their own paths independently of the changes or in perverse relation to them, as with the reclaiming of dialect as a sophisticated language for lyric poetry in the face of its gradual disappearance from everyday usage ('poesia neo-dialettale'). But the more emblematic figures were those artists or intellectuals whose *oeuvre* and public existence reflected and inflected the dramatic evolution in the broader culture.

Take, for example, the extraordinary career of the poet and film-maker Pier Paolo Pasolini, certainly one of the most fertile and stimulating figures at work between the 1940s and 1970s. A sketch of Pasolini's notion of cultural practice as it evolved over three decades almost reads like a template for the time. During the war, Pasolini began writing arcane dialect poetry in Friulan, drawing on the rich Italian (and indeed European) lyric tradition and contributing to small, local literary journals in Friuli, Bologna, and later Rome. In other words, he embarked on a wholly traditional initiation into the traditional literary-humanist 'high' cultural élite. Following his indirect involvement with the Resistance and his encounter with Marx and Gramsci, his notion and practice of culture shifted in the late 1940s. He now aspired to the role of 'organic' intellectual working for a 'national-popular culture' giving space and voice to dialect culture, popular song, and the subproletariat of Rome's shanty towns (the *borgate*). In the 1960s, whilst never abandoning his position in the cultural élite and the rhetorical protection it afforded him, he moved into the mass medium of film and then in the early 1970s also into mass-circulation journalism, taking as his maxim a determination 'never be afraid of *where* you say what you have to say'. In the process, he adopted, if only as a means to mounting a devastating 'apocalyptic' critique of it (*Scritti corsari*, 1975; *Lettere luterane*, 1976), an all-embracing, anthropological understanding of 'culture' as the sum of habits and customs of the entire society around him.

As well as illustrating the changing conceptions and arenas of culture, the example of Pasolini points to another factor governing the entire trajectory of post-war 'high' culture in Italy and giving it its unique colouring: its politics. The cultural élite of the 1940s was indissolubly bound up with the legacy of the anti-Fascist Resistance, and thus, its dominant ideology was of the left. It was a heterodox Marxist culture, close to the PCI although often in uneasy or openly hostile relation to it, and it finally died in the early 1990s along with the PCI itself and so many of the founding assumptions of post-war Italy. Crucially, being aligned with the Left in this period of centre-right Cold War government meant being by definition counter-hegemonic, and indeed the cultural élite derived much authority and vitality from its status as a culture of opposition or critique. However, this also led to complications and contradictions. The conservativism of 'high' culture—its hostility to modernization and 'progress' and its dedication to preserving its own aura and traditions—sat uneasily with an ideology of radical, even revolutionary change. Furthermore, as large sectors of society embraced consumerist mass culture, leftist artists and intellectuals (much like their Catholic counterparts) were often pushed into one of two extreme responses, famously formulated by Umberto Eco as either 'apocalyptic' rejection or optimistic 'intergration' (*Apocalittici e integrati*, 1964). For the former, this meant the end of the Gramscian ideal of the 'organic' relation to class and society, and the return to a didactic, disorganic detachment; for the latter, a loss of perspective and critical vision.

Given what has been described thus far, the public history of post-war 'high' culture in Italy can be plausibly mapped as a dual movement in the history of the left-leaning cultural élite: first its formation, centred on the years immediately after the war but reverberating for decades beyond, and then its contradictory encounter from the 1950s onwards with modern, consumerist mass culture. There are of course many other histories which cannot be forced into this template, in particular the 'private' histories of individual artists or more strictly aesthetic trends. Geographies too can be obscured by a history of intellectual formations of this kind, and regional or urban identities continue to play an important role in this period as in all others of Italy's history (e.g. the Sicilian novel from Brancati to Bufalino; the Roman milieu of Moravia, Morante, and Pasolini; the Turin of 'Arte Povera'). Some of these other histories will be mentioned in counterpoint to the central model in what follows, although others, such as the rich history of lyric poetry (from late Montale, Mario Luzi, and Vittorio Sereni to Attilio Bertolucci and Sandro Penna; from Giovanni Giudici, Amelia Rosselli, and Vittorio Sereni to Valerio Magrelli and Patrizia Valduga) are unjustly neglected.

The Resistance and its aftermath

The left-wing cultural élite has its origins in the radical Fascism and anti-Fascism of the 1930s and its apotheosis in the extraordinary moment of artistic and intellectual creativity in the mid-1940s known as neo-realism. After this, neo-realism became the obligatory point of reference in literature, cinema, and to an extent the visual arts at least until the convulsions of 1968–9 and the aftermath. The sheer energy of neo-realism can in large part be explained by the rapidity of the turn to anti-Fascism after the late 1930s, particularly among young former Fascists (e.g. Elio Vittorini, Vasco Pratolini, Roberto Rossellini). This is evident in a series of works foreshadowing neo-realism before the fall of the regime in 1943: Vittorini's *Conversazione in Sicilia* and his anthology of American literature *Americana* (both 1941); Renato Guttuso's extraordinary paintings

Fuga dall'Etna (1940) and *La Crocifissione* (1941); Luchino Visconti's *Ossessione* (1942). But the Resistance of 1943–5, dominated by the PCI and other left-wing or liberal formations, was the catalyst that transformed these disparate precursors into a burst of creativity and public *impegno* (social commitment), and also into a subjective and affective experience of great intensity for its protagonists. In its wake, after 1945, a cluster of works appeared which seemed to offer a direct response to recent collectively shared events and a vision of the future that Italy might now build for itself.

In the cinema the dominant figures were Rossellini (*Roma città aperta*, 1945; *Paisà*, 1946; *Germania anno zero*, 1947), Vittorio De Sica and Cesare Zavattini (*Sciuscià*, 1946; *Ladri di biciclette*, 1948, *Umberto D*, 1952), Visconti (*La terra trema*, 1948), and Giuseppe De Santis (*Caccia tragica*, 1947; *Riso amaro*, 1948). Although ideologically and temperamentally very different, all their films had in common a more or less politicized (i.e. Marxist) moral humanism, a tendency towards a bare and apparently uncomplicated film style, and a narrative dealing with war and/or the poor and marginalized of contemporary society. Although unsuccessful at the box office (with the significant exception of *Roma città aperta*), swamped as they were by the dumping of Hollywood films that had not been released in Italy since 1938, the image they presented of Italy and the hopes they raised for renewal made them subject to political controversy and also to broad popular assimilation.

Roma città aperta, the first and most important of all these films, is a good example of how a vision of the future is encoded in a film about the war. In it, an idealized and tragically redemptive Resistance—formed of an alliance between Catholics (Don Pietro played by Aldo Fabrizi), Communists (the unassuming hero Francesco), and the Common Woman (Pina, famously embodied by Anna Magnani)—prefigures a similar alliance as the source of strength for a better future, a new Italy. As the film ends, the child gang who have secretly risked their lives for the anti-Fascist cause walk away from the scene of Don Pietro's execution by the Nazis and the camera pans to show them set against the skyline of St Peter's. The city, the nation, indeed the future will be theirs.

Literary neo-realism was both less successful and coherent aesthetically than its cinematic counterpart and more directly, intellectually engaged with the problem of its relation to politics and society. Like neo-realist cinema, it had pre-war precursors, such as Vittorini's and Pavese's interest in the poetic realism of contemporary American writing, Moravia's psychological-bourgeois realism (starting with *Gli indifferenti*, 1929), or Ignazio Silone's peasant realism in his exile works *Fontamara* (1933) and *Pane e vino* (1936). After the war, Resistance narratives provided the core element of neo-realist writing. The critic Maria Corti argued in an influential essay that their narrative technique—concrete and oral, local and everyday, documentary and episodic—was formed specifically in the dozens of clandestine Resistance pamphlets of 1943–5 and beyond which would include stories of the partisan war in this style. Italo Calvino, looking back in 1964 on his Resistance novel *Il sentiero dei nidi di ragno* (1947), saw this as only part of the story, recalling above all else the intense subjective and collective experience of both the Resistance and the neo-realist years:

Rather than as my own work I read [*Il sentiero*] now as a book born anonymously from the general climate of the time, from a moral tension, a literary taste in which our whole generation saw itself after the end of the Second World War.

The literary explosion of those years in Italy was, before it was a matter of art, something physiological, existential, collective. . . . More than anything else it was a what you might call a sense of possibility hanging in the air. And soon lost.

Despite the conjunction of specific forces (1930s trends filtered through the Resistance and Resistance story-telling), and despite the large number of war memoirs or chronicles published in the immediate post-war years by 'amateur' writers, many of which adhered closely and naturally to a neo-realist mode (e.g. Pietro Chiodi's *Banditi*, 1946; Renata Viganò's *L'Agnese va a morire*, 1949), the major writers associated with neo-realism all had problematic relations with it. Vittorini's *Conversazione in Sicilia* (1941) and *Uomini e no* (1945), Carlo Levi's *Cristo si è fermato a Eboli* (1945), Pavese's *Il compagno* (1947), *La casa in collina* (1948), and *La luna e i falò* (1950), Calvino's *Il sentiero dei nidi di ragno* (1947): all of these seem to break cardinal rules of neo-realism (although these were never set prescriptively) by being variously too lyrical or symbolic, too autobiographical and pathetic, too comic or simply too literary. Even Beppe Fenoglio, commonly acknowledged as the most important writer to emerge specifically from the Resistance, often wrote in an eccentric Anglo-Italian that seems the opposite of realist, and in any case was mostly published posthumously, too late to be at the heart of the neo-realist moment (*I ventitré giorni della città di Alba*, 1952; *Una questione privata*, 1963; *Il partigiano Johnny*, 1968). Perhaps the work that captured best of all the sense of elation and fear of the war, although it pointedly avoided the Resistance to deal instead with the black market and deportation to Germany, was Eduardo de Filippo's play *Napoli milionaria!* (1945).

A genuinely distinct realism with a subject-matter detached from the specificities of the Resistance was forged by Vasco Pratolini in his chronicle-narratives set in working-class Florence (*Il quartiere*, 1944; *Cronache di poveri amanti*, 1947). Indeed, it is no coincidence that Pratolini, along with the 'purest' of the neo-realist film-makers, Visconti, was at the centre of the key debates in 1955 when each produced a work that challenged the worn-out nostrums of neorealism by tackling the historical roots of contemporary Italian society in a turn to what their defenders saw as a new critical historical realism (Pratolini's *Metello* portrayed union unrest of late nineteenth-century Florence; Visconti's *Senso* lavishly recreated the costumes and intrigue of Risorgimento Venice).

Neo-realism and *impegno* were vague terms and much energy was expended in looking for ways to put them into practice. Special mention needs to be made of Vittorini's vibrant journal *Politecnico*, if only because of the very famous public falling out it provoked with Palmiro Togliatti over the duty of the committed writer to his party. *Politecnico* (September 1945–December 1947) offered in lively prose and typography news and debate on a wide range of international trends in literature, politics, sociology, political theory, theatre, cinema, and art. Vittorini claimed for the committed intellectual the role of eclectic cultural progressive, a figure whom he crucially distinguished from the political progressive. His allegiance to the party was preceded by a version of that ecumenical humanism that animated so much of the neo-realist moment: '[to be] not of the party but with the party . . . because I love the world, I love life, I love men' (1946). Vittorini's refusal to 'be the piper of the revolution' ('suonare il piffero della rivoluzione') signalled a crisis in a certain model of *impegno* almost as it was being born, so that although the Left continued to hold sway over artists and intellectuals, after *Politecnico* their role was more often that of the fellow-traveller, 'scrittore scomodo' or 'heretic'. The convulsions in the Soviet Union and international communism in 1956 were to deal an even graver blow to relations between intellectuals and the PCI, as indeed would the events of 1989 later.

The heyday of neo-realism finished as the post-war hiatus came to an end in or about 1948. About this time Vittorini abandoned *Politecnico*; *Fronte nuovo* artists clashed with Togliatti and non-figurative work increasingly took centre stage in the visual arts; Rossellini moved boldly into a cinema of bourgeois alienation; Pavese committed suicide. Neo-realism persisted for several years as a point of debate and as a standard for the left-leaning literary culture, even as Cold War 'Zhdanovist' rigidities set into PCI cultural policy. One reason for this continued mutual exchange between the party and intellectuals, despite unresolved tensions between them, was the extraordinary impact on the Left of the posthumous publication of Antonio Gramsci's prison letters and notebooks from 1947 onwards (*Lettere dal carcere*, 1947; *Quaderni del carcere*, 1948–51). Gramsci laid great emphasis on an analysis of literature as a tool for understanding the dialectic of history (Dante, Manzoni, Pirandello), but more importantly still, he set more store than any major Marxist thinker before him on the figure of the intellectual and his so-called 'organic' relation to the party and/or class he represented.

Other trends

As Ann Caesar has convincingly argued, one fundamental development in Italian literature (although less so in film or art) obscured by a history of public *impegno* is the extraordinary growth in women's writing. In the 1940s and 1950s, a great deal of important writing by women appeared, often focusing on private, autobiographical or fantasy worlds rather than politics and the public world: these included Natalia Ginzburg's family narratives *Tutti i nostri ieri* (1952) and later *Lessico famigliare* (1963); Elsa Morante's rich, complex narratives of isolation and fantasy *Menzogna e sortilegio* (1948) and *L'isola di Arturo* (1957); Anna Banti's intimate and baroque dialogue-cum-imagined-autobiography *Artemisia* (1947); Anna Maria Ortese's chronicle of Naples *Il mare non bagna Napoli* (1953). These and others looked forward to an even greater expansion in women's writing after the 1970s, in part as a contribution to the feminist movement of those years (e.g. Dacia Maraini, Giuliana Morandini, Oriana Fallaci) and in part in the 1980s as a withdrawal from the militancy of that movement into more literary concerns of memory, history and psychology (e.g. Francesca Sanvitale, Francesca Duranti, Paola Capriolo).

Closer to neo-realism, but excluded from it in a number of ways, were war narratives which went too far beyond the template of Resistance-dominated, committed writing. By far the most important of these was Primo Levi's harrowing and lucid account of his months in Auschwitz, *Se questo è un uomo* (1947), famously turned down by the left-leaning publisher Einaudi. Many other deportees, whether Jewish, political, or military, also had difficulty publishing their memoirs. In a slightly separate category were accounts of the Russian front (by Nuto Revelli and Mario Rigoni Stern) and the grotesque mix of decadent high society and brutalizing Nazi violence in Curzio Malaparte's *Kaputt* (1944).

Other writers stood beyond the ambit of neo-realism for reasons of politics or cultural politics. Not being a Marxist was sufficient motive for marginalization, so that for example Ignazio Silone—a former colleague of Gramsci and Togliatti and now a socialist and increasingly Christian figure—was all but ostracized in Italy as he became a figure of considerable moral authority in Europe in the wake of his inclusion in the influential collection by apostate communists *The God that Failed* (1950). Even more beyond the pale was the aristocrat Giuseppe Tomasi di Lampedusa, whose posthumous historical novel *Il gattopardo* (1958) was one of the first bestsellers in Italian publishing. It was the subject of a furious debate over its portrayal of Sicily, class, and the Risorgimento with its smooth, studiedly old-fashioned narrative technique. Lampedusa was turned down by Vittorini at Einaudi and accepted at Feltrinelli by Giorgio Bassani, another writer whose nostalgic and sentimental autobiographical fiction seemed to mark a return to the values of the nineteenth-century novel and was accused of turning the Fascist period into nothing more than personal memory, local colour, and historical background (*Il romanzo di Ferrara*, in six volumes, 1956–72).

After neo-realism

In the cinema of the 1950s neo-realism was to an extent absorbed by the commerical cinema, in comedies or so-called *neo-realismo rosa*, and in this transitional phase, emergent film-makers like Fellini made a number of films (*I vitelloni*, 1953; *La strada*, 1954) caught between realism and fantasy (a balance also struck by Italo Calvino during the 1950s with his trilogy of fables *I nostri antenati*, 1952–9). A gamut of revisionist realist styles was to emerge in the early 1960s, in Visconti's epic analysis of migration and the economic miracle, *Rocco e i suoi fratelli* (1960), Pasolini's 'sacred' realism (*Il vangelo secondo Matteo*, 1964), the documentary realism of Francesco Rosi's *Salvatore Giuliano* (1961), and Gillo Pontecorvo (*Battaglia d'Algeri*, 1966). Visconti also pursued his decadent or analytical (depending on your point of view) historical film-making (from *Il gattopardo*, 1963, to *L'innocente*, 1977), and for others too, the interrogation of history came to the fore as a means to a committed cinema. Bernardo Bertolucci in particular, with a series of sophisticated films reworking twentieth-century Italian history from a Marxist-cum-Freudian perspective, marked the passage to a younger generation, in ambivalent conflict with their fathers (*Il conformista*, *Strategia del ragno*, both 1970; *Novecento*, 1976). This was of course also the generation that animated the movements before, during, and after 1968, for whom the 'fathers' were precisely the Resistance and the neo-realist generation.

Largely thanks to Gramsci's influence, the question of the role of the intellectual remained a crucial point of reference for the literary élite throughout the 1950s and beyond. For example, Vittorini, who set aside his creative work and his intellectual militancy to commit himself to work for the publisher Einaudi, there created a series, 'I gettoni', which published what one might loosely call realist or committed works by young writers (including Calvino, Fenoglio, Sciascia, and Cassola). Of these, the most interesting in terms of *impegno* was undoubtedly Leonardo Sciascia, whose combination of devoted observation of his native Sicily and a passion for the Enlightenment and its values of justice and reason produced an *œuvre* of striking narrative intensity and political subtlety, whether he tackled the mafia

(*Il giorno della civetta*, 1961; *A ciascuno il suo*, 1966), the murky conjunction of criminality and Christian Democracy (*Todo modo*, 1974),
torture and the Inquisition (*Morte dell'Inquisitore*, 1967), or the
murder of Aldo Moro (*L'affaire Moro*, 1978).

The 1950s saw other routes away from neo-realism towards the
1960s avant-garde. Perhaps the most important of these was the
Bolognese journal *Officina* (1955–9), co-edited and animated by Pasolini, among others. In Pasolini's own poetry and narrative of these
years (*Ragazzi di vita*, 1955; *Le ceneri di Gramsci*, 1957), he attempted
to transcend the stylistically and poetically naïve realism of the 1940s
and *Officina* did something similar in its literary-critical project,
returning to nineteenth-century models and forging a new conjunction of poetics and ideology. The key term for this in his essays in
Officina was 'sperimentalismo', and although there was bitter mutual
hostility between him and the emerging poets of the new avant-
garde, there is an undoubted consonance between their experimental-
isms in these years. Also involved on the fringes of *Officina*, as he had
been with *Politecnico*, and responsible for pushing many beyond
Gramsci towards other Marxist thinkers (Lukács, Brecht, the Frank-
furt School) was the essayist and poet Franco Fortini, whose radically
negative politics and intellectual rigour were to make him a beacon
for the 1968 movements.

The long 1960s

The student and industrial unrest of 1968–9 marked a watershed in
Italy as important as that of 1945–8. In many ways it represented a
final convulsive agony for the committed but still essentially élitist
subculture thrown up in the 1940s. Its roots can be seen in the
course of the preceding decade which witnessed the economic miracle (1958–63), the social and economic transformations of the
1960s, and the commericalization of the culture industry. What is
more, as Umberto Eco has pointed out, 'Nineteen sixty-eight, in
other countries, lasted one year or a little more (in the United States
it began in 1967). In Italy it lasted ten years.' In other words, the
history of 1968 is also the history of the decade of extremism,
terrorism, and social reform which followed it and found some

reflection in literature and cinema, perhaps for the last time in a direct way.

The decade before 1968 saw an opening out of intellectual horizons, so that the dominant Crocean or indeed Crocean-Gramscian philosophical idiom began to be superseded by an eclectic mix of phenomenology, semiology and structuralism, sociology, psychoanalysis, and anthropology. These influences came together in the 'Gruppo '63' (named after its first major meeting in Palermo in 1963) or *neo-avanguardia*, which was born out of the journal *Il Verri* and a group of young linguistically and formally experimental poets including Edoardo Sanguineti (*Laborintus*, 1956; *Erotopaegnia*, 1961), Antonio Porta, and Elio Pagliarini. The group also included Umberto Eco, who began to apply semiology to the serious study of mass culture in a highly influential move; the novelist Alberto Arbasino whose *Fratelli d'Italia* (1963) was the most ambitious novel of the 1960s youth culture in Italy; the maverick and ludic Giorgio Manganelli (*Hilarotragoedia*, 1964; *La letteratura come menzogna*, 1967); and Nanni Balestrini, who moved emblematically from avantgardist experiment to the extreme politics of *Vogliamo tutto* (1971). Certain other writers, although not part of the movement, also experimented with multiple languages and formal and visual play: the most important of these was the poet Andrea Zanzotto. All these writers were influenced by the recent republication and lionization of the 'Joycean' plurilinguistic works of Carlo Emilio Gadda (*Quer pasticciaccio brutto de via Merulana*, 1957; *La cognizione del dolore*, 1963).

The Gruppo '63 had close links with the vibrant world of experimental art, music, and architecture of the 1960s, especially in Milan (see, for example, the 1964 Milan Triennale). There was for a period a constant dialogue between journals, groups, and individual creators. *Il Verri*, for example, published special issues on 'Informale' and Action painting, and on the 'Arte Povera' movement of Mario Merz and Michelangelo Pistoletto (inspired by conceptualists such as Lucio Fontana and Piero Manzoni). Many of the formal concerns of these interconnected groups came together in the cinema of Michelangelo Antonioni, especially the tetralogy with Monica Vitti (*L'avventura*, 1960, *La notte*, 1961, *L'eclisse*, 1962, *Deserto rosso*, 1964), and *Blow-Up* (1966). Antonioni's was a cinema of empty spaces and empty time, enigmatic subjectivities reduced to fragmented perceptions of objects and disrupted meanings. It has been described as a 'reflection on rather than a reflection of the world', and this captures nicely the intellectual influences that converged in him, from realism to phenomenology to metaphysical art.

Antonioni's cinema also captured an element of that critical ideological position towards the world which the 1960s experimentalists continued to share with their predecessors, even if their critique was now mediated through a destabilization of language and subjective perceptions. Others were to tackle the changes in society and culture more directly. In the years leading up to 1968, the cultural arena was becoming commercialized in a wholesale way not seen before. Mondadori launched the first mass-selling paperback series in Italy, the 'Oscar', in 1965. Book prizes (especially the Strega, Viareggio, and the newcomer Campiello) were increasingly used as marketing tools. Authors such as Calvino, despite his real enthusiasm for the modern (evident in his increasingly formalist and science-driven writing, from *Le cosmicomiche*, 1965, onwards), remained nostalgically attached to an earlier, more innocent way of making literature:

Now that writing is a regular profession, that the novel is a 'product' with its 'market', its 'demand' and 'supply', its hyped launches, its successes and its routine, now that all Italian novels are 'of a reasonable middling standard' and are part and parcel of the mass of superfluous goods of a society too easily satisfied, it is hard to recall to mind the spirit [of the 1940s] with which we were trying to set up a narrative built from scratch with our own bare hands. (1964 preface to *Il sentiero dei nidi di ragno*)

From 1959 to 1966, Calvino co-edited with Vittorini a journal called *Il menabò*, which was a sort of *Politecnico* for the 1960s. It tackled the new literary, philosophical, and socio-economic currents from a constructive but critical perspective. Its most influential issue was perhaps the fourth, on 'Industry and Literature', a key modern theme reflected in a current of industrial novels such as Paolo Volponi's disturbing *Memoriale* (1962) or the more idiosyncratic *La chiave a stella* (1978), a collection of stories about a peripatetic industrial rigger by Primo Levi. Even Fellini's cinema, although predominantly a cinema of Jungian fantasy and autobiography, took a satirical look at the superficialities of modern culture to often devastating effect, from *La dolce vita* (1959) to his final film *La voce della luna* (1990).

As mentioned earlier, several new realisms also emerged in cinema to tackle the issues of modernization or modernity. Particularly characteristic of the time, because of its focus on an angry (and here sick) youth destroying the established norms around it (here his family), was Marco Bellocchio's *I pugni in tasca* (1965). In general youth, newly educated and prosperous, its energy harnessed in militant cultural groupings, was the driving force behind the upheavals of the decade. Already from the mid-1960s, certain of the groups were moving away from cultural politics and into extreme leftist militancy (*Quaderni rossi, Classe operaia*). In 1968, as the youth movement became physically rather than formally violent and ever more politicized, the 'high' cultural versions of these youthful groups lost all sense of coherence and cohesion. *Quindici*, one of the most vital journals of the late 1960s, collapsed in the face of events in 1969, and with its demise the new avant-garde was at an end.

The early and mid-1970s were played out in response to the events of 1968–9 and they present a confused mix of ever more extreme militancy alongside consolidation of the culture market. Several of the key figures of the *neo-avanguardia* 'intergated' with television, publishing, and academia. Pasolini, having lambasted the students in 1968 as more bourgeois than the police who beat them up, maintained and broadened the critique before his murder in 1975, seeing consumerist modernity as a homogenizing cultural 'genocide'. By contrast, the comic playwright Dario Fo moved out of conventional theatre and into a militant co-operative, producing protest plays ('drama as newspaper') and consciously setting himself in the subversive tradition of the medieval *giullare* (*Mistero buffo*, from 1969; *Morte accidentale di un anarchico*, 1972). Radical political groups, newspapers (*Lotta continua, Il manifesto*) and publishers sprang up, with unclarified links to the terrorism of these years, and the student community remained a volatile and active force, exploding into unrest once more in the 1977 *movimento*, during which a series of young writers, directors, and intellectuals of the 1980s were formed (e.g. Nanni Moretti, Pier Vittorio Tondelli, 'cyberpunk'). Beyond student *contestazione* and the violence of the 'anni di piombo', movements of social reform—especially feminist issues of psychiatric reform, divorce and abortion—took over much of the militant energy of the 1960s. This carried on a process of liberalization and loosening of moral taboos begun in the early 1960s coinciding with the liberal papacy of John XXIII and the Second Vatican Council. It is reflected in women's writing—both fictional and documentary—of these years, but also in a trend towards sexually explicit cinema, as porn but also as 'art' in work by Bertolucci, Pasolini, Liliana Cavani, and others.

Postmodernity, retrenchment, and diversification

The decades after the 1970s are inevitably hard to codify and describe, but one very telling coincidence allows us to mark a moment of transition: the almost simultaneous publication of the two most important 'postmodern' works of literature in Italian, Italo Calvino's *Se una notte d'inverno un viaggiatore* (1979) and Umberto Eco's massive bestseller *Il nome della rosa* (1980). In a remarkable consonance of themes, both texts sought to combine formal play—taken to an extreme in Calvino's case—with a gripping genre narrative, whilst at the same time adumbrating a wide range of issues thrown up by structuralism and semiology, reader-reception theory and related fields. A similar postmodern tinge can be identified in the artistic trend known as the *transavanguardia* (Sandro Chia, Enzo Cucchi, Mimmo Paladino), which turned away from minimalism towards a figurative, colourful, and eclectic exuberance (influenced by late De Chirico among others). The status of these moves as a reaction to the failure of the grand ideological and intellectual projects of the post-war decades becomes clear in the philosophical manifestation of postmodernism in Italy, Gianno Vattimo's (and other's) 'weak thought' (*Il pensiero debole*, 1983), which embraced plurality, uncertainty, and subjectivity as positive alternatives to foundational absolutes (such as Marxism).

Italian cinema of the 1980s suffered greatly from the death or ageing of several great *auteurs* and the unhealthy concentration of production power in the hands of the new televisual entrepreneurs. As often in the past, the comic tradition remained a stronghold of talent (Moretti, Roberto Benigni, Maurizio Nichetti, Massimo Troisi). A rich example of cinematic postmodernism was Nichetti's *Ladri di saponette* (1989), which comically reworked an icon of neo-realism (*Ladri di biciclette*) as a degraded product for commercial television. Where *Ladri di biciclette* was direct, authentic, and socially committed art, *Ladri di saponette* is slick, complex, parodic, and confusingly multi-layered. It remains a work of protest of sorts (against the damage done to cinema by television and advertising), but a formal and tonal abyss divides it from De Sica and the 1940s notion of *impegno*.

Beyond the postmodern trend, the 1980s saw a certain retrenchment in the public role of the artist and intellectual, to an extent prompted by the death of a number of significant post-war figures: Calvino (died 1985), Primo Levi (1987), Sciascia (1989), Moravia (1990), and Natalia Ginzburg (1991). At the same time, the book market largely flourished, translating a great deal of foreign work and offering a liberating, de-politicized pluralism of narrative forms and styles. These included the women writers referred to earlier; historical novels (Eco, Roberto Pazzi, and Dacia Maraini); Antonio Tabucchi's beguiling worlds of deceptive appearances and unspoken meanings; Gianni Celati's studiedly banal chronicles; Sebastiano Vassalli's sparkling enquiries into self and history; Roberto Calasso's encyclopaedic meditations on myth. The two most subtle and substantial literary stylists of the time were the Sicilian 'baroque' pair, Gesualdo Bufalino and Vincenzo Consolo, whereas the two most flamboyant were Pier Vittorio Tondelli and the inventive, but mannered Aldo Busi, both dealing openly with their homosexuality. Despite his early death from AIDS in 1991, Tondelli was the initiator and mentor of an explosion of 'young writing' in the 1980s (e.g. Andrea De Carlo, Daniele Del Giudice, Sandra Petrignani), editing anthologies of under-25 authors and launching a journal of new writing, *Panta*. Tondelli's journalism, collected in *Un weekend postmoderno* (1990), gives a vibrant picture of the international cultural eclecticism of his generation fed by pop-music, literature, cinema, and night-life. In a different tenor, the youth-driven literature market continued to flourish in the 1990s with, for example, the *succès de scandale* of an anthology of young writers influenced by the extreme violence and glib irony of horror cinema and American trash culture (*Gioventù cannibale*, 1996).

In the 1990s, if only because of the extraordinary political events that brought Silvio Berlusconi to power for almost a year, to the disbelief of many within and without Italy, signs of a new political vigour emerged in some writing and cinema (e.g. Moretti's *Aprile*, 1998, which, however, turns into the story of Moretti's abandonment of politics for fatherhood), but stronger still were the signs of consistent, high-quality, 'genre' products, evident, for example, in Italy's success abroad in a sort of equivalent of the English 'heritage' film (*Nuovo cinema paradiso, Mediterraneo, Il postino*) or in the intelligent film-making of younger directors such as Mario Martone or Francesca Archibugi. The vital tensions that governed the history of *impegno* and its encounter with modernity from the 1940s to the 1980s are no longer in place, leading some bastions of the intellectual élite to millennial laments such as Alberto Asor Rosa's recent nostalgic evocation of 'a literary civilization that once existed and now is no more'.

Conclusion

Patrick McCarthy

From Robert Gordon's chapter one firm conclusion may be drawn about post-1945 Italy: this has been a great period of high culture. It is worth affirming this, at the risk of stating the obvious, because Italians extend their habitual (and not altogether convincing) self-criticism to their culture. But the cinema of Fellini and Antonioni outdoes the best that the French *nouvelle vague* has to offer, while more recent directors, even if their work is less easily exported than Fellini's, offer excellent insights into difficult problems like the social movements of the 1970s (Francesca Archibugi's *Verso Sera*) or the relationship with post-1989 central Europe (Gianni Amelio's *L'America*) or the great theme of Gordon and Gundle, the decline of a specifically left-wing culture (Nanni Moretti's *Caro Diario* and *Aprile*). As the dust settles on the controversial, exasperating figure of Giorgio De Chirico, he will be seen to be as original in his later postmodernist incarnations as he was in his early paintings of dreamlike *piazze*. One might also suggest that, if the fascination with Pasolini ever declines (which seems unlikely!), it will allow more attention to be paid to extremely good but overshadowed poets like Sandro Penna.

The end of the war saw a revival of that most Italian of art forms, the opera. True, there was little new opera written but in that respect Italy was no different from France or Germany. There was a revival at popular and élite level of Verdi and other musicians whose work the Fascists had tried to annex but who remained national figures. The first public building rebuilt in Milan was La Scala and one might claim that the post-war began when Toscanini once again conducted in it. Massimo Mila, as well as writing about music for l'*Unità*, published his research on the young Verdi, while controversies about singers like Callas filled newspapers for decades to come. At the very least they were more interesting than arguments about Grandi or Ciano.

Unexpected moments of optimism emerge from these chapters: Salvatore Lupo expresses his conviction that the Mafia, ineptly led by the militaristic Corleonesi, can now be defeated. Since Lupo's chapter was finished, Giuseppe Piromalli, a leading boss in the '*ndrangheta*, has been captured. An intriguing mixture of the traditional and the modern and very much the kind of Mafioso whom Lupo depicts, Piromalli preyed off the container port of Gioia Tauro, while living in an underground hideout stocked with Dom Perrignon champagne but also containing several altars decked out with plastic statues of saints.

In his own way Piromalli was paying tribute to the strength of popular Catholicism. Meanwhile preparations for the beatification of Padre Pio were in full swing. The Church lost a parliamentary vote on fertility treatment for unmarried couples but won a more important vote rejecting third-party donors. It was affirmed that the term 'practising' Catholic had no meaning any longer but that the Church retained two areas of strength: the prayer groups with their tendency towards mysticism and the volunteer groups who work in social projects such as the integration of immigrants. Although neither is orthodox in the traditional sense, both demonstrate that the Church retains enough energy to avoid finishing like the Anglican Church.

Over Italian society as a whole hangs a huge question-mark: can it make the effort of modernization that its hard-won role as a leading EU nation demands? The more austere governments of the post-'1992 period, culminating in Prodi's two tough deflationary years, 1996–8, have given it the opportunity to try. How will it fare? Economically and socially, past experience would suggest that it will thrive. Yet this effort will require modifying Italy's strong points: the small enter-prises and family capitalism. Once more there is no one model for success in the so-called global universe. But a larger stock market seems essential and it will require greater transparency and a freer flow of information, for which the prerequisite is more and more varied trust. Trust, outside the boundaries of the family and local communities, has historically been in short supply in Italy. Another prerequisite is bigger companies that can withstand foreign competition, which means corporate mergers. some of which will be the result of hostile take-over bids.

Both of these developments are under way in the form of Roberto Colaninno's bid for Telecom and the formation of big banking groups like San Paolo di Torino-IMI which then bid for the Banca di Roma. These trends mark the sunset of Enrico Cuccia's world: his creation of 'Chinese boxes' where a few well-bred capitalists hid their own and one another's shares and controlled their companies with minority holdings. Can Italian capitalism really dispense with Cuccia? Can it invent pension firms, like the Anglo-Saxon companies that own so much industry and turn it over to management teams which they then fire if they do not produce rapid profits?

If the Italian economy is capable of finding a new synthesis of its traditions and of the free market and if Italian society learns to disclose secrets and to trust (which is less likely), the task still remains of creating a political system strong enough to allow the Italian government to bargain successfully within the EU and to co-operate in governing the Euro, in negotiating with the United States (over greater issues than bananas), and in guiding Europe in the global economy. But, as Pasquino explains, the referendum of 18 April 1999 failed to obtain a quorum, which indicates that the electorate is disillusioned by the post-1992 movement of attempted change

Without electoral reform, however, D'Alema's vision of a stronger Italy playing a significant role in Europe and even in other regions like the Middle East will remain a grand illusion. In the Kosovo crisis Italy's perfectly reasonable view that the NATO bombing was not an adequate method of ending Serbia's persecution of the ethnic Albanians was not expressed as the foreign policy of a leading European nation. Rather it was an illegitimate discourse, that is maintained for shabby reasons of domestic politics and in contradiction with the automatic acceptance of American initiatives which is expected of Italy.

D'Alema has, of course, the task of truly making the ex-PCI into a party of government. This is essential if politics is to be reshaped into the alternation of the centre-right and the centre-left in power. It leads D'Alema, however, into the classic Togliattian error of being too conciliatory towards the Church and the USA. A bolder stance, which aimed at legitimization by the electorate and which included a willingness to try out new organizational structures that are different from the traditional party, would give D'Alema more power to shape governmental policy.

Meanwhile the right languishes under the leadership of Berlusconi, whose very natural preoccupation with not going to goal takes up a lot of his energy, sharpens his rivalry with Fini, and prevents the Right from taking advantage of its in-built superiority in the country. The PPI, interested only in retaining its share of power under the old rules, is waging a vigorous campaign for a Catholic president; Romano Prodi is heading for a golden and useful exile in Brussels, while the small parties defend the system of proportional representation which allows them to continue their shadowy existence. The old system gained a boost when Andreotti was found innocent on two charges of collaborating with the Mafia (1999) and when the death of Bettino Craxi brought an unexpected wave of sympathy (January 2000).

This adds up to a set of problems which a mere change in voting methods cannot banish. An unreformed political class has resisted— with considerable success—attempts to transform it. It takes for granted short-lived governments that are replaced at the first sign of difficulty by other, equally weak governments. With certain exceptions like the directly elected mayors, this class is living in the pre-1992 period along with the very disappointing Forza Italia which, significantly, spawned the least austere government of the 1990s.

Even with the reinforcements provided by the two anti-system parties—Rifondazione comunista and the Lega—such a political class could not survive without the connivance of some part of the electorate. In our opinion this is provided by the (in some respects) admirable tendency of Italians to treat politics as theatre, to enjoy charisma but quickly to grow bored with it and to emphasize the magic elements in the language, gestures, and behaviour of politicians. No other European country can equal Italy for politics as spectacle—in what other country would a friendly parliamentarian go to Moscow to fetch Ocalan and to offer him to the prime minister as a pre-Chistmas present?—but, as with all theatres, there is a price to be paid.

Certain tasks can only be performed by the state, even if one accepts that the great age of the nation-state is over. The creation of infrastructure, the training of skilled labour, and the laying down of the rules for economic activity will not be undertaken by the private sector. Certainly power should be devolved to the grass roots but this cannot easily be done in the absence of a state self-confident enough to act as arbiter among regions and interests. Nor can 'Europe' replace the national authorities. By definition the EU is a collection of nation-states and it relies on them to perform many functions, including the ever more difficult allocation of welfare. No one except the Italian government can undertake pension reform.

One feels that the Prodi government's obsession with Europe distracted the electorate from the need to reform the process of government in Italy. Yet, just as the 1992 crisis began with the revelation of bad government, so the reform movement will only be complete with the establishment of better government. Europe should be a spur to this undertaking rather than a pretext for ignoring it.

Until this reform is complete Italy will continue to be a country where one lives well, entertained by the novels of Daniele Del Giudice, by the top models who act as hostesses in the San Remo festival and by the prowess of 'La Juve', not to mention by the spectacle of Fausto Bertinotti quoting from Che Guevara in Kurdish at the RC congress, by the verbal antics of Francesco Cossiga and by the tactical skills of D'Alema. Which is to say that one is living very well indeed but not in an Italy that is performing up to its potential.

Further reading

Introduction

Ginsborg, Paul (1990), *A History of Contemporary Italy: Society and Politics, 1943–1988* (Harmondsworth: Penguin).

Hood, Stuart (1983), *Carlino* (Manchester: Carcanet, 1st pub. London: Hutchinson, 1963).

Lepre, Aurelio (1993), *Storia della prima repubblica* (Bologna: Il Mulino).

Pavone, Claudio (1991), *Una guerra civile: un saggio storico sulla moralità della Resistenza* (Turin: Bollati Bollinghieri).

Woolf, Stuart J., (ed.) (1972), *The Rebirth of Italy* (New York: Humanities Press).

1. Italian society transformed

Acquaviva S. S. and Santuccio, M. (1976), *Social Structure in Italy: Crisis of a System* (London: M. Robertson).

J. Bailey (ed.) (1992), *Social Europe* (London: Longman).

M. Barbagli (1990), *Provando e riprovando. Matrimonio, famiglia e divorzio in Italia e in altri paesi occidentali* (Bologna: Il Mulino).

—— *et al.* (1988), 'La mobilità sociale in Italia', special number, *Polis*, 1/8.

Baranski, Z., and Lumley, R. (eds.) (1990), *Culture and Conflict in Postwar Italy* (Basingstoke: Macmillan).

Cavalli, A (1996), 'Il prolungamento della giovinezza in Italia: Non bruciare le tappe', in A. Cavalli and O. Galland (eds.), *Senza fretta di crescere. L'ingresso difficile nella vita adulta*, (Naples: Liguori editore), 31–44.

Ciancullo, A. and Fontana E. (1995), *Ecomafia* (Rome: Editori Riuniti).

Deaglio, M. (1991), *La nuova borghesia e la sfida del capitalismo* (Bari: Laterza).

Diamanti, I. (1996), *I mali del nord. Lega, localismo e secessione*, (Rome: Donzelli).

Gallino, L. (1971), 'Italy', in M. Archer and S. Giner (eds.), *Contemporary Europe: Class, Status and Power* (London: Weindenfeld & Nicolson).

Ginsborg, P. (1990*a*), *A History of Contemporary Italy: Society and Politics, 1943–1988*, (Hrmondsworth: Penguin).

—— (1990*b*), 'Family, Culture and Politics in Contemporary Italy', in Baranski and Lumley 1990, 21–49.

Ginsborg, P. (ed.) (1994), *Stato dell'Italia* (Milan: Il Saggiatore Mondadori).

—— (1998), *L'Italia del tempo presente. Famiglia, società civile, Stato , 1980–1996* (Turin: Einaudi).

Lepore, A. (1995), *Storia della prima Repubblica* (Bologna: Il Mulino, 2nd edn).

Lumley, R. (1990*a*), *States of Emergency: Cultures of Revolt in Italy, 1968–1977* (London: Verso).

—— (1990*b*), 'Challenging Tradition: Social Movements, Cultural Change and the Ecology Question', in Baranski and Lumley, 1990, 115–36.

Martinelli, A. (1998), 'Introduction' to A. Martinelli *et al.*, 'Social Trends in Italy, 1960–1990' (unpublished ms).

Mendras, M. (1997), *L'Europe des Européens* (Paris: Gallimard).

Pasolini, P.-P. (1975), *Scritti corsari* (Milan: Garzanti).

Picchieri, A. (1973), 'Le classi sociali', in N. Tranfaglia, (ed.) *Il mondo contemporaneo. Storia d'Italia* (Florence: Nuova Italia), i., 88–106.

Pizzorno, A. (1980), *I soggetti del pluralismo. Classi, partiti, e sindacati* (Bologna: Il Mulino).

Reyneri, E. (1997), *Occupati e disoccupati in Italia*, (Bologna: Il Mulino).

Richards, C. (1995), *The New Italians* (Harmondsworth: Penguin).

Ricossa, S. (1976), 'Italy, 1920–1979', in C. M. Cipolla (ed.), *The Fontana Economic History of Contemporary Europe* (London: Collins/Fontana), i. 266–322.

Rusconi, G.-E. and Scamuzzi, S. (1981), 'Italy Today: An Eccentric Society', special number of *Current Sociology*, 291.

Sabel, C. F. (1982), *Work and Politics: The Division of Labour in Industry* (Cambridge: Cambridge University Press).

Sales, I. (1993), *Leghisti e sudisti* (Bari: Laterza).

Schizzerotto, A. *et al.* (1993), 'Le classi superiori', special number of *Polis*, 1/93.

Slater, M. (1979), 'Migration and Workers' Conflicts in Western Europe', *Comparative Social Research*, 2: 71–92.

Stella, G.-A. (1996), '*Schei*'. Dal boom alla rivolta: il mitico nordest (Milan: Baldini & Castoldi).

Sylos Labini, P. (1975), *Saggio sulle classi sociali* (Bari: Laterza).

—— (1995), *La crisi italiana* (Bari: Laterza).

Therborn, G. (1995), *European Modernity and Beyond: The Trajectory of European Societies, 1945–2000* (London: Sage).

Zanetta, A.-M. (1997), *Le nuove famiglie* (Bologna: Il Mulino).

2. Evolution of the economy

Amatori F. (1997), 'Italy: The Tormented Rise of Organizational Capabilities between Government and Families', in A. Chandler F. Amatori, and T. Hikino, *Big Business and the Wealth of Nations* (Cambridge, Cambridge University Press).

Bagnasco A. (1977), *Tre Italie: la problematica territoriale dello sviluppo* (Bologna: Il Mulino).

Best, M. H. (1990), *The New Competition: Institutions of Industrial Restructuring* (Cambridge: Polity Press).

Fauri, F. (1995), 'Italy in International Economic cooperation: the Franco-Italian Customs Union and the Fritalux–Finibel Negotiations? *Journal of European Integration History*, 1/2.

—— (1996), 'The Role of Fiat in the Development of Italy's Car Industry in the 1950s', *Business History Review*, 70/2.

Maddison, A. (1991*a*), *Dynamic Forces in Capitalist Development* (Oxford, Oxford University Press).

—— (1991*b*) 'A Revised Estimate of Italian Economic Growth', *BNL Quarterly Review*, 171: 115–41.

—— (1995), *Monitoring the World Economy, 1820–1992* (Paris: OECD).

Ministero del Tesoro (1988), *Il debito pubblico in Italia, 1861–1987* (Rome: Istituto Poligrafico dello Stato).

Putnam, R. (1993), *Making Democracy Work* (Princeton: Princeton University Press).

Rossi, N. Toniolo, G. (1996), 'Italy', in N. Crafts and G. Toniolo (eds.), *Economic Growth in Europe since 1945* (Cambridge, Cambridge University Press).

Rossi, N., Sorgato, A., and Toniolo, G. (1996), 'I conti economici italiani: una ricostruzione statistica, 1890–1990', *Rivista di Storia Economica*, 10/1.

Sforzi, F. (1990), 'The Quantitative Importance of Marshallian Industrial Districts in the Italian Economy', in F. Pyke, G. Becattini, and W. Sengenberger (eds.), *Industrial districts and interfirm Cooperation in Italy* (Geneva, ILO).

SVIMEZ (1961), *Un secolo di statistiche italiane: Nord e Sud, 1861–1961* (Rome: 1961).

—— (1998), *Rapporto 1998 sull'economia del Mezzogiorno* (Bologna: Il Mulino).

Zamagni V. (1986), 'Betting on the Future: The Reconstruction of Italian Industry, 1946–1952', in J. Becker and F. Knipping (eds.), *Power in Europe? I* (Berlin New York: Walter de Gruyter).

Zamagni, V. (1992), 'The Italian "Economic Miracle" Revisited: New Markets and American Technology', E. Di Nolfo (ed.), in *Power in Europe? II* (Berlin: Walter de Gruyter).

—— (1993), *The Economic History of Italy, 1860–1990* (Oxford: Clarendon Press: paperback 1997).

—— (1995), 'American Influence on the Italian Economy (1948–58)', in C. Duggan and C. Wagstaff (eds.), *Italy in the Cold War: Politics, Culture and Society, 1948–58* (Oxford: Berg).

—— (1998), 'How to Lose the War and Win the Peace', in M. Harrison (ed.), *The Economics of World War II: Six Great Powers in International Comparison* (Cambridge: Cambridge University Press).

3. Political development

Bufacchi, V., and Burgess, S. (1998), *Italy since 1989: Events and Interpretations* (London: Macmillan).

Bull, M.J. (1996), *Contemporary Italy: A Research Guide* (Westport, Conn.: Greenwood Press).

—— and Rhodes, M. (eds.) (1997), *Crisis and Transition in Italian Politics (London: Frank Cass).*

Della Porta, D. (1996), Movimenti collettivi e sistema politico in Italia 1960–1995 (Rome-Bari, Laterza).

Gilbert, M. (1995), *The Italian Revolution: The End of Politics Italian Style ?* (Boulder, Colo.: Westview).

Ginsborg, P. (ed.) (1994), *Stato dell'Italia* (Milan: Il Saggiatore/Mondadori).

—— (1998), *L'Italia del tempo presente. Famiglia, società civile, Stato 1980–1996* (Turin: Einaudi).

Gundle, S. and Parker, S. (eds.) (1996), *The New Italian Republic: From the Fall of the Berlin Wall to Berlusconi* (London New York: Routledge).

Hine, D. (1993), *Governing Italy: The Politics of Bargained Pluralism* (Oxford: Clarendon Press).

LaPalombara, J. (1998), *Democracy Italian Style* (New Haven London: Yale University Press).

McCarthy, P. (1995), *The Crisis of the Italian State: From the Origins of the Cold War to the Fall of Berlusconi* (New York: St. Martin's Press).

Mershon, C. and Pasquino, G. (eds.) (1995), *Italian Politics: Ending the First Republic* (Boulder, Colo.: Westview).

Pasquino, G. (ed.) (1995), *La politica italiana. Dizionario critico 1945-1995* Rome Bari: Laterza).

4. Italy and the world since 1945

Andreatta, Beniamino (1993), 'Una politica estera per l'Italia', *Il Mulino*, 5 (Sept.–Oct.), 881–91.

Andreotti, Giulio (1989), *Gli USA visti da vicino* (Rome: Rizzoli).

Chabod, Federico (1951), *Storia della politica estera italiana, 1870–1895*, 1. *Le premesse* (Bari: Laterza).

Cossiga, Francesco (1997), 'Geopolitical Interview: The "Pro-American Lobby" in Italy', in *LiMes: What Italy Stands for*, Significant Issues Series (Washington, DC: CSIS).

Ferraris, Luigi Vittorio, *et al.* (1996), 'Quel che resta dell'atlantismo', *LiMes* 4.

—— (1997), 'Geopolitical Survey: The Sixth Fleet is the Real Thing', in *LiMes: What Italy Stands for*, Significant Issues Series (Washington, DC: CSIS).

Hamilton, Alexander, (1982), 'The Federalist No. 70', in *The Federalist Papers* (New York: Bantam).

Harper, John L. (1986), *America and the Reconstruction of Italy, 1945–1948* (Cambridge: Cambridge University Press).

Ilari, Virgilio (1993), 'Il bel paese a stelle e striscie', *LiMes*, 4.

Panebianco, Angelo (1993), 'Il paese disarmato', *Il Mulino*, 5 (Sept.–Oct.); *LiMes*, inaugural issue (1993), 7–8.

Prodi, Romano (1998), interview with Marco Marozzi, *La Repubblica*, 19 Dec.

Romano, Sergio (1981), 'Irréalité de la politique extérieure de l'Italie?', *Politique Étrangère*, 2.

Romero, Federico (1994), 'Europe as a Tool of Nation-Building: The Culture, Language, and Politics of Italy's Post-War Europeanism', typescript, courtesy of the author.

Sulzberger, C. L. (1970), *The Last of the Giants* (New York: Macmillan).

US Department of State (1952–4; 1955–7; 1958–60), *Foreign Relations of the United States* (Washington, DC: Government Printing Office).

Suggestions for further reading

Bosworth, R. J. B., *Italy and the Wider World, 1860–1960* (London: Routledge, 1996).

DI Nolfo, Ennio, '"Power Politics": The Italian Pattern,' in Di Nolfo (ed.), *Power in Europe?*, ii (Berlin: Walter de Gruyter, 1992).

Harper, John L., *America and the Reconstruction of Italy, 1945–1948* (Cambridge: Cambridge University Press, 1986).

Holmes, John, 'Can Italy Change Yet Remain Stable?', *Mediterranean Quarterly*, 4/2, (spring 1993).

Kogan, Norman, *The Politics of Italian Foreign Policy* (New York: Praeger, 1963).

McCarthy, Patrick, *The Crisis of the Italian State* (New York: St Martin's Press, 1995).

Merlini, Cesare, 'Italy and Europe,' in Jonathan Story, *The New Europe* (Oxford: Basil Blackwell, 1993).

Miller, James E., *The United States and Italy, 1940–1950: The Politics and Diplomacy of Stabilization* (Chapel Hill, NC: University of North Carolina Press, 1986).

Spotts, Frederick, and Wieser, Theodore, *Italy: A Difficult Democracy* (Cambridge: Cambridge University Press, 1986).

Willis, F. Roy, *Italy Chooses Europe* (New York: Oxford University Press, 1971).

5. Italian environmental policies in the post-war period

Benevolo, L. (1998), *L'architettura nell'Italia contemporanea* (Bari: Laterza).

Benvegnù, C. (1993), 'Lo sviluppo del centro industriale di Priolo', Diss., Faculty of Architecture, University of Venice.

Cederna, A. (1995), *Scritti dal 1953–1995* [from *Il Mondo, Corriere della Sera, La Repubblica*] (Turin: Einaudi).

Conti, L. (1979), *Visto da Seveso* (Milan: Garzanti).

Fontana, E. and Miracle, L. (1998), Rapporto Ecomafia—1998 (Edizioni Ambiente).

Legambiente, (1996), *Porto Marghera*, report.

6. The Church in post-war Italy

Alberigo, Giuseppe (1981), *Chiesa conciliare* (Brescia: Paideia Editrice).

Baget Bozzo, Gianni (1977), *Il Partito cristiano e l'apertura a sinistra* (Florence: Vallecchi).

—— (1996), 'Andreotti: un destino per la DC e il paese', *Chiesa in Italia. Annale de 'Il Regno'*.

Cavallari, Alberto (1966), *Il Vaticano che cambia* (Milan: Mondadori).

Di Nolfo, Enrico (1978), *Vaticano e Stati Uniti, 1939–1952* (Milan: Franco Angeli).

Donati, P.-P. (ed.) (1987) *La società civile in Italia* (Milan: Mondadori).

Garelli, Franco (1991), *Religione e chiesa in Italia* (Bologna: Il Mulino).

—— (1992), 'Incongruenza e differenziazione della religiosità in Italia' *Chiesa in Italia*.

Gaulle, Charles de (1956), *Mémoires de guerre: L'Unité, 1942–1944* (Paris: Plon).

Gedda, Luigi (1998), *18 aprile 1948* (Milan: Mondadori).

Gentilone, Filippo (1998), *La chiesa post-moderna* (Rome: Donzelli).

Kertzer, David (1980), *Comrades and Christians* (Cambridge: Cambridge University Press).

Milani, Don Lorenzo (1957), *Esperienze pastorali* (Florence: Libreria Editrice).

Penco, Gregorio (1977), *Storia della Chiesa in Italia* (Milan: Edizioni Jaca).

Pius XII (1995), *Mystici corporis Enchiridion delle Encicliche* (Bologna: Edizioni dehoniane).

Pompei, Gian Franco (1994), *Un ambasciatore in Vaticano: Diario 1969–1977* (Bologna: Il Mulino).

Rossi, Emilio (1956), *Il pensiere politico di Jacques Maritain* (Milan: Edizioni di comunità).

Spinosa, Antonio (1992), *Pius XII l'Ultimo Papa* (Milan: Mondadori).

Szule, Tad (1995), *Pope John-Paul II* (New York: Simon and Schuster).

Tarantini, Nadia (ed.) (1994), *Maria Goretti, un delitto che parla ancora* (Rome: L'Unità).

Tardini, Domenico (1960), *Pio XII* (Rome: Tipografia Poliglotta Vaticano).

Tatò, Antonio (1988), 'Catholic Communists, 1938–1946', in Leonard Swidler and Edward James Grace (eds.), *Catholic–Communist Collaboration in Italy* (Lanham, Md.: University Press of America).

Winowaka, Maria (1955), *Il vero volto di Padre Pio* (Paris: Edizioni Paoline).

Suggestions for further reading

Alberigo, Giuseppe, (ed), *History of Vatican II* (Maryknoll, NY: Orbis, 1995).

Carroll, Michael P., *Madonnas that Maim* (Baltimore: Johns Hopkins University Press 1992).

—— *Veiled Threats: The Logic of Popular Catholicism in Italy* (Baltimore: Johns Hopkins University Press 1996).

Hebblethwaite, Peter, *John XXIII: Pope of the Council* (London: Geoffrey Chapman, 1984).

—— *Paul VI: The First Modern Pope* (New York: HarperCollins, 1993).

Mulazzi Giammanco, Rosanna, *The Communist–Catholic Dialogue in Italy* (New York: Praeger 1989).

Logan, Oliver, 'Pius XII, *romanità*, Prophecy and Charisma', *Modern Italy*, 3/2, (Nov. 1998), 237–48.

Poggi, Gianfranco, *Catholic Action in Italy* (Stanford, Calif.: Stanford University Press, 1967).

Stacpoole, Alberic, (ed.), *Vatican II by Those who Were There* (London: Cassell, 1986).

7. The Mafia

Allum, P. A. (1975), *Potere e società a Napoli nel dopoguerra* (Turin: Einaudi).

Arlacchi, P. (1983), *La mafia imprenditrice. L'etica mafiosa e lo spirito del capitalismo* (Bologna: Il Mulino).

—— (1992), *Gli uomini del disonore* (Milan: Mondadori).

Barbagallo, F. (1997), *Napoli fine Novecento: politici, camorristi, imprenditori* (Turin: Einaudi).

Barone, G. (1993), 'La cooperazione agricola dall'età . . . giolittiana al fascismo', in O. Cancila (ed.), *Storia della cooperazione siciliana* (Palermo).

Blok, A. (1986), *La mafia di un villaggio siciliano, 1860–1960* (Turin: Einaudi).

Caciagli, M. (1977), *Democrazia cristiana e potere nel Mezzogiorno* (Florence: Guaraldi).

Cervigni, G. (1956), 'Antologia della "fibia", *Nord e sud*, 16.

Chubb, J. (1982), *Patronage, Power and Poverty in Southern Italy: A Tale of Two Cities* (Cambridge: Cambridge University Press).

Commissione parlamentare antimafia (1972), *Documentazione allegata alla relazione conclusiva* (Rome).

Crainz, G. (1997), *Storia del miracolo italiano. Cultura, identità transformazioni fra anni cinquanta e sessanta* (Rome: Donzelli).

Deaglio, E. (1995), *Raccolto rosso* (Milan: Feltrinelli).

De Masi, E. (1963), 'Sopraluogo nella Sicilia della mafia', *Nord e sud* (Oct.)

Hess, H. (1970), *Mafia* (Rome/Bari: Laterza).

Hobsbawm, E. J. (1966), *I ribelli* (Turin: Einaudi).

Lodato, S. (1992), *Dieci anni di mafia* (Milan: Rizzoli).

Lupo, S. (1996a), *Storia della mafia. Dalle origini ai giorni nostri* (Rome: Donzelli).

—— (1996b), *Andreotti, la mafia, la storia d'Italia* (Rome: Donzelli).

—— (1997), 'Di fronte all mafia: consenso, passività, resistenza', in AAVV, *Mafia e società italiana. Rapporto '97*, ed. L. Violante (Rome/Bari: Laterza).

Rapporto Malausa, in Commissione antimafia, *Relazione sulle risultanze acquisite al Comune di Palermo* (Rome: Donzelli).

Sabetti, F. (1993), *Politica e potere in un comune siciliano* (Cosenze: Pellegrini; 1st pub. 1984).

Scarpinato, R. (1996), 'Caratteristiche e dinamiche degli omicidi esequiti e ordinati da Cosa nostra', *Segno*. 176.

8. Sport

Hoberman, John M. (1984), *Sport and Political Ideology* (Austin: University of Texas Press).

Lanfranchi, Pierre, (1991), 'Bologna: "The Team that Shook the World"' *International Journal of History of Sport* (Dec.), 336–345.

Mosse, George L. (1974), *The Nationalization of the Masses: Political Symbolism and Mass Movements in Germany from the Napoleonic Wars through the Third Reich* (Howard Ferting: New York.).

Pivato, Stefano, (1994), *Les enjeux du sport* (Tournai: Casterman.).

Suggestions for further reading

De Grazia, V., *Consenso e cultura nell'Italia fascista* (Rome Bari: Laterza, 1981).

Hoberman, J., *Politica e sport. Il corpo nelle ideologie politiche del '900* (Bologna: Il Mulino, 1988).

Marchesini, D., *L'Italia del Giro d'Italia* (Bologna: Il Mulino, 1996).

—— *Coppi e Bartali* (Bologna: Il Mulino, 1998).

Mosse, George L., *La nazionalizzazione delle masse. Simbolismo politico e movimenti di massa in Germania (1815–1933)* (Bologna: Il Mulino, 1975).

Papa, A., and Panico, G., *Storia sociale del calcio in Italia. Dai club dei pionieri alla nazione sportiva (1887–1945)* (Bologna: Il Mulino, 1993).

Pivato, S., *Sia lodato Bartali. Ideologia, cultura e miti dello sport cattolico* (Rome: Edizioni Lavoro, 1985: 2nd edn. 1996).

—— *L'era dello sport* (Florence: Giunti/Casterman, 1994).

Porro, N., *Identità, nazione, cittadinanza. Sport, società e sistema politico nell'Italia contemporanea* (Rome: Edizioni Eam, 1995).

Pratolini, V., *Cronache dal Giro d'Italia (maggio–giugno 1947)* (Milan: Lombardi, 1992).

9. Memory and identity: popular culture in post-war Italy

Abruzzese, Alberto (1997), *Lo splendore della televisione* (Milan: Costa & Nolan).

Baldazzi, Gianfranco (1989), *La canzone italiana del Novecento* (Rome: Newton Compton).

Chambers, Ian (1986), *Popular Culture: The Metropolitan Experience* (London: Methuen).

Eco, Umberto (1990), 'A Guide to the Neo-Television of the 1980s', in Zygmunt Baranski and Robert Lumley (eds.), *Culture and Conflict in Postwar Italy* (London: Macmillan).

Ellwood, David W. (1992), *Rebuilding Europe: Western Europe, America and Postwar Reconstruction* (London: Longman).

Fortichiari, Antonio, and Mayer, Isabella (1997), 'Filogamo: "Boccio molti cantanti ma promuovo i tre presentatori e spero che mi mandino un saluto"', *Gente*, 25 Feb.

Gramsci, Antonio (1975), *Quaderni del carcere*, ed. Valentino Gerratana (Turin: Einaudi).

Hall, Stuart, and Jefferson, Tony (eds.), *Resistance through Rituals: Youth Subcultures in Postwar Britain* (London: Hutchinson).

Hebdidge, Dick (1979), *Subculture: The Meaning of Style* (London: Methuen).

Ginsborg, Paul (1990), *A History of Contemporary Italy: Society and Politics, 1943–1988* (Harmondsworth: Penguin).

Suggestions for Further Reading

Abruzzese, Alberto, *Lo splendore della televisione* (Milan: Costa & Nolan, 1997).

Anania, Francesca, *Davanti allo schermo: storia del pubblico televisivo* (Rome: NIS, 1997).

Baldazzi, Gianfranco, *La canzone italiana del Novecento* (Rome: Newton Compton, 1989).

Borgna, Gianni, *Storia della canzone italiana* (Milan: Mondadori, 1992).

Chambers, Iain, and Curti, Lidia, 'A Volatile Alliance: Culture, Popular Culture and the Italian Left' in *Formations of Nation and People* (London: Routledge & Kegan Paul, 1984).

Fantini, Lorenzo, *Fare casting* (Milan: Feltrinelli, 1996).

Forgacs, David, 'National-Popular: Genealogy of a Concept' in *Formations of Nation and People* (London: Routledge &Kegan Paul).

—— 'Cultural Consumption, 1940s to 1990s', in David Forgacs and Robert Lumley (eds.), *Italian Cultural Studies: An Introduction* (Oxford: Oxford University Press, 1996).

Ginsborg, Paul, *A History of Contemporary Italy: Society and Politics 1943–88* (Harmondsworth: Penguin, 1990).

—— *L'Italia del tempo presente: famiglia, società civile, Stato 1980–96* (Turin: Einaudi, 1998).

Gundle, Stephen, L'americanizzazione del quotidiano: televisione e consumismo nell'Italia degli anni Cinquanta', *Quaderni storici*, 21 62 (1986), 561–9.

—— 'From Neorealism to *Luci rosse*: cinema, politics, society 1945–85', in

Zigmunt Baranski and Robert Lumley (eds.), *Culture and Conflict in Postwar Italy* (London: Macmillan, 1990).

—— *I comunisti italiani tra Hollywood e Mosca: la sfida della cultura di massa, 1943–91* (Florence: Giunti, 1995).

—— 'Fame, Fashion and Style: The Italian Star System', in Forgacs and Lumley, *Italian Cultural Studies* (1996).

—— 'Italy', in James Coleman and Brigitte Rollet (eds.), *Television in Europe* (Exeter: Intellect, 1997).

Marsili, Marzia, 'De Gasperi and Togliatti: Political Leadership and Personality Cults in Post-War Italy', *Modern Italy*, 3:2 (1998), 249–61.

Veltroni, Walter, *I programmi che hanno cambiato l'Italia* (Milan: Feltrinelli, 1992).

10. *Impegno* and the encounter with modernity: 'high' culture in post-war Italy

Asor Rosa, Alberto (1998), 'Il triangolo di Narcisi', *La Repubblica*, 21 Feb.

Caesar, Ann (1996), 'Post-War Italian Narrative: An Alternative Account', in David Forgacs and Robert Lumley (eds.) (1996), *Italian Cultural Studies* (Oxford: Oxford University Press), 248–60.

Calvino, Italo (1991), 'Prefazione 1964 al *Sentiero dei nidi di ragno*', in *Romanzi e racconti*, i (Milan: Mondadori), 1185–1204.

Corti, Maria (1978) *Il viaggio testuale* (Turin: Einaudi).

Eco, Umberto (1964), *Apocalittici e integrati* (Milan: Bompiani).

Suggestions for further reading

Asor Rosa, Alberto, *La cultura*, in *Storia d'Italia*, vi. *Dall'Unità a oggi* (Turin: Einaudi, 1975).

Baranski, Zygmunt, and Lumley, Robert (eds.), *Culture and Conflict in Postwar Italy* (London: Macmillan, 1990).

Baranski, Zygmunt, and Pertile, Lino (eds.), *The New Italian Novel* (Edinburgh: Edinburgh University Press, 1996).

Bobbio, Norberto, *Ideological Profile of Twentieth Century Italy* (Princeton: Princeton University Press, 1995).

Bondanella, Peter, *Italian Cinema: From Neo-Realism to the Present* 2nd ed. (New York: Continuum, 1990).

Braun, Emily (ed.), *Italian Art in the Twentieth Century* (Munich: Prestel Verlag, 1989).

Brunetta, Gianpiero, *Storia del cinema italiano dal 1945 agli anni ottanta* (Rome: Editori Riuniti, 1982).

Caesar, Michael, and Hainsworth, Peter (eds.), *Writers and Society in Contemporary Italy* (Leamington Spa: Berg, 1984).

Celant, Germano, *et al, The Italian Metamorphosis, 1943–68* (New York: Guggenheim Museum Publications, 1994).

Duggan, Christopher, and Wagstaff, Christopher (eds.), *Italy in the Cold War: Politics, Culture, Society 1948–1958* (Oxford: Berg, 1995).

Ferretti, Giancarlo, *Il mercato delle lettere* (Turin: Einaudi, 1979).

Ferroni, Giulio, *Storia della letteratura italiana. Il novecento* (Turin: Einaudi, 1991).

Forgacs, David, *Italian Culture in the Industrial Era: 1910–1980* (Manchester: Manchester University Press, 1990)

—— and Lumley, Robert (eds.), *Italian Cultural Studies* (Oxford: Oxford University Press, 1996).

Luperini, Romano, *Il Novecento. Apparati ideologici, ceto intellettuale, sistemi formali nella letteratura italiana contemporanea* (Turin: Loescher, 1981).

Romano, Massimo, *Gli stregoni della fantacultura* (Turin: Paravia, 1979).

Sorlin, Pierre, *Italian National Cinema* (London: Routledge, 1996).

Chronology

1943 JULY Allied landings in Sicily.
Mussolini overthrown.

SEPT. Armistice with the Allies.
King and Badoglio flee to Brindisi.
German troops occupy Northern and Central Italy.
Pope Pius XII remains in Rome.
Mussolini, rescued, sets up Republic of Salò.
Resistance begins.

1944 MAR. Palmiro Togliatti returns from USSR and makes Salerno speech.

1945 APR. Liberation from Nazis.

DEC. Alcide De Gasperi becomes head of a coalition government that includes the Communists.
Roberto Rossellini, *Roma città aperta*, starring Anna Magnani.
Elio Vittorini, *Uomini e no*

1946 JUNE Referendum on monarchy: 54 per cent choose republic.
Election to Constituent Assembly. DC as largest party.
Piaggio introduces the Vespa.
Mediobanca founded

1947 MAR. Concordat inserted into new constitution with PCI support.

MAY Communists and Socialists excluded from government.

1948 JAN. New Constitution comes into force.

APR. 18th Elections. DC wins an outright majority of seats.

JULY Attempt to assassinate Togliatti.
Gino Bartali wins Tour de France.
Giuseppe de Sanctis, *Riso amaro* starring Silvana Mangano.

1949 MAR. Parliament votes to join NATO.
Fausto Coppi wins Giro d'Italia and Tour de France
Turin soccer team killed in plane crash.

1950 MAY Founding, after split, of Catholic union, the CISL.

AUG. Founding of bank to develop South, the Cassa per il
mezzogiorno.
In the context of infallibility, Pope declares Mary's
Assumption to be an article of faith.
Canonization of Maria Goretti.

1951 JAN. First Sanremo song festival.

1952 Italo Calvino, *Il Visconte Dimezzato.*

1953 JUNE Elections: DC wins but without outright majority.
Founding of ENI

1954 OCT. Trieste rejoins Italy.
Federico Fellini, *La strada*, starring Giulietta Massina.

1955 Fiat launches 600 car
Pasolini and Bologna friends found review *Officina.*

1956 JUNE Togliatti supports, with many reservations, Krushchev's
report on Stalin. However, PCI supports Soviet invasion of
Hungary in October. Italo Calvino leaves party.

1957 Fiat launches 500 car.
Giangiacomo Feltrinelli publishes *Dr Zhivago.*
Pasolini, *Le ceneri di Gramsci.*

1958 Italo Calvino, *La speculazione edilizia* and *La nuvola di
smog e la Formica Argentina.*

JULY Elections: DC largest party. Amintore Fanfani forms
government.

OCT. Angelo Roncalli elected pope after death of Pius XII.
Feltrinelli publishes Tomasi di Lampedusa's *Il gattopardo*, after Einaudi refuses it.

1959 Fellini, *La dolce vita*.

1960 MSI Congress in Genoa. DC Prime Minister, Tambroni, wants to bring Neo-Fascists into government. Popular resistance. Demonstrators killed in Reggio-Emilia. Tambroni resigns.
Luchino Visconti, *Rocco e i suoi fratelli*.
Michelangelo Antonioni, *L'avventura*.
Olympic Games held in Rome. Livio Berrutti wins 200 metres.

1961 Antonioni, *La notte*.
Pasolini, *Accattone*.

1962 FEB. Fanfani forms the first centre-left government.
OCT. Second Vatican Council opens.
NOV. Nationalization of electrical industry.

1963 Italo Calvino, *La giornata di uno scrutatore*.
APRIL Election: DC loses votes but remains largest party.
JUNE Death of Pope John XXIII; election of Paul VI.
Natalia Ginzburg, *Lessico famigliare*

1964 JULY General de Lorenzo attempts *coup d'état*.
AUG. Togliatti dies, huge funeral, painting by Renato Guttuso.
Sergio Leone, *Per un pugno di dollari*.
Death of Giorgio Morandi.

1966 Florence flooded. Chiesa di Santa Croce damaged, many paintings and sculptures lost.
Antonioni, *Blow-up*, starring Vanessa Redgrave.
Gillo Pontecorvo, *La battaglia di Algeri*.
Italy loses to North Korea in World Cup.

1967   First wave of student protest against university reform and Vietnam War.

Death of Totò.

Death of Primo Carnera, only Italian to win the world heavyweight boxing title.

Nino Benvenuti wins world middleweight title.

1968 MAY Elections. PSI vote down.

       JULY Paul VI's encyclical *Humanae vitae*.

Massive student protest and violent clashes with police.

1969 DEC. Divorce Law passes.

Bomb in Piazza Fontana, Milan, sixteen people killed.

Autunno caldo: wave of strikes, unions challenged from below.

Dario Fo, *Mistero buffo*.

1970 MAY Statuto del Lavoro passed.

June First regional elections.

Fo, *Morte accidentale di un anarchico*.

1972 MAY Elections. MSI vote increases.

1973 OCT. Berlinguer proposes the historic compromise.

1974 MAY Divorce referendum, 59 per cent vote to keep divorce.

Brescia: bomb kills six people.

       AUG. Bomb on Italicus train kills twelve people.

1975 JULY Local elections: Left wins major cities.

Wage indexation introduced.

First Armani women's collection.

Montale receives Nobel Prize.

Pasolini killed outside Rome

1976 JUNE Elections. PCI's highest ever vote—34.4 per cent.

Government of national solidarity formed, no Communist ministers, Giulio Andreotti prime minister.

1977   Movimento del '77 prevents union leader, Luciano Lama, from speaking at Rome. Then takes over Bologna.

1978   MAR.   DC leader, Aldo Moro, kidnapped by Red Brigades. Killed in May.

       MAY   Abortion law passed.

       JUNE   President Leone (DC) forced to resign on corruption charges. Sandro Pertini (PSI) replaces him.

       OCT.   John-Paul II elected pope.
              Death of Giorgio De Chirico.
              Leonardo Sciascia, *L'affaire Moro*.

1979   JUNE   Election: PCI loses 5 per cent. End of national solidarity.
              Italy enters EMS.
              Italo Calvino, *Se una notte d'inverno un viaggiatore*.

1980   MAY   National Health Service set up.

       AUG.   Bomb at Bologna railway station kills eighty-five people.

       SEPT. Fiat lays off 14,000 workers; metalworkers strike;
              Berlinguer speaks at factory gates; march of 40,000;
              victory for management.

       NOV.   Earthquakes in South. PCI gives up historic compromise for 'alternative government'.

1981   MAY   Referendum retains abortion.
              Scandal of P2 Masonic lodge breaks.
              Divorce of Treasury and Bank of Italy.
              Death of Montale.
              Retrospective of De Chirico at National Gallery of Modern Art.

1982   JULY   Italy wins the World Cup.

       SEPT. General Carlo-Alberto Dalla Chiesa killed by Mafia in Palermo.

1983   JUNE   Election: DC vote falls. Craxi prime minister.

1984   Dispute between PSI and PCI over wage indexation.

JUNE Berlinguer dies after speaking to crowd in Padua. Huge
funeral. PCI largest party in European elections.
Alessandro Natta secretary.

1985   Referendum prohibits wage indexation.

JUNE Francesco Cossiga elected president.

SEPT. Death of Calvino.

1987 JUNE Election: PCI slumps to 26.6 per cent.

1989 JUNE European elections: PCI holds under Achille Occhetto
secretary.

NOV. PCI Central Committee votes to reform the party.

1990   Italy hosts the soccer World Cup, loses to Argentina.
Intense internal debate in PCI. Bologna congress. Pietro
Ingrao, memorable speech in support of 'no'.

1991   PCI splits at Rimini congress into non-communist Partito
Democratico della Sinistra and Rifondazione comunista.

1992   Start of *Mani Puliti* (Clean Hands) investigation in Milan.

APRIL Elections: DC and PSI do badly. Rise of the Lega. Giuliano
Amato becomes prime minister. Oscar Luigi Scalfaro
elected president.
Two leading judges killed by Corleonesi wing of Mafia.

SEPT. The lira forced out of EMS.

1993   Referendum votes 'yes' to electoral reform.
Direct election of mayors in cities. PDS-based coalitions
win in Turin, Genoa, Venice, Rome, and Naples.

1994   Berlusconi launches Forza Italia. Polo of FI, Lega, and ex-
fascist Alleanza nazionale defeats the Progressisti, a
coalition based on PDS. Occhetto resigns and Massimo
D'Alema becomes PDS secretary. Berlusconi forms a
government.
His team AC Milan win European Champions Cup.
Italy loses to Brazil in final of World Cup.

DEC.   Berlusconi forced out as prime minister.
       Nanni Moretti, *Caro diario.*

1995   Lamberto Dini leads 'technical' government.
       Romano Prodi challenges Berlusconi.

1996   Prodi's Olive Tree coalition defeats Polo. Prodi as prime
       minister. Ex-Communist ministers.
       Nanni Moretti, *Aprile.*

1998   Cyclist Marco Pantani wins the Tour de France and the
       Giro d'Italia.

MAY   Italy admitted to founding group of the EU's monetary
       union.

OCT.   Prodi loses a vote of confidence and resigns as prime
       minister. D'Alema replaces him.

1999   *La Vita è bella* is nominated for seven Oscar awards and is
       the highest-grossing foreign film ever in the USA.

MAR.   NATO bombs Serbia. D'Alema supports attacks.
       Criticism from Catholics and Left.

APR.   Referendum to abolish the 25 per cent of House seats
       awarded by proportional representation fails to achieve
       quorum.

2000   Pope John-Paul II proclaims 2000 a Holy Year. Pilgrims
       overrun Rome.

JAN.   Bettino Craxi dies.

Index